WHO NEEDS HOLLYWOOD

Michael –
God Bless!

Joe C

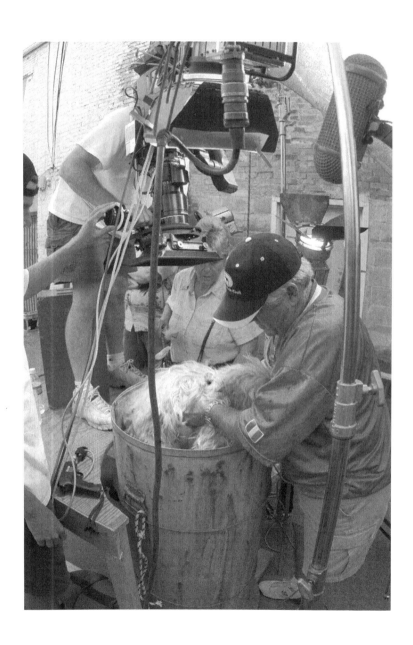

For Michael —
A story of tenacity and perseverance
that led us to know the lovable,
little dog, Benji....

Woof!

Joe Mitchell

2012.

WHO NEEDS HOLLYWOOD

The Amazing Story of a Small Time Filmmaker
Who Writes the Screenplay, Raises the Production Budget, Directs,
and Distributes the #3 Movie of the Year

JOE CAMP

14 HANDS PRESS

Also by Joe Camp

National Best Seller
The Soul of a Horse
Life Lessons from the Herd

The Soul of a Horse Blogged
The Journey Continues

The Benji Method
*Teach Your Dog to do what
Benji Does in the Movies*

Coming:

Born To Be Wild
The Soul of a Horse

The Soul of a Happier Healthier Horse
No Stalls – No Shoes – No Sugar

For more: www.14handspress.com

All photos by Tony Demin - www.tonydemin.com

Copyright © 2010 by Joe Camp - All rights reserved.

Published in the United States by 14 Hands Press,

an imprint of Camp Horse Camp, LLC

www.14handspress.com

Library of Congress Control Number: 2010908081

Library of Congress subject headings

Camp, Joe

Who Needs Hollywood / by Joe Camp

Motion pictures – Production and direction

Motion picture authorship

Motion picture producers and directors – United States – diaries

Benji (motion picture)

ISBN 978-1-930681-00-2

First Edition

What Readers and Critics Are Saying About Joe Camp

"Joe Camp is a master storyteller." *THE NEW YORK TIMES*

"This book is absolutely fabulous! An amazing, amazing book. You're going to love it." *JANET PARSHALL'S AMERICA*

"One cannot help but be touched by Camp's love and sympathy for animals and by his eloquence on the subject." *MICHAEL KORDA, THE WASHINGTON POST*

"The Hollywood glamour days are almost secondary, the theatrical drama virtually anti-climactic. In a strange, strong, compelling sense, the book is not about the making of a Hollywood movie. It is about faith....having faith in what you can do, in hanging on. The conscientious reader wanting much more than the typical Hollywood celebrity story need not despair or search any longer. He or she will find it in what Camp has written." *JACK L. KENNEDY, THE JOPLIN INDEPENDENT*

"I wish you could *hear* my excitement for Joe Camp's new book. It is unique, powerful, needed." *DR. MARTY BECKER, BEST-SELLING AUTHOR OF SEVERAL CHICKEN SOUP FOR THE SOUL BOOKS AND POPULAR VETERINARY CONTRIBUTOR TO ABC'S GOOD MORNING AMERICA*

"Joe Camp is a gifted storyteller and the results are magical. Joe entertains, educates and empowers, baring his own soul while articulating keystone principles of a modern revolution in horsemanship." *RICK LAMB, AUTHOR AND TV/RADIO HOST "THE HORSE SHOW"*

"This book is fantastic! It has given me shivers, made me laugh and cry, and I just can't seem to put it down!" CHERYL PANNIER, WHO RADIO AM 1040 DES MOINES

"Joe Camp is a natural when it comes to understanding how animals tick and a genius at telling us their story. His books are must-reads for those who love animals of any species." MONTY ROBERTS, AUTHOR OF NEW YORK TIMES BEST-SELLER THE MAN WHO LISTENS TO HORSES

"Joe speaks a clear and simple truth that grabs hold of your heart." YVONNE WELZ, EDITOR, THE HORSE'S HOOF MAGAZINE

"Joe Camp has done it again. He grabs our attention right away, makes us laugh, cry, and believe in the possibility of all good things. A smart man, with a true gift of storytelling, Joe Camp brings us along for the ride, inspiring this reader to stay true to her passions. We laugh, struggle and cry with him. A really good read!!!!! Thanks, Joe!!" MARJORIE SAMUELS - READER

"I got my book yesterday and hold Joe Camp responsible for my bloodshot eyes. I couldn't put it down and morning came early!!! Joe transports me into his words. I feel like I am right there sharing his experiences. And his love for not just horses, but all of God's critters pours out from every page." RUTH SWANDER – READER

"I love this book! It is so hard to put it down, but I also don't want to read it too fast. I don't want it to end! Every person who loves an animal must have this book. I can't wait for the next one !!!!!!!!!" NINA BLACK REID – READER

"I LOVED the book! I had it read in 2 days. I had to make myself put it down. Joe and Kathleen have brought so much light to how horses should be treated and cared for. Again, thank you!" *ANITA LARGE – READER*

I LOVE the new book… reading it was such an emotional journey. Joe Camp is a gifted writer." *MARYKAY THUL LONGACRE – READER*

"I was actually really sad, when I got to the last page, because I was looking forward to picking it up every night." SABINE REYNOSO - READER

"*The Soul of a Horse Blogged* is insightful, enlightening, emotionally charged, hilarious, packed with wonderfully candid photography, and is masterfully woven by a consummate storyteller. Wonderful reading!" HARRY H. MAC-DONALD - READER

"I simply love the way Joe Camp writes. He stirs my soul. This is a must read book for everyone." *DEBBIE K - READER*

"This book swept me away. From the first to last page I felt transported! It's clever, witty, inspiring and a very fast read. I was sad when I finished it because I wanted to read more!" *DEBBIE CHARTRAND - READER*

"This book is an amazing, touching insight into Joe and Kathleen's personal journey that has an even more intimate feel than Joe's first best seller." *KATHERINE BOWEN – READER*

For Carolyn and Kathleen, my two incredible wives
Without whom I would be so much less

THE PHOTOGRAPH ON THE COVER

Kathleen hates it. Because I look grumpy and grouchy. I love it. It makes me laugh because that's pretty much how I look throughout any production. Nothing ever seems to go right. And I always feel that I'm one of the few on the set who really cares about what we're supposed to be trying to accomplish. I'm not, of course, but knowing that doesn't seem to abate the *feeling*. Being both the producer and director has always been a lonely gig for me, and the photo seems to speak to that as well. Okay, perhaps this is all too esoteric for a book cover, but it is interesting because Kathleen and I are rarely this far apart on *any*thing. Neither of us can remember what I might've been observing at the moment but we do agree that something wasn't measuring up to what I had seen while writing the screenplay. A safe bet. It almost never does. And that's the point of the photograph. It speaks the truth. Thanks Tony.

A light breeze rippled the tall grasses around the aging gray mansion. A single Indian Paintbrush danced a bit and then, again, grew still. I knew how it must feel, out there by itself. This was going to be a lonely vigil. The risk and responsibility were all mine and the weight of it scared me a little, but I wouldn't have it any other way. This was *my* time! I had worked and waited forever, it seemed, for this moment. And now it was here. The cameras were about to roll.

— Joe Camp

FOREWORD

A wise elder once said, "You can't tell a book by its cover."

He or she must have been referring to Who Needs Holly-wood.

If you want or expect a namedropping foray through Tinsel Town, or a nice cute tale about dogs by the guy in 1974 who forged the first Benji movie almost with his bare hands, you won't be too disappointed as author Joe Camp does throw in a few names and battles with stereotypical Hollywood forms and other more conventional devices.

But the Hollywood glamour days are almost secondary, the theatrical drama virtually anti-climactic. In a strange, strong, compelling sense, the book is not about the making of a Hollywood movie. It is about faith....having faith in what you can do, in hanging on.

It also is a love story, for Joe's first wife Carolyn, a college sweetheart who died too young but believed in him and for his present wife Kathleen. It is about strength and memories and family and remembering what his dad taught him about talent and perseverance long before he approached movie making. It is about the importance of little things like trust, observation, caring, really observing, questioning, mentoring, and doing something one believes in with someone one cares about, not just making money for the sake of the coins collected. It is not a pompous, presumptive, egocentric piece about success on the surface but more about feeling and finding and forming. Camp's previous best seller, The Soul of a Horse used a similar approach: horse training as a way to explore the real human soul. Camp occasionally gives us some clues about himself and his motivation for life, not just a springboard for screenplays and books. He writes, for example, "Given a choice, I simply prefer to believe, rather than doubt, what people tell me. I prefer faith to suspicion. So, I tend to thwart what little intuition I might have with an assumption that people are largely caring, honest, intelligent and understanding."

Sometimes, we literally have trouble seeing things from others' points of view. It was hard to convince potential backers that Benji could act, that he was the star. A Dallas newspaper reviewer never mentioned the pooch when on the set to do a story; "big people" had to be the star." Camp, however, finally sold the idea that emotions and feelings can be transmitted and revealed via a small canine.

The conscientious reader wanting much more than the typical Hollywood celebrity story need not despair or search any longer. He or she will find it in what Camp has written.

Jack L. Kennedy
August 31, 2010
for The Joplin Independent

PREFACE

I remember the moment as if it were yesterday. We were driving home from my part-time job at Bob's Camera Store and I had been thinking a lot about the future. How was a sixteen-year-old supposed to know what to do with his life; which way to point? There were so many things to consider, and college was barely a year away. As we rounded the corner from Highland onto Southern, I turned to my dad.

"How am I supposed to go about choosing a career? Where do you start?"

His response was profound, and not of the times, and for some reason that surprised me.

"Do what you would do if you didn't have to earn any money at it whatsoever," he said. "Only then will you be passionate about your career, and happy."

Those words changed the direction of my life forever, ratifying a dream that I had only thought of, at the very best, as wholly irrational. I hope this book will do the same for you.

CONTENTS

WHO NEEDS HOLLYWOOD

INTRODUCTION

I've found that two of the most exciting, extraordinary things you can do with your life is to realize your dreams, and to help others do the same. It not only breeds happiness and a feeling of enrichment, it tends to make the world a better place. And why else are we here, but to leave things a little better than we found them?

That is the effort of this book.

It is, I hope, a book of promise for all those who have battled the odds for things held dear and, perhaps, surrendered too quickly to those indolent, oft-spoken assurances: *You can't do that! That's impossible! Give up! Quit! Sit down! Shut up! Go away!*

In a world scarred by chaos and upheaval, where astonishingly the wasteful poisons of war, racism and hatred continue to reopen and infect old wounds, where the crumbling character of our business, political, and religious leaders stutter across each day's headlines, why, pray tell, should we pause to digest a small-time ad guy's struggle against the system for a fluffy, four-legged dream of superstardom?

Perhaps because, in the experience, there's still hope that the human spirit can rise above the doom and gloom in which it seems to so often dwell. The unknown, the uncelebrated can still mount a white horse, charge off into the distance and accomplish things worthwhile, and hold his or her head high in the process. And, in an industry where sex and violence are seemingly the only sure routes for selling movie tickets, that small-time ad guy can still turn a family-safe floppy-eared notion into a worldwide phenomenon that brings joy and happiness to the hearts of millions.

I will be pleased if you find these pages interesting and entertaining. But my fondest hope is that you might find yourself inspired and equipped to follow your own dreams; to strike out against the odds; to adventure into uncharted waters with passion, honesty and integrity; and to leave the world a better place for the effort. This work, then, would truly be my most treasured achievement.

1

THE HARVEST

"The possible's slow fuse is lit by the imagination."
Emily Dickinson
Poems

I grabbed Carolyn's hand as we stepped off the train. A nervous chill of anticipation skittered up my spine. People were rushing past us, anxious to get on with their morning, and we timidly tried to keep up. Someone spoke, and smiled, then spoke again and hurried off. The words meant nothing, but we smiled back just the same.

I was bristling with excitement. Gone were the miseries of the long, sleepless flight over. Gone were the first flashes of Milano, seen as a drowsy blur of television stations and newspaper reporters. Now, after a good night's sleep on a long train ride, my senses were alive and tingling again and the whole feeling was like I had dozed off in Dallas and awakened here.

It was our first trip abroad and my first time out of the country except for three days in Nassau and a few hours in Juarez. So, maybe you can imagine. I mean, anywhere would've been terrific, but we weren't just anywhere. We were in Rome!

The Eternal City. Born nine hundred years before Christ. Home of Cato, Nero, Constantine and the Caesars. A magical place where it is said, you can actually hear the breathing of the centuries; a state of mind for classical study and romantic dreams; a place that most of us only read about in books and see in movies.

And here it was, coming at me as a splash of bright sunlight at the end of a crowded train terminal.

Rome. As in Italy.

We emerged into the Piazza del Cinquecento and it took our breaths away. Mouths agape, we stood for a long moment, feeling every bit like hillbillies come to town. Then suddenly my heart stopped.

There before me, across the piazza, ten thousand miles from home, forty feet wide on a huge billboard, was my small, scruffy notion of a dog conceived in the shower one morning back in Texas. *Benamino!* Our first movie was taking Rome by storm.

What an extraordinary feeling! The whole world seemed to grind to a stop. Everything froze in place for a moment as the realization sank in. We had been working incredibly hard, running, seemingly, at light speed for more than two years, raising money, writing script, shooting the picture, promoting, distributing. Always looking forward to the next problem, the next market, the next plateau; never really slowing down enough to look back at what had been accomplished. To fully realize, to absorb, to enjoy.

Somewhere behind us a woman shrieked. Carolyn and I spun around. A wave of humanity was surging, racing, screeching frantically toward the terminal entrance. I was certain that some terrible disaster had befallen us, until, out of the melee, I heard the jubilant yelp of a small child. "Benamino! Te amo!"

Benji and his trainer were just emerging into the piazza. I turned to Carolyn and she smiled. She must have known what I was feeling. Emotions were rushing at me like a river. I wanted to reach out and hug everybody in sight. Instead, I burst into tears. Carolyn slipped her arm around my waist and we turned back to the billboard and just stood there for a very long time.

Even today, I'm still in awe of Benji's success. As I attempt to recapture and recount the adventure, I think I understand it, intellectually, but, emotionally, I find it all terribly hard to believe. Yet, here I am, the silly, sometimes sobbing proof that the old fashioned American dream is alive and well. The warranty that you can accomplish whatever you want to accomplish, no matter how impossible it might seem, if you want it bad enough to work hard enough to achieve it. To make the right choices and stick with them. Those choices I was taught early on, yet I'm still mystified that they work. But they do.

The trick, of course, is that it's not always an easy road, or a short one. I thought I knew what I wanted to do with my life when I was eight years old. I was certain I knew by the time I was sixteen.

I was thirty-four before I was doing it.

2

Raison d'etre

"We are such stuff as dreams are made on..."
William Shakespeare
The Tempest

I turned my head to the side and brushed away the tears with my shoulder, then turned back to the screen. They were all dancing off into the sunset singing *Zip a Dee Do Dah,* and I didn't want them to go. Uncle Remus, and Bobby Driscoll, and Luana Patten, and Brer Rabbit and Brer Fox.

I knew my Dad would be waiting outside to pick me up, but when the final fade out came, I didn't budge. I stayed glued to my seat. I wanted to see the beginning again, to see the names that flashed on the screen. These were the days when you could sit in a theater all afternoon for the price of one ticket. The shows were continuous because most people paid little attention to starting times. They just showed up whenever it suited them, then stayed through the next showing until they got back to the part where they came in.

There was a preview, a cartoon, and a newsreel that showed President Truman with the first television set to be installed in the White House, then, once again, the bright, happy music that signaled the opening of Walt Disney's *Song of the South.* I was mesmerized as the picture came up and all those names began to pass before me. I wanted to be one of them. I don't think it really mattered which one; that wasn't the point. It was an eagerness to be a larger part of such a delicious experience. Not just a kid in the audience.

It would've been nice, I supposed, to be Bobby Driscoll since, during the preceding hour-and-a-half, I had fallen hopelessly in love with his young co-star, Luana Patten.

I wasn't sure what *Directed by* meant but it sounded important, and it was the last name on the screen, so maybe that's who I'd like to be. Especially if that was the person in charge of making me feel so good.

A hand touched my shoulder.

"Haven't you passed where you came in?" my Dad whispered.

"I was just coming," I said. And we walked up the aisle together.

"Daddy?" I whispered. "You know when it says 'directed by' on the screen? What does that mean?"

"It means he's the boss."

I tugged on his hand, pausing to glance back at the screen. It was confusing because I had thought Walt Disney was the boss, but *Song of the South* was directed by somebody else.

"Come on, let's go!" he whispered sternly.

I blinked, and imagined the words on the screen. Then the screen disappeared as the doors swung shut. Daddy was dragging me from the theater.

The words had looked good, I thought. Real good. *Directed by Joey Camp.*

***

It was a fine fall morning in Paris, crisp and clear, and Benji was quite full of himself, cavorting near the fountain, playing with the children who had inexplicably materialized out of nowhere at the first whiff of a movie star. Their faces radiated, and they took turns gently stroking his head. Those Benji chose to favor with a big sloppy lick exploded with laughter, and one young girl ran to her mother, screeching in French that she would never wash her face again.

A younger boy, perhaps eight, stood alone, apart from the crowd, a conspicuous shyness depriving him of the fun. I slid away from the camera, walked over and took the boy's hand and lead him through a jungle of groping arms to what I imagine was his first kiss ever from an international superstar. He beamed up at me and for that moment, in his eyes, I was King of France, maybe the world. For this was no ordinary canine. This was the embodiment of all the emotions he had felt while snuggled in a dark corner of a theater somewhere in Paris, living Benji's desperate struggles as if they were his very own.

How well I understood. The smile I returned was genuine, for this was the best reward of all. The very best.

3

CAUSES AND EFFECTS

"Courage is the resistance to fear, the mastery
of fear - not the absence of it."

Mark Twain

Tears were streaming down my face.

But you must fight the assumption that I break down and bawl every time the wind shifts. These are simply the moments one tends to remember. That I can cry at all probably comes as a shock to many because it's rarely seen. Even as a kid, I usually managed to keep it all locked up until I could reach the darkest region of the nearest closet.

On this cold, dismal January afternoon, I had finally come to battle with my parents over where I would be attending college, less than a year away, and they were winning. No, that's not quite true. They had won. The battle was really over and I was buried deep in the familiar back corner of my closet between a suitcase full of magic tricks and a pair of shoes caked with dried mud.

I had wanted UCLA. *The* film school. My parents wanted Ole Miss, aka the University of Mississippi. No film school. Their reasoning, unfortunately, was depressingly sound, which begot the struggle confounding me at the moment. Could they possibly be right?

I hadn't been what you would call a social whirlwind during my high school years. We had moved to Memphis as I was beginning the seventh grade and I was dropped into the literal middle of a twelve-year school, one that began in the first grade and ended, with most of the same students, twelve years later. It was not a transient community so most of the cliques were formed early on. If you weren't there by spring break of the first grade, you were already an outsider. And I stumbled in six years later.

In Jackson, Mississippi, my fifth and sixth grade years had been a different story. I entered the fifth grade in a brand new school, full of brand new students, in a brand new neighborhood. An even start. Nobody knew who to reject yet, so I made sure it wasn't me. The final bell hadn't rung the first day before I had evaluated the entire class, picked out the shakers and movers and brought them together into a solid group to which I indelibly affixed myself.

It wasn't easy for a kid with no clearly defined outstanding attributes. I was mediocre in sports and only a B student, plus or minus. A penchant for tactics was beginning to emerge, but I certainly didn't have the guts to attack class politics. So I picked out a few others who did and helped them along, riding just under the crest, occasionally rising to the top for brief moments, like when Lola and I won the sixth grade dance contest.

But it didn't take long to learn that things were going to be different in Memphis. The circle at the top, populated with kids from one of the most exclusive residential areas in town, had long since been knitted solid. No penetration there. It was a new and intimidating experience so I rationalized it all away as trivial and unimportant, gathered up a small group of stragglers and, together, we shuffled through the next six years, if not as social outcasts, definitely as social periphery. And that was my parents' primary concern.

I don't mean social in the provincial sense. Mom and Dad simply realized, even when I didn't, that I enjoyed making things happen, and that could rarely occur from the outside looking in. Not that the years at East High in Memphis were entirely in deficit. There was juggling and magic enough to win the school talent contest. I discovered cameras and became photographer for the annual. Employment at a movie theater and a camera store dispensed knowledge from both sides of the lens, and my friends and I wrote, filmed and acted in numerous, no-budget eight-millimeter spectaculars. My dream was still at the forefront. But my parents were perceptive enough to realize that those years in high school weren't, for the most part, terrific. I was out of the mainstream. And I had done very little to change the way things were because courage was not my strong suit. Not even close.

They could see all that, those cruel, hard-headed, unyielding parents of mine. And they felt I could use a confidence builder, another fifth grade experience. An even start, in an arena not quite as intimidating as Los Angeles and UCLA. At the time, Ole Miss had, on campus, just under 3,000 students. Oxford, Mississippi had a population of 4,500.

Their proposition was: "Go to Ole Miss for two years, then, if you want to transfer to UCLA, we'll try to work it out."

"Two years," my Dad said. "Do it for us."

My dream was slipping away. I was convinced that the old show business stigma was at fault. What my parents wanted, I was certain, was to steer me away from movie making into a legitimate profession. I had no concept of what they were really trying to do and I was fraught with wonder about what was to become of me over the next two years. What manner of skullduggery did they have up their unified sleeve to keep their only son from embarrassing the entire family tree.

I sighed heavily and shrugged. "It's your money."

Then I strolled nonchalantly off to my closet.

The dried mud caked on the shoes wedged beside me was from the creek bed, east of town where four friends and I had filmed what was to be our last eight-millimeter epic. I broke off a

clump and crumbled it between my fingers. I had wanted the film
to be so good and it had turned out so bad. There was so much to
learn, and now there was nowhere to learn it. At least for two years.
Of course, what I was really afraid of was me. Was my desire for a
career making family films strong enough to survive two years
without nourishment? What if I got caught up in the mean-aver-
age-norm and wound up a banker, or an engineer?

It was a revolting thought, yet there was something disturb-
ingly warm and comfortable about it. Lack of risk, I supposed,
which comes back to courage. I wondered how many of life's decisions would be made for that reason. Not many, I hoped. It didn't
taste good.

I broke off another clump of mud, tossed it across the closet
into a trash can and, with that gesture, bid filmmaking adieu.

Little did any of us know that the decisions made on that cold,
cloudy January afternoon would insure the very dream I thought I
was losing.

***

I strolled out of the dorm into another magnificent Mississippi
springtime, my second at Ole Miss. The redbuds and dogwoods
were bursting forth with color, the air was scented with jonquils
and jasmine, and I was having the time of my life. Back again,
firmly entrenched, just under the crest of the wave, I was right in
the middle of everything that was happening and everything that
seemed important.

The luck of the draw my freshman year had bestowed upon
me a roommate predestined to be a ranking man about campus. A
word from him and I was asked to pledge one of the best fraterni-
ties; I helped direct his successful campaign for freshman cheerleader, later varsity cheerleader, and I was his co-chairman on the

school spirit committee during the pinnacle years of Ole Miss' football fame. The mass of waving flags still seen today in the student cheering section began under our regime, Roy's and mine.

I was making up for lost time, quietly happy that my parents had talked me into Ole Miss. Concern about the future had given way to present delight. The business school was good and I was generally pointed toward an advertising major, only because it seemed the least innocuous of the available options. Any thoughts about moviemaking had been properly tucked away in the fantasy lobe of my brain. Real people don't make movies, they go into business, or become engineers or physicists or whatever. How else can one be considered sane and stable in the eyes of one's peers? That was important back then.

At least it was until MGM came to town.

Overnight, with no advance notice, while I was dreaming up strategy for the upcoming elections and planning fraternity beach parties at Sardis Lake, a bona fide, big-time Hollywood production dropped right into my lap. Old symptoms sprang from their dusty hideaways. My heart began to race and my breathing became erratic. Robert Mitchum, George Hamilton, George Peppard, Eleanor Parker, Luana Patten—the Luana Patten from Song of the South—Vincente Minnelli, Denver Pyle, Dub Taylor, Everette Sloan, Yvette Mimieux, a huge crew, trucks, lights and cameras, all descended upon Oxford, Mississippi to shoot a motion picture entitled Home from the Hill.

Because someone at MGM had decided that a Mississippi town looked more like a Texas town than any town in Texas, all order suddenly sputtered and spewed out of my life.

Old passions came clawing to the surface. I had never been on a real movie set. Never even close, even though we had lived in Los Angeles for almost six months when I was a kid.

I was ten years old at the time, and the move from Little

Rock, Arkansas was the single most exciting thing that had ever happened to me. I was absolutely certain I was on the way to fame and fortune. My Dad had been transferred on three previous occasions during my young life, but this was the one that counted. This one was going to land me right in the middle of a glamorous, Hollywood movie studio.

Slight miscalculation.

It landed me right in the middle of El Segundo, about as far west as you can get in Los Angeles without falling into the ocean. On the weekends, we often visited friends in Westwood and I remember whiling away the hours wandering around the edges of the UCLA campus, entranced with its size and beauty, wondering if maybe that's where I might go to college.

Dad's route from El Segundo to Westwood would take us through Culver City, by one of the MGM back lots. It was really just a big, open field with nothing whatsoever on it except a huge— I mean gigantic—rotting billboard picturing a fading assortment of old buildings. It turned out to be a backdrop painting of Atlanta used during the filming of Gone With The Wind. I was obviously impressed because my friends heard about it for years, but that was as close as I ever came to a movie set.

I did manage to see a few stars up close in the Hollywood Santa Claus Parade and even spoke to Dale Evans and touched her horse. But the biggest thrill came after the El Segundo Centennial Parade when Spade Cooley, astride a beautiful chestnut stallion, took a short cut through our backyard and paused long enough for his horse to poop right next to my swing set. I roped it off and charged admission for weeks.

Who is Spade Cooley?

It doesn't matter. It was the close personal contact that was important, not the size of his name.

We left Los Angeles on a cold New Year's day in 1949, after standing for hours in an unusually icy wind watching the Rose Parade. We had assumed we were going to be in California for the rest of our lives. It was Dad's last planned transfer, so there was no hurry. There would be time to do everything we wanted to do. Then an offer came from another company, a terrific offer Dad couldn't turn down. I was called into a family conference and asked if I would be willing to trade Los Angeles for Jackson, Mississippi.

"Jackson, Mississippi??"

I choked. "Sure, whatever." I forced a smile, and headed for the nearest closet.

After the parade, a huge lump formed in my throat as we climbed into our '47 Nash sedan, packed to overflowing for the trip east. It was the first time I could remember being really sad about leaving a place. Later that day, a violent snowstorm smacked into us as we crossed the border into Arizona and it stayed with us all the way to Pecos, Texas. The excitement helped me forget what I was leaving behind. But not the dreams. I was certain I would be back.

Now, more than a decade later, Hollywood was coming to me.

Not, unfortunately, to me personally, but MGM's arrival in Oxford, a mere two months from the end of my second collegiate year, was clearly a sign laden with hidden meaning. And I was there, front and center, the night filming began. It was the first of two planned nights on the Oxford town square, filming in a corner drugstore and around the obligatory Confederate soldier who was perched high atop his stone column on the south side of the courthouse, his back disdainfully turned to the north. That first night's filming was scheduled from 6:00 p.m. until 6:00 a.m. And they needed extras!

I did everything but jump into the assistant director's lap but he managed to ignore me completely. Still I stayed into the wee hours, trying to catch a glimpse of the director at work. I'm sure any Hollywood director would have been impressive, but this wasn't just any Hollywood director. This was Vincente Minnelli.

The same Vincente Minnelli who, only three days before, had accepted an Academy Award for his direction of Gigi. The same Vincente Minnelli who had directed Zigfield Follies, Father of the Bride, On a Clear Day You Can See Forever, and was nominated for An American in Paris!

And, yes, the same Vincente Minnelli who had been married to Judy Garland and was father of a pert little thirteen-year-old daughter named Liza, with a z.

Across the square, on the courthouse lawn, several of Hollywood's finest character actors sat around the base of the Confederate monument in dusty jeans and sweat-stained cowboy hats. They whittled away at sticks of wood and gossiped with one another about the goings-on in town. That was the scene. Denver Pyle and Dub Taylor (both featured in at least half the westerns ever made) were among the group. But they were so far away, I could hear nothing and see very little of what was happening. But I took careful note of how they were dressed.

I spent much of the next day grubbing up a pair of jeans and scavenging a beat-up western hat and a pair of boots from friends around town. I also found out as much as I could about the story and the planned sequence of shooting. That night the day's work paid off. I was selected as an extra.

I had been told that most of the filming was to be inside the drugstore, so, of course, that's where I wanted to be. It was a tiny little cubicle and Vincente Minnelli would be in there directing. I could watch his every movement and hear his every word.

When the assistant director first pointed at me, my heart leaped into my throat, but I stepped ever so casually out of the crowd and maneuvered myself into the interior of the chosen group. That way, I figured, I would have time to determine whether they were first populating the inside of the drugstore or the sidewalks outside. Then I could jump to the front, or hide in the back, accordingly.

Naturally, I was the first one selected. Must've been the outfit. So why did they send me so far off down the street to be a mere passerby? An outside passerby.

The second assistant director scattered us along the sidewalk west of the drugstore while the first assistant worked inside. "Terrific outfit," the second assistant said to me. "We've had trouble finding enough western hats in town."

He lifted mine from my head. "That's a nice one. Looks like a Stetson." His face went blank when he saw it was a Davis. The inscription on the band read: Cotton Bowl - Ole Miss vs TCU. I had borrowed it from Claire Smith, the Athletic Director's daughter.

"Any more of these around?!" he asked.

"Probably not," I replied. "Too long ago."

He plopped it back on my head and grumbled, "Someone should've thought of hats when they decided not to shoot in Texas." Then he wandered off up the street.

At the time, the only important thing was that a rapport had been established, if not with me, at least with my hat. To somebody in an official capacity, I was no longer just one of the crowd. That would surely prove valuable in the days to come.

For the moment, however, I was still outside the drugstore and most of the work would be going on inside. A chill fluttered into a shiver as I tried to focus on the problem. What I was contemplating was heady stuff for one so timid. I had been told to walk up the sidewalk and turn the corner at the drugstore. The girl walking with me was to wave goodbye and cross the street. A half block after my turn, well out of camera range, I was supposed to stop and listen for "Cut", then hurry back to my original position and prepare for another take.

On the first full rehearsal, we walked up the street, waved goodbye, and I turned the corner. But I didn't continue on down the sidewalk. I strolled casually into the drugstore where four of the stars were in conversation at the soda fountain. My heart was pounding and I think my breathing had stopped altogether. I paused at a counter right behind the four actors and fiddled with some ladies' cosmetics. No one seemed to notice. Outside, the second assistant was probably having cardiac arrest, but inside, everyone was calm except Mr. Minnelli. Apparently he was getting less than he wanted from one of the young stars at the counter. I was reasonably sure the second assistant had his hands full outside and I hoped to get to the first assistant to confirm that he liked my action before the second got to him and kicked me, and Claire's hat, right off the set.

As the scene ended, I tensed for the attack, but Minnelli snared his assistant and spent several agonizing minutes going over things he wanted done. I kept peering over my shoulder, expecting any moment to be yanked back out onto the sidewalk, tied to the confederate monument and lashed with a whip. Then suddenly I realized that the first assistant and Mr. Minnelli were looking at me. Minnelli was gesturing toward the door.

I could imagine what he was saying. "Where did that idiot come from?!" I started to turn and run. Minnelli went back to his actors and the A.D. stalked toward me, taking long deliberate strides, each one filled with importance and meaning. I replaced the mascara stick in its rack and turned to face him. Doom was upon me.

"Mr. Minnelli would like for you to already be inside when the scene starts. But not here at the cosmetics. It's not that kind of picture. Here, by the film. There'll be a sales clerk with you and you'll pretend to be discussing a purchase."

I tried to hide my gasp of ecstasy. For a brief moment, I felt lightheaded and heard only part of what he said next, something about my hat, then he hurried off to other business.

The two nights scheduled for shooting on the square turned into a full week, most of it in the drugstore, and I spent many luxurious hours watching Vincente Minnelli fret and frustrate, coax and cajole, and sometimes explode all over the foursome at the soda fountain. He would shoot take after painstaking take, sometimes into the twenties and thirties, in an effort to extract the performance he wanted from each actor. In the process, unfortunately, I think he also set up a subconscious pattern that ruined me for life; a seeming obsessive drive to use as much film as is humanly possible; to never stop with take six when take seven might be better. I call it pari-mutuel moviemaking. If you go to the window enough times, you're bound to hit a winner somewhere in the bunch.

Insecurity wasn't Vincente Minnelli's problem, however. Two of the four young people he was directing in this scene had practically no experience at all. The one he was spending the most time with was Yvette Mimieux, a rank beginner. She had been signed to a studio contract right out of college and this was her first movie. I was concerned, on more than one occasion, that it might be her last.

George Hamilton was twenty and this was his second picture, but I don't imagine his first really prepared him for the likes of Minnelli. It was a low-budget, experimental re-make of Dostoevski's Crime and Punishment. George Peppard had only made two movies but he was older at thirty, and had spent several years on Broadway.

The seasoned veteran of the group was Luana Patten. At

twenty, she was going into her thirteenth year of acting in movies, having made her screen debut when she was eight. I think she cornered even more gawks around town than Robert Mitchum because she was exquisitely beautiful; and once again, I was helplessly infatuated. Both with the lady and the knowledge that this was the same face I had been so in love with when I was eight years old watching her in Song of the South.

Seeing her here, now, up close; being able to talk with her, however ineptly, rekindled the happy tears of those first movies and flooded my memory with so many movies that had stirred my emotions. So many times I had wished upon Mr. Disney's star that I could be the one who so instinctively understood the needs, the positive needs, of this thing called human emotion. To be able to cause someone to feel as good as I felt leaving so many of those films, had to be the greatest feeling in the world.

Working from dusk till dawn sometimes made it difficult to stay alert, but I tried to soak up as much of Mr. Minnelli as I could and, as the nights wore on, I even began to experience some of his frustrations, imagining myself in his shoes, pacing, pointing, dueling, directing. He was concentrating so on his actors that he probably didn't notice, but one of the extras had been instructed to climb off a stool at the soda fountain, leave some money on the counter and exit the drugstore. It was easily the worst piece of acting I had ever seen and I'll never forget how badly I wanted to leap across the drugstore and show him how to do it.

His place at the counter was right next to one of the actors, very prominent on camera. In the middle of the scene he would get up, reach into his pocket and without ever looking at the money he withdrew, slam it down on the counter and walk out.

At least glance at it, I thought. Count it out. Something!

I don't know why this particular incident has stuck with me so, and remained so vivid, but it was a precursor of things to come. I am, today, a compulsive perfectionist, probably to a fault. But I wasn't aware of it then. At least not until then. And I can see, looking back, that this was the beginning of a period when things began to change. For the next couple of years, priorities toppled with escalating speed. And for the first time in my life, deplorably late I'm afraid, I was beginning to see the value of learning. What it can do for you, where it can take you, the horizons it can expand. The most powerful catalyst was yet to come, but I was now, at last, an eager prospect.

Robert Mitchum wasn't scheduled for any of the drugstore scenes but, occasionally, out of boredom I suspect, he would saunter in and entertain the troops with his sarcasm and bawdy one-liners. He was only forty-two at the time but Home from the Hill was his sixty-second motion picture! And his affection for alcohol was already well established. He had driven down from Memphis, according to the campus newspaper, in a rented car with a built-in bar. I always wondered who at the campus newspaper had been in his car, and why. During those long nights, he would slide in, survey the campus lovelies arranged around tables at the rear of the drugstore—Ole Miss had more than its share of beautiful young ladies in those days, fielding two Miss Americas in as many years—then he'd move right in and sit across from his selection, shooing others away if necessary. Anyone who interrupted usually received an x-rated jab to the eardrum. That sort of response was also the price for an autograph. One had to be something of a masochist to ask because he would invariably bitch like a banshee as he scribbled his name.

The company always broke to feed the cast and crew around midnight, which we thought was a pretty terrific gesture of goodwill until we learned it was required by the union. One night an elderly lady walked up to our table and asked where Mr. Mitchum was sitting. I tried to explain to her that it might be in her best interest not to bother him while he was eating, but she promptly told me to answer her question and keep my opinions to myself, which I promptly did.

The entire table watched in anticipated horror as this nice little old lady tottered across the restaurant toward the shock of her life. Whispers danced from one table to the next and, as she reached out and tapped this most scurrilous of the visiting movie stars on the shoulder, a hush settled across the room. He turned, listened, glanced at the floor for just the right length of time, then stood up smiling, took off his hat and was nothing short of the perfect gentleman, signing the lady's autograph and even thanking her for asking.

You could've heard a pin drop as she walked away. The entire room was in shock. Mitchum took his seat, making no attempt to hide the devilish smile that curled up in one corner of his mouth. He knew exactly what he had accomplished. And he was so good at it, I had to laugh. He owned the room, lock stock and barrel. He was the star. And no one in Grundy's Restaurant that midnight would ever doubt it.

Later that morning, he would prove it again. His first scene was to be shot just outside the drugstore. A long one, with no coverage. It all had to work in one shot. He was to drive his car across the square, park in front of the drugstore, swagger over to the Confederate monument—Robert Mitchum, like John Wayne, never merely walked—and have a conversation with Denver Pyle, Dub Taylor and the boys who were still jawin' and whittlin'. He would ask if anyone knew where his boy (George Hamilton) was, there would be a full page of dialog on the subject, then the entire group would pile into Denver's pickup and drive off.

After spending a week watching Vincente Minnelli shoot take after take of basically simple little shots with the group in the drugstore, I decided there was not enough time on the calendar, nor money in Hollywood, to ever get this one to the director's satisfaction.

They got it on take two!

It would've been take one had the clock in the courthouse tower not gonged the hour right in the middle of the dialog.

These were old line professionals at work and they were incredible to watch. The scene was alive from the roll of the camera, and purely electric from the moment Mitchum stepped out of his car.

Because it went so quickly, we got off too early that morning for our usual trek to the Mansion Restaurant. I don't remember how it got started, or why I was brought into the fold, but throughout the week, after wrap each morning, Denver and several of the character actors around the monument would traipse off to eat steak and eggs, and they would always ask a couple of us locals to join them.

At first, it was embarrassing because steak is something we rarely saw during school years, certainly never for breakfast. "Everybody eats steak for breakfast in Hollywood," one of the actors prodded. So, we all ate steak. Who, after all, could resist eating a real Hollywood breakfast with real Hollywood actors and hearing all those real Hollywood stories? Six mornings in a row!

I was being paid ten dollars a night for being an extra, reduced, after deductions, to something like eight dollars and fifty cents. As I remember it, that barely covered the steak and eggs each morning, if you didn't count the tip.

I imagine Denver and the boys had a good laugh with such stories when they returned to Hollywood. The offset came sixteen years later, when I was preparing a motion picture comedy about camels in the pre-Civil War cavalry. We wanted Denver for a prominent roll and he was kind enough to come in and read for the part—many stars and well-known character actors won't do that after reaching a certain point in their careers. As he walked into the room, I sprang out of my seat, hurried over to him, and reached for his hand.

"Great to see you again!" I exclaimed. I turned to Ben Vaughn, our co-producer. "Denver and I ate many a breakfast together a few years back."

His smile sputtered and his eyes went blank. He hadn't the vaguest idea what I was talking about. Of course I didn't really expect him to. I would've been surprised if he'd remembered, but I couldn't resist letting him struggle with it for a while.

He made no attempt to fake it and, finally, when I let him off the hook, he shook his head and said, "I remember the picture, but I'm sorry, I don't remember you at all. Are you sure it was me you ate breakfast with?"

With a smashing blow to the chops he had won the last round. I must've looked devastated because he only let me dangle for a moment before saying, "Unless, of course, you were that strange, skinny kid with the cowboy hat from the Cotton Bowl."

He was terrific in our picture, and for the second time, a delight to be around.

All in all, I think that week of seemingly endless nights as an extra in the drugstore cost me at least ten dollars. But I suppose I would've paid much more. It was, after all, part of my education.

The more formal part, meanwhile, suffered serious setbacks during those seven days, but only Political Science never fully recovered. It was a delicate balancing act, trying to do justice to why I was there, in school, and still spend as much time as possible on the set.

The filming continued around town for almost four weeks. Then one day they were gone, as clean as if they had never come, leaving virtually nothing behind except a hollow, empty feeling in the pit of my stomach. And, of course, sorority row's collection of bawdy Robert Mitchum autographs.

When Home from the Hill finally came out, almost a year later, the drugstore scene had been cut from the film and left, in its entirety, on the editing room floor. I never forgave Yvette Mimieux for that. Yvette had been cleverly and completely eliminated from the picture. Gone. Poof! As if her part had never even been written. And she took my big scene with her!

I couldn't help thinking about the cost, and the time and effort that went into that week of nights in the drugstore. Plus her other scenes!

The amazing thing was that none of them were missed. So why, I wondered, couldn't that decision have been made before all the expense and effort?

I never found out why she was cut. A few months before the film was released, she was named "Deb Star of the Year" on a television special and I wondered if the studio felt that her part in Home from the Hill was too embarrassingly small after the deb star treatment. Or if Vincente Minnelli just didn't like her performance.

Or maybe, I speculated, Yvette's and my screen debut had been cut because of the atrocious performance of that kid at the soda fountain who had slammed his money on to the counter without looking at it.

I knew I should've said something.

There were campus elections to keep me busy, and fraternity parties, and soon, final exams. But the events of those weeks when MGM was in town wouldn't shake loose. They were tasty memories that stirred the adrenaline whenever they surfaced.
I wondered why. Maybe it was chemical. Something in my biogenetic construction. So many other people had been totally unimpressed with the fact that a movie company was in town. My

roommate was one. He thought I was nuts. I don't believe he once left campus to see what was going on. And Carolyn was always as blasé about the business as if she were making her living as a grocery clerk. But I still gawk at movie stars. My heart still races when I walk on to a set. And whenever I see a motion picture that moves me, I still can't stop with the simplicity of enchantment, I am compelled to reach further, for the exhilaration that creation for others can, itself, create.

Joe Camp, certified loony.

No contest.

The highs come from strange, yet wonderful places.

Can anyone watch Doctor Zhivago without being moved? Not many, I suspect, which is probably why blank faces grasping for some thread of understanding of just what in God's name it is I'm trying to communicate, usually come tumbling into the fold when I talk about the rush that engulfed me the night I spent 176 minutes in a Montreal screening room... watching Doctor Zhivago... sitting next to Omar Sharif.

I blinked at the stained, once creamy enamel that was still trying, in vain, to cover the ceiling plaster of the dorm room. Thoughts were exploding in my head like fireworks, rapid-fire and random, careening off the stained, once creamy plaster walls and racing back to smack me in the face. Anxiety and impatience were writhing and kicking away at comfort and security. At Ole Miss, I kept telling myself, I was content, happy, a part of whatever somebody, somewhere, sometime ago said was important. At worst, I was a moderate-sized fish in a small campus pond, probably well on my way to becoming part of the Mississippi establishment. But none of it made my heart race, nor made me feel so alive and eager as what I had just been through.

And none of it scared me quite so much either.

I rolled over on my side. The gray metal desk, chafed and scarred from years of sophomoric abuse, seemed to shudder under the weight of homework undone. It would have to wait. This was an important decision, maybe the most important I would ever make.

What if it's only infatuation, I thought to myself. Intimacy with a recent memory, like a summer romance that seems real for a moment, then is quickly forgotten. I drifted back eleven years, to a garage in Little Rock, Arkansas. I was standing on a platform that had been painstakingly constructed by nine-year-old labor. It was flanked by beautiful chenille bedspreads strung on ropes and wires so they would open and close like curtains on a stage. Above was a maze of spaghetti, intricately rigged so one person could draw both bedspreads from a single spot, essential because it was a one-kid show.

I'll never forget how crushed I was when some of the neighbors who bought tickets didn't show up for the performance. I'm sure they meant well. A dime of encouragement for that cute little kid down the street. But it wasn't their money I wanted as much as their presence in the audience on show night; a characteristic that Carolyn always said, with chagrin, didn't change much over the years.

In Jackson, my Dad and I had once spent weeks building a functioning miniature stage. It took up more room than a good-sized desk. He thought it was terrific, at first, but with each succeeding house move, it seemed to become less and less wonderful. It was an intricate configuration of curtains, teasers, tormentors, light battens, tiny floodlights, spotlights, colored lights, flying backdrops and a host of little plastic people who participated in Christmas pageants, big band tours, and Shakespearean plays.

Big B Productions was the official name for the group of friends I put together in high school to challenge Hollywood's moviemaking prowess. I don't remember why the letter "B" was in the name, but I like to think I was being prescient. With Buddy Scott as co-producer, we made five films, the longest running on for almost fifteen minutes. These were days before videotape, or even magnetic striping on eight-millimeter film, so most of our movies were silent, with sub-titles. Our only sound epic had to be recorded separately on a tape recorder, which, of course, never ran in sync with the projector. Strangely, my clearest, most vivid memories do not come from writing, directing, photographing, or editing each production, but from sitting for hours dipping loops of film into some foul-smelling black liquid to create fade-outs and fade-ins between scenes.

Then there was magic. I had studied and performed from the time I was eleven right up until the day all six of my white doves decided, en masse, they were quite tired of sitting on a magic wand thank you and went on a rampage through the house, leaving feathers and droppings on every item of furniture and decor that my Mother considered priceless.

No, I concluded, I think I'm hooked. These memories do not have the feel of a flimsy summer romance.

I rolled over on my back and gazed up again at the chipped and stained dormitory ceiling. The conclusion held little comfort for my natural instinct to cluster with the known. I was not programmed to go off alone, to follow an individual course, to abandon the natural inclination to be one of the pack.

Here we are back again at courage.

It seems I've spent a great deal of my life at that particular precipice; being pulled and torn by opposing forces. Fear and intellect saying be careful, be sane, be one of the group. Stick with something sure, where you'll be judged by what you already know, not what you have yet to learn. Countered by the passion to strike out alone, to create and see the results of creation in the faces of an audience, to feel it in their hearts. To take full responsibility for the work created and have such direct contact with its effect that there can never be any doubt about how it's going; because it's there to see, and feel, and measure.

Then I remembered my Dad's advice when I had asked how in the world I was supposed to choose a career. "Do what you would do if you didn't have to make any money at it whatsoever," he had said.

I rolled out of bed, dropped into the gray metal chair at the gray metal desk, picked up a pen and began to write.

"Dear UCLA..."

***

It was a large room, as hotel rooms go, on a corner, with huge oversized windows, but they didn't help. It was still dark and depressing, an ancient molding memory of a more glamorous day. For a night, maybe two, it might've been a passable place to stay, but it had been my home now for almost seven weeks.

Outside, daylight was evaporating into dusk and the windows were all open to the fresh air and the noises of the city. It was an ineffectual effort to conquer the odor of the room. Not so much an odor, I suppose, as a dankness, inbred for almost half a century, a living part of the room's very fiber.

This was the summer after my sophomore year, my summer in Dayton, Ohio. I was working for Proctor and Gamble on a field advertising crew, their corporate label for a group that tramples through residential neighborhoods passing out free samples of whatever product they happen to be testing at the moment. This particular summer, it was Mr. Clean, a liquid household detergent. Each of us would begin with a case of 32 six-ounce glass bottles—heavy glass bottles—and trudge through a neighborhood placing the bottles in plastic sacks along with a handful of coupons, then hanging the sacks on the front doorknobs of every house on the street.

Early on, we found that a coupon thief was following us around, stealing the coupons out of the sacks, so company order was to ring the doorbell and personally hand the sack to whoever answered. If no one came to the door, we were to remove the coupons from the sack, press a foot against the bottom corner of the door, forcing it open just enough to slide the coupons between the door and the weather-stripping. Invariably, every time I attempted this, an incredulous homeowner would appear out of nowhere to find me wrestling with their door, obviously trying to break into their home.

This was my introduction to advertising and whereas an instinctive desire to stay out of jail did improve my communication skills, it was clearly not the kind of job my Dad had advised me to find. In fact, it made me wonder if I should keep his advice under wraps. Such a philosophy could cause the demise of Proctor & Gamble's entire Field Advertising Department.

The phone rang. It was one of the guys on the crew recruiting bodies to go hear Kai Winding blow some jazz. "I'm really tired," I lied. "Thanks anyway." I hung up the phone and glanced across the room at the unopened envelope propped against the gallon-sized peanut butter jar on the dresser.

Get it over with, I thought.

I climbed off the bed and walked over to the dresser, spread some peanut butter onto a piece of stale bread, then picked up the envelope and held it up to the window. It had arrived that afternoon with a batch of other mail from my folks. A mere glance at the return address stirred the butterflies in my stomach. Office of Admissions, University of California at Los Angeles.

I propped it back against the jar, twisting it just enough to catch the waning light from outside. I wasn't ready yet. These things take time.

It was a strange feeling. I knew why I didn't want to open it. I was no longer sure what I wanted it to say. And until I was sure what I wanted it to say, I couldn't possibly know how to react. Should I be elated or disappointed? I needed to know.

Here, alone, in a graying, dismal hotel room, further away from home—and further north—than I had ever been before, I was, at last, at the moment of truth. Which road would I follow? Which road did I want to follow? My emotions and intellect were flip-flopping, trading places at random.

I was on my own for the first time in my life. Really on my own, away from family, friends and familiar situations. The first time, I suppose, without someone close by I could lean on. Most of the guys on the crew were good people to work with, but I couldn't call one of them a close friend. The boss was the only college graduate and he was older, with his feet firmly planted on the first rung of the corporate ladder. For me, this was experience. More education. For everyone else, it was a living. I was getting by, but I didn't much care for it. It was a lonely summer. With very little to look forward to but September.

I longed for the comfort of campus life at Ole Miss. But I chastised myself for the feeling, and wondered if this had been my parents' plan all along. Get him comfortable and let nature take its course. It was hard to decipher because they had never really discouraged my drive to entertain. In fact, for the most part, they had encouraged it. Their son, the magician, was on display whenever there was a gathering of friends or business associates. I was hired to perform at club functions and formal parties. And they would beam with pride whenever I would amaze their crowd with a minor miracle.

I never stopped to ponder what all of that meant. I just gobbled it up, loving each and every minute of it.

And that, of course, was an important clue. But not a new one. Throughout my life there had been that passion to entertain, to be loved by many, found, without exception, within every person I've ever met who is in this business by choice. It had always been there; on that makeshift stage in the garage at nine, playing the saxophone at eleven, doing magic, making movies and producing miniature extravaganzas with little plastic people. Yet, until recently, I had never noticed the pattern, or at least, hadn't recognized it. But surely my parents had.

If so, I don't think they ever accepted it beyond avocation. Entertaining is okay for a nice hobby but, of course, a career is a serious matter. One must think of security, advancement and such. That's the way they were brought up, and the way they lived. That's what they knew, and how they felt. High-risk was not part of their vocabulary. They didn't have these crazy drives, so comfort and safety was a good solution for them.

Inexplicably, it was not totally without appeal for me, or at least for part of me. That's the funny thing about most of us crazies who wind up in this business. We desire the attention, the focus of the masses, the opportunity to entertain, and at the same time, we're scared to death of it. We're afraid to reach for it because to reach is, per chance, to fail. And for me to transfer to UCLA meant reaching for a goal where failure is the norm, not the exception.

I wondered if UCLA would be as lonely as working in Dayton.

The view would be better, I thought, remembering those days as a child when I walked the edges of the campus in Westwood.

But I'd be starting in the middle again. Like junior high in Memphis. An outsider trying to nuzzle into pre-formed clusters.

Good grief, Joe! Grow up! I thought.

I reached for the envelope.

Wait a minute. What about Carolyn?

The envelope slid through my fingers and clunked onto the dresser.

The day before I left Memphis to fly to Dayton, a few of the guys and I were searching for a way to celebrate my departure. Mother commented that she had seen an article in the paper about a sorority from Ole Miss that was in town for a meeting of some kind. There was no further discussion. We piled into the car and made immediate haste to the appropriate Holiday Inn. To discover so large a group of unescorted ladies had to be a sure way to begin a terrific evening.

It was indeed. In fact, it turned out to be a sure way to begin a lifetime. We tromped through the Holiday Inn courtyard out to the pool and I quickly scanned the marvelous group of young ladies before us for the best-looking familiar face. It belonged to Carolyn Hopkins. We had exchanged occasional "hellos" around campus, but that was about all we knew of one another. I descended quickly and encircled her with barbed wire. She produced dates for those who didn't find something to their liking around the pool and the entire group—I think we filled three cars—embarked upon a night that can only be described as the one to remember.

I don't know exactly when it happened because it wasn't a textbook case; you know, the moment she walked into the room I knew kind of thing; love at first sight, and all that. In fact, it wasn't the least bit like I expected it would be. No crash, bang, smash! It was slow, and sneaky. I left the Holiday Inn in the early evening with a girl I barely knew and returned some twelve hours later with someone I felt I had known forever, someone for whom I felt very deep, rich affection.

And then I left for Dayton.

Letters flew back and forth that summer like machinegun fire, but none of them said very much. We fenced and danced around our feelings, I suppose, because distance made the magic of our one evening together seem fragile, more illusory than real, like a bubble that might burst at any moment. Neither of us would declare what we thought we felt for the other, but it was clear that we both wanted more time together. If I transferred to UCLA, we might never have it.

I licked the peanut butter from my fingers and walked to the window. The garish flashing neon of downtown Dayton had vanquished the gray calm of dusk. This is stupid, I thought. What ever happened to black and white?! It was the first time I had ever suspected that absolutes don't really exist. I suppose because it was the first time I had faced a major fork in the road with such strong feelings about both sides. There wasn't a clear-cut answer and I suspected this was the way it was going to be from now on. For every black there would be a white, for every pro a con, for every if a but, for every maybe a maybe not; creating tapestry after tapestry of muddled shades of gray. There must be an easier way to deal with it all than wallowing around in confusion, being pulled and torn first one way, then another.

I glanced across the room at the pieces of a jigsaw puzzle spread out on the coffee table. I hadn't worked on it for days. It had sort of become part of the decor, like when you know something's there but you don't really see it. The room was dark, the walls blinking red and green reflections of the neon signs outside, yet the puzzle seemed somehow different, distinct, each piece clear and well-defined. And quite suddenly I knew.

Jigsaw puzzles are solved by the process of elimination. Spread the conflicts of a problem out onto a table, like the pieces of a puzzle, and the same philosophy could apply. Approach each disparity one at a time and assess it, exactly as you would a piece of the puzzle. Weigh one against the other, eliminating those that don't fit, that don't measure up, until only the priority is left, standing alone, as the only piece that fits. A simple sorting through the issues to get to the bottom line. Then putting aside the other issues, not to waver in pursuit of the priority until the goal is achieved or is confronted with new and different issues.

Insight! Another first. I felt like I had crossed some sort of threshold. It seemed a stupidly simple but perfectly logical way to approach life's problems, to find solutions, to make decisions. The discovery of that evening is burned indelibly into my memory and I still use it every day. As a process, it has never failed to work. Break a problem down to it's smallest components then start the reconstruction, the process of elimination. More often than not, when you're looking for those pieces that fit, the solution steps up and reveals itself.

I turned and gazed back out the window at the kaleidoscope of blinking neon, trying to clear my mind. Which was more important, job security or passion? Would I do better at something I desperately wanted to do or something that provided me safety. The answer was obvious.

Which would better equip me to pursue my goal, the comfort of campus life at Ole Miss, or the education I could get at UCLA?

Again, no contest. Or so it seemed at the moment.

What about the school spirit committee? And the fraternity? I had been elected Social Chairman for next year. Were these priority pieces of the puzzle? I put them back in the box.

Friends? No, the real ones I'd never lose.

And Carolyn?

I took a deep breath.

If we were right for each other, we'd find a way. We only had one date, for God's sake. It would hardly be rational to toss away the career I wanted most because of one date.

I took another deep breath. The only piece remaining on the

table was pointing west. It made me feel good to know. I reached for the envelope and ripped it open.

The letter began, "We are sorry to inform you..."

That moment, looking back, was one of the two most devastating times in my life, before Carolyn died. But it had to happen exactly the way it did or you would've never heard of Benji, and I wouldn't be writing this book.

Look fool, God was saying, *there are a lot of things you need, but an education in film is not one of them! Among other things, you need to know how to advertise and sell!*

That's not even close to the message I thought I was receiving.

4

THE LEARNING CURVE

*"If a man empties his purse into his head,
no man can take it from him."*

Benjamin Franklin

Rejection is always painful, no matter from whence the source. It aches deep down in the soul. Even today, there's a particular icy, enigmatic January I retreat to whenever the chorus of negative voices gets too loud, when I begin to lose faith in myself, when the pressure begins to win. It's the flag I wave when I begin to believe, against all logic, that the naysayers might be right, that hope has vanished. Because during this particular January, I learned, for all its worth, that experienced, intelligent, successful people can be very, very wrong. It's a month I'll never fully understand, but have resolved to never forget. Within a matter of days, the original stockholders abandoned our fledgling Mulberry Square Productions and left it for dead, legally and finally... and Hollywood said a categorical *no* to *Benji*.

On that warm July evening in Dayton, Ohio, as I read the rejection letter from UCLA, I learned something important about myself. I discovered how very much I hate to lose. Especially when it's my fault; when the difference between winning and losing is completely within the limits of my control.

I suppose it's strange finding this out so late—I was twenty at the time—but I hadn't been in many competitive situations, or, at least, hadn't lost enough of them to know. Probably because I tended to avoid direct competition and seek out sparsely populated arenas in which to excel. I mean, how many magicians or jugglers do you have in your neighborhood?

This time, however, I had reached out, competing with thousands of other kids, and I had lost. And it burned like a hot poker in the pit of my stomach because there was no one to blame but me. I was rejected at UCLA because my grade average was three-tenths of a point under what they required for out-of-state transfers.

Somewhere it says that we reap what we sow. Surely this is one of the great truths of the universe. Very little of what we do doesn't come back to haunt or help us at one time or another, and one semester of spirited emphasis on play and late nights on a movie set had blown my chances at UCLA.

I was angry, but it was a productive mad because I resolved that it would never happen again. That I would never again, knowingly, undercut my potential. That whatever I was to do, I was going to do it as well as it could be done. I had emerged from the experience a different person and I was anxious to be on the attack.

A direct thrust into the study of motion picture was no longer a possibility so I stuck with what appeared to be the next best thing: advertising, reasoning that I might be able to work my way into the production of television commercials someday, and from there, who knows? Two years later I finished with a straight *A* average in my major, one straight *A* semester, three semesters on the honor roll, two on the Dean's list, a beautiful wife and a baby on the way.

Carolyn and I were married in August after our junior year and, once again, it was totally different than I ever expected it would be. No rush and gush. We didn't go racing into each others' arms when I returned from Dayton. In fact, we pretty much ignored each other for the first few months. I really don't know why. I'm sure it was mostly my fault since boys still did the asking in those days but, gradually, in a manner I'd like to think was more meaningful than sudden rapture, we were slowly and inexplicably drawn back together. The relationship seemed to fuel solely upon itself and it grew so naturally that we didn't even recognize the existence of a relationship at first. So quietly and unobtrusively did it take hold that I was actually surprised to find myself realizing one Saturday afternoon that I didn't want to go out with anyone else. Carolyn was helping us decorate for a fraternity luau party to which, incidentally, I had invited one of her sorority sisters.

I watched her all afternoon, hanging flowers, clowning with the other guys and tried to convince myself that I should leave well enough alone. The compass heading I was rounding up to was full of dangerous and uncharted waters. So, of course, I promptly took her out and asked her to wear my fraternity pin.

She accepted, we kissed, then I felt obliged to tell her that I already had a date for the party. With Sylvia Fowler. Being the conscientious person that I was—conscientious, in this context, meaning cowardly—it would be unforgivable to break a date with Sylvia a mere two hours before I was to pick her up. Whatever were we to do? I supposed we could wait until tomorrow to get pinned. Unless, of course, Carolyn had an idea.

Sylvia was a freshman, Carolyn explained innocently, the corners of her delicious mouth wrinkling, almost imperceptibly, into a foxy little smile. A mere pledge. It was the calling of such lowly types to be ecstatic when informed that they had the rare opportunity to contribute to the happiness of an upper class member.

She straightened her sweater.

"Now get that pin off your shirt and put it where it belongs. I'll be ready at eight."

As I look back over the whys and wherefores of our success with Benji, one thing is undeniably clear. For everything to have happened the way it did, I *had* to go back to Ole Miss. For more reasons than marketing.

Carolyn was at the top of that list. She claimed direct responsibility for my academic improvement those last two years and, claimed or not, her impact on all that happened afterward was substantial and vital. Not the woman *behind* the man, but the marvelously bright and able woman *beside* the man.

Of course, there were pitfalls. In abundant supply. We often looked back to that day when we decided we were right for each other and wondered how we could've ever made such an obvious mistake; a natural result when two people work as closely together as we did. But the pluses always outweighed the minuses.

Against overwhelming odds. The fact is we were too much alike to have made the distance. We had too many problems. We worked too many hours together, we were constantly in each others' business and we were both as hard-headed as the quartet on Mount Rushmore.

Still, right up to Carolyn's unexpected death in December of 1997, we were desperately in love. Not that I always deserved it, but that's another book. Thank you so very much, God, for sending me back. I could never have made it without her.

***

"So, how good a writer are you?"

I wriggled uncomfortably in my chair and searched for an answer among the discord of ad reprints, sketches, tearsheets, copy scripts, snapshots and headlines cluttering the walls. Finally, I sighed and confessed, "I don't guess I'm a writer at all."

The speaker was Dolores Williams, a spunky, diminutive fireball of a lady, about fifty-eight, without a trace of gray in her hair, or her manner. She would flit, like a hummingbird, all over the room just to make a single point. She'd stand up, sit down, pound the desk, and then stalk off to a window only to turn abruptly at just the right moment to emphasize a word. Writing was like that to her. Each word, each phrase needed to be placed and constructed for emphasis and inflection. "Communication is not just to the intellect," she would preach. "To last, it must reach the emotion. It must wave its arms and pound the desk!" Then her face would drop and her eyes would soften and reach out as she whispered, "Or it must lure you into a quiet corner and speak softly."

In early Spring, well before graduation, I had written sixty-three letters to advertising agencies all over the country. Only twenty-eight had responded. Of those, ten offered interviews; one in Philadelphia, eight in New York, and the McCann-Erickson office in Houston. The eight in New York placed new college graduates in the mail room where they could expect to stay for at least a year, sometimes two or three. Four even required a master's degree for mail duty. Only two of the agencies interviewed had any kind of formal training program, one in Philadelphia, and the one I accepted in Houston.

"How do you know you aren't a writer?!" Dolores blared across the desk. "Have you ever written?"

If advertising was to be my stepping stone, this was the chance of a lifetime. The training program at the Houston office of McCann-Erickson took one college graduate every two years and placed the individual in each department of the agency for a period of time to determine for which type of work he or she was best suited. Dolores Williams' office was my first stop. She had a month to find out if I could write.

I had, of course, struggled through my share of themes and term papers. And, in college, there was a short-lived sports column for the campus newspaper. But I would never pretend that any of that was real *writing*.

"It doesn't matter," Dolores said. "Whether you can write or not, at this moment, is not the point. It's what you can do when I get through with you that counts."

I had never really considered writing; never thought much about it. A writer was some sort of mystical something-or-other who holed-up or hid out somewhere and magically translated thoughts, emotions and feelings into words in a form and manner that transcended the words themselves and became, once again, thoughts, emotions and feelings. The process was beyond mere mortals.

Thank goodness for Dolores Williams.

She exploded all the myths and showed me that writing is labor, not magic. And that if I worked at it hard enough, even I, on occasion, could put a few decent words together. She also taught me that the written word is where everything begins. Every advertisement, every radio commercial, every TV spot starts with the same blank piece of paper. Nothing happens until somebody writes something. "If you want to have any degree of control over the work you do, and thereby your destiny, learn to write," she preached. How right she was. I now preach the same thing to every young person I meet.

The first things I wrote for Dolores were better than I expected. Not good, she said, but not bad. It was mostly copy for ads selling the benefits of natural gas over electricity. She worked with me and taught me, virtually full-time for a month, then part-time when I moved on to other departments. She kept dragging me back. We would tear ideas apart, piece them back together, and, once again, rip them to shreds. She saw something in me that I didn't even see myself and she was determined to pull it out.

I hadn't been at the agency five months when she recommended that I be taken off the training program and placed into copy-contact work. I was delighted, but I still didn't consider myself a writer. I was a junior account executive, who also, almost parenthetically, did some writing.

It's strange. If you can fix a sink, you can call yourself a plumber. Pass the state CPA exam and you can call yourself a CPA. If you have a degree in physics, I suppose you can call yourself a physicist. But just putting words on paper doesn't make you *a writer*. There's an intangible qualitative element involved, but there's no set criterion upon which to judge it. Except, maybe, your own. And I have yet to live up to mine, so, even now, I'm hesitant to say, "Yes, I am a writer."

The introduction to business and marketing that I received at McCann-Erickson would one day prove to be a pivotal piece of the Benji puzzle. But no more so than Dolores Williams, who forced me to work with words and explore ideas. Had it not been for her, I might never have discovered writing at all.

Or the doors it could open.

Conversation had evaporated into the aroma of liver and onions that lay heavy over the room. We hadn't yet struck a common denominator. I couldn't think of a single thing to say, so I stuffed enough food in my mouth to eliminate the opportunity altogether. For several long minutes we just sat listening to each other chew.

"So," Erwin finally said, wiping an errant bit of Jello from his chin, "do you also write copy?"

"Some," I mumbled through a mouthful of loathsome calf's liver. "But what I'd really like to try sometime is a screenplay." As I listened to myself speak, I wondered where such nonsense was coming from. Motion picture dreams notwithstanding, I hadn't, in my entire life, given a second's thought to ever writing a screenplay. But suddenly it seemed so logical. And, certainly, it was the literary thing to say. I mean, no one writes advertising copy as an end in itself, but only as the means to an end. You know, a way to pay bills until the *serious* stuff starts selling.

Erwin swallowed. "I tried a short story once but everyone who read it threw up."

Perhaps they were eating calf's liver, I thought.

"Too much prose," Erwin chirped. "A screenplay would be more visual. Maybe we should take a crack at one together."

The thought stirred my adrenalin. It was a new slant on an old dream. A new challenge, but an old, familiar tingle of excitement that fired the blood and made it flow faster. A writer! I was already picturing myself in a belted, tweedy sports jacket, puffing a crooked pipe, ambling thoughtfully through the brilliant autumn colors of a peaceful New England wood. And what was it Delores Williams had taught me? Without a script, nothing gets produced. And the person with the script, the *good* script, can usually wrestle the control, if he or she wants it.

"Let's do it," I said. "Let's write a screenplay."

Harland thought we were nuts.

Erwin and Harland were free-lance commercial artists, sharing a studio that was, for all practical purposes, the art department of the advertising agency I had gone to work for in Dallas.

The prickling excitement of those first days at McCann-Erickson had dissipated with the merger of Standard Oil of New Jersey into Humble Oil, the agency's largest client. We had moved from a picturesque, tree-shaded old house on Lovett Boulevard to the twenty-second floor of the Exxon building in downtown Houston. The move was accompanied by planeloads of employees from New York and a new highly structured pecking order that put an end to any hopes of sliding sideways into the television commercial production department.

The agency in Dallas was smaller, more like the original McCann. And the city had a rapidly growing commercial production industry.

My first day on the new job, Erwin and Harland had invited me to join them for lunch in the basement cafeteria of the Dallas Federal Savings Building. It was a small, no-frills lunchroom for tenants only, cold and austere. It reminded me of several school cafeterias I had known in the past, but it soon became our collaborative writing studio.

"Shall we start with movies or TV?" Erwin queried.

"Let's start at the book store," I said.

We bought and exchanged a half-dozen thick tomes on motion picture and television writing. After consuming several, it became apparent that television offered fewer variables for beginners—thus a more measurable learning experience—than writing for motion pictures. So, when the new fall television season began, we divided up the three networks and set out in search of a series we'd like to write for.

The books also advised us to find an agent. But the same books would go on to say that no agent worth his or her salt would take on a new writer until said writer had sold something.

Catch 22.

CBS was my assignment, so each night during premiere week, Carolyn and I would race through dinner, to get Joey into bed, to get to the couch by seven o'clock, to see what the network with the big eye had to offer. On Wednesday night, a silly but ingratiating little invertebrate entitled *Green Acres* plopped up on the screen. It starred Eddie Albert and Eva Gabor as a snooty, citified couple from New York who had decided to abandon the traffic and tall buildings and take up nature on a small, run-down farm in the country. The reverse of *The Beverly Hillbillies,* down the road from *Petticoat Junction.* All three shows were from the same production company, the latter two having already cut their teeth in previous seasons, gobbling up big numbers in the Nielsen Ratings.

Shortly after the first commercial break, Eddie and Eva stumbled on to the local fruitcake who would become their handyman. I almost fell out of my chair. It was a fraternity brother from Ole Miss!

"It can't be," Carolyn said.

But I was certain. Nobody else in the world looks and talks like Tom Lester."

How ironic! This was the same Tom Lester who, back at the Sigma Nu house, would have surely been voted least likely to ever accomplish anything. And he was co-starring in a television series! I loved it! "Oh ye of little faith," I wanted to scream to Coker, Bones, Travis and Little John back in Mississippi. Don't ever count anybody out!

I called Roy, who was now back at Ole Miss in his first year of law school. Then Erwin and Harland. Then I sat down and composed a telegram of congratulations to Tiger—that's what he was called around campus. I had no idea where it should go, so I sent the same telegram twice. Once to CBS in New York and again to CBS in Los Angeles. The lady at Western Union thought I was nuts, but it didn't matter. Tiger Lester was a TV star!

I was flip-turning jubilant. For him. And for us. Less than a week before, I had been a junior advertising executive with a ten-year-old dream, but now, at last, things were about change.

At Ole Miss, Tiger had failed to make a C average either of his first two semesters, so he was still a pledge when I was a pledge. Usually two semesters were all that were allowed. If you didn't make it by then you were dropped from the fraternity roles, unless there were extenuating circumstances. Tiger had been reprieved, I had guessed early on, purely for the entertainment of certain of the good brothers. They *did* enjoy making fun of him. He was at least six-feet-four-inches tall and couldn't have weighed an ounce over a hundred and sixty pounds. He was constantly trying new concoctions to gain weight. He chewed protein pellets like candy, stashed by the thousands in a huge jug in his room. He lifted weights and exercised religiously. He couldn't stand bugs of any kind, or worms, and he let everyone know it, so the inevitable was a daily occurrence. He was, it seemed, the perpetual focus of somebody's joke, or was being razzed about one thing or another. The tickling puzzle is, he didn't seem to mind. He would laugh right along with those who taunted him, even at himself. Somewhere along the line, I suppose he decided it was worth it, just to be one of the boys. And, indeed, he was, in a bizarre sort of way. I even suspect he enjoyed the attention. His eccentricities certainly encouraged it.

Tiger was a hard core Southern Baptist, a lay preacher I believe, and he wasn't at all shy about telling the more rank of our ranks how quickly they were all going to hell. Yet, by contrast, he loved fraternity parties and was an incredible dancer. He'd collar the hottest lady on the floor and they'd wind up putting on such a show that everyone else would stop to watch, all clapping and cheering them on.

One day, several soon-to-be-doomed brothers called Tiger into a room and gathered around a small trunk. They quietly informed him that they had God in the trunk and asked Tiger to let him out. He went racing, screaming down the hall.

His collegiate major was pre-med, and he studied hard, but with little success because—as we all discovered later—pre-med simply wasn't where he wanted to be. It wasn't a goal he truly cared about. It wasn't his passion. So it follows that he would never manage the grade point necessary for entrance into medical school. He wound up in Oklahoma, teaching for a while, until the day he decided that his dream to be an actor was only a fantasy because he considered it so.

"What dream to be an actor??" I questioned him later.

"It's been there forever," he said. "I just never told anyone. I was afraid they'd laugh at me."

I was astonished. We all knew Tom Lester. He was an open book. But not, obviously, as open as we had thought. He had tricked us well, for he, too, like all the rest of us, had a point beyond which he would not risk scorn. A private hideaway in the soul for his most personal dreams and passions. A place from which intruders were forever barred.

Tiger was in Hollywood less than six months, acting in a student workshop, when Paul Henning showed up one night to see his daughter perform. Henning was the creator and producer of *The Beverly Hillbillies* and executive producer of *Petticoat Junction* and a new series entitled *Green Acres*. Some months later, Henning told me that, from the very first, he had felt Tom Lester was one of the freshest, most sincere, most unique personalities he had ever met in Hollywood.

The part of Eb had been written for a much older actor, sort of a crotchety old hick, but Mr. Henning began to work on Jay Sommers, the creator and producer of the series, to convince him to take a look at Tiger. Some of the dialog would have to be rewritten, but Henning was convinced that the freshness Tom Lester could bring to the show was the kind of magic they always sought, but rarely found.

In less than two weeks, Tiger was a co-star on a television series destined to be a huge hit. It would run for six years, capture the number eleven spot in the ratings in its first season and the number six spot the following year, beating out both its rural predecessors.

The day my telegrams arrived—he received both of them—he dropped me a five-page thank you note, and shortly thereafter I called him and we spent an hour bringing each other up to date on post-collegiate exploits. I finally told him that we wanted to write a speculative script for *Green Acres* and he was excited that I, too, had foolish dreams. He said there would be no trouble getting the producer to read it. The next day, he put copies of several scripts in the mail for us to study.

5

PROVOKING OPPORTUNITY

"Nothing comes from nothing."

Lucretius
On the Nature of Things

We skulked through the side entrance of the Adolphus Hotel and slithered along the ornate walls of the lobby, stumbling over a chair and an ash stand, before the front desk finally came into view. A wrinkled, withered old lady huddled in a plump, overstuffed chair watched us with a suspicious eye.

"Where's the envelope?" Erwin whispered.

I handed it to him.

"Wish me luck," he said. He glanced at the envelope, took a deep breath, then, ever-so-casually, meandered off toward the desk.

I turned my back. I couldn't watch. Harland chewed on his lower lip. We were both teetering on the fringes of shock. Erwin Hearne, the conservative Southern Baptist of the group, was about to commit fraud. More or less.

The desk clerk smiled as Erwin approached and handed him the envelope. "This should be placed in Mr. Dana's box," Erwin said with casual confidence. Then he turned to leave, pausing to look back just in time to see exactly which box the envelope went into.

There was no message in the envelope. Merely a blank piece of paper. The maneuver was a ruse to get Bill Dana's room number. We weren't at all sure that our two previous messages had been delivered and we were going to personally hand carry the next one to his room and shove it under his door.

Bill Dana was appearing nightly at the Adolphus show room. His comic characterization of the frightened astronaut Jose Jimien-ez was the rage of the country and he was drawing big crowds wherever he went. More important to us, Bill Dana was a writer. He had spent years writing for television before he started perform-ing, and his presence in Dallas was a rare opportunity. If we could weasel our way in to see him, we could pick the brain of one of the best, most experienced television comedy writers in the business.

There were so many questions. And maybe he would even cri-tique a bit of our script.

We had spent three months studying the material from *Green Acres*, developing a story, and writing that first ever teleplay. It was almost finished the day we stepped off the elevator on the four-teenth floor of the Adolphus Hotel and stole quietly down the hall to slip four yellow pages under Bill Dana's door. An hour with someone like Bill Dana could catapult us light years down the road to brilliance. Mistakes could be avoided, insight bequeathed. And - dare we think of it? -- if he liked our work, he might, just possibly, one never knows, do something to help us.

"Which side should face up?" Erwin asked.

I snatched the pages away from him, gazed down the long empty hallway, inhaled all the courage I could hold, and tiptoed off toward room number 1408. It was not my style to be the one out front, but this was too important. If the pages didn't get pushed under the door just right, someone might think it was a piece of trash. And this was our last chance. It was already Friday, and Dana's engagement at the Adolphus ended Sunday night.

The first attempt had been a simple note, left in his box at the front desk. It introduced us as fledgling television writers and beseeched him to take an hour out of his busy schedule to talk with us. Anytime, at his convenience.

That was a week before. We never heard from him.

Next, a colorful piece of artwork went into the box—it's nice to have two artists on the team—depicting three pained, miserable writers isolated in the mid-section of a United States map, insulated from the wealth of professional experience available on both coasts. We were all three waving placards boldly advertising our phone numbers.

Again, there was no response. No phone call.

The four pages that went under his door was a short television script in which three young hopefuls paced around an office discussing the pros and cons of whether or not Bill Dana was going to call.

FADE IN:
Joe paces across the room, from the window to the door, then back again. He pauses to gaze out at the Adolphus tower less than two blocks away. Erwin sits by the phone. Harland looks up from his doodling.

> HARLAND
> *Forget it. He's not going to call. He doesn't care.*

Joe spins from the window.

> JOE
> *He does care! He's a nice man! He'll call.*

> ERWIN
> *He may have forgotten the phone number.*

> JOE
> *How could he forget a number like 742-8773??*

> HARLAND

It is a dramatic number. And deep. I mean
intellectually. Don't you think?
    (raises a hand into
    the air and bellows
    dramatically)
742-8773!!!

                    JOE
I know he'll respond. Helping new writers
*is a **passion** of his. Besides, he doesn't*
want my death on his conscience.

Etcetera, ad nauseam, for four pages.

We wrote our home numbers into the script, to cover Saturday and Sunday, then we spent the rest of the day and the entire weekend glued to our telephones. To no avail. There was no call from Bill Dana. His two-week stint at the Adolphus was up and we assumed our futures in show business were once again balanced exclusively upon Tiger's tall but spindly shoulders.

It was late Monday morning when the call came in. I was sitting in a copywriter's office, neck deep in the problems of an upcoming campaign. The soft, throaty voice of the receptionist wafted through the halls, beckoning me to pick up line three. I punched the blinking button and said, "Hello."

"Joe Camp?"

"This is he."

"This is Bill Dana."

Silence.

Something horrible had happened to my vocal chords. And my brain. I was frozen in a gasp. The copywriter across the desk must've assumed I was in cardiac arrest.

"Did you faint?" Dana asked politely.

The thinnest of vibrations rattled from my throat. "Yes. I think so."

He said he was leaving for the airport in a couple of hours and wondered if we could accomplish anything by phone.

Courage, Joe, I charged myself, and I dove in with both feet, explaining how we were only two blocks away and could be there in five-minutes and it would mean so much to us if he could just spare a little time. We wanted him to see something we had written and we couldn't do that by phone and...

"Okay, cease already! You win. Come on over. Room 1408."

"We know," I said.

It's not easy to hang up the phone when you're so high off the ground.

"That was Bill Dana," I tried to say casually.

"Is that a client?" asked the copywriter.

Bill Dana is Jewish.

Virtually everyone in the entertainment business is Jewish.

The Feldmans, Weintraubs, Goldmans and Steinbergs are everywhere.

But I had never thought much about it, so I missed the humor in Dana's greeting to us when three glaring WASPs, all chalky pale and more or less blond, strolled through his hotel room door.

"Vell, you sure don't *look* like comedy writers."

Erwin fell on the floor laughing. I sank into a puddle of despair, assuming we had failed our first test.

Dana didn't notice. He looked like he had been run over by a truck. He had a massive hangover and if he felt anything at all like his appearance, taking time to see us was more of a benevolence than any group of strangers could possibly deserve.

He spent over an hour answering our questions, asking and answering a few of his own, and, in general, filling our pockets with treasured gems of advice.

On stealing material: "Don't. It doesn't pay. But if you do, which you will, don't mess around. Steal *big*. Steal from Shakespeare."

On how many pages does a script make? "How can anyone answer that? Consider this line: *And the Indians took the fort*."

Pause.

"You tell me how long that one line will take on the screen, I'll tell you how long to make the script."

On which shows to write for: "Write for shows that'll do you some good. Shows that get Emmys, or big ratings, or at least a semi-intelligent audience. In other words, don't do Gilligan's Island. If that one ever turns up with any of the above, get out of the business."

He asked to see something we'd written. I had no idea how he might feel about *Green Acres*, so I handed him the script, wrapped in a rambling explanation of why we had chosen that particular series. It wasn't necessary. He had never seen the show. He had been working nights since Fall.

He thumbed through the script, reading a page here, two pages there, then he dropped it back onto the coffee table. "Good stuff," he said, yawning. "Inventive. Send me a copy when you're finished. And maybe some springboards for *Get Smart*. Don Adams and I are close. I'll feed 'em to him in a salad one night."

Suddenly I felt dizzy.

Bill Dana had, quite casually, without flourish, hurled a blistering thunderbolt into our lives. The lights dimmed, the overture began! A moment before, we were just three ad guys with a silly notion, pacing outside the castle walls, begging, pleading for nothing more than a peek inside. Seconds later, the gates stood open, we were bid to enter, and our notion didn't seem so silly anymore. Still, I had to ask.

"What are springboards?"

A springboard, he told us, is a one paragraph suggestion of a story line. It's the unique premise upon which your story is to be built, it's the twists, and the resolution. It's everything you need to make a producer want to buy it. All in three sentences or less.

"It is," he concluded, "the most difficult writing you'll ever do."

Days later, our heads were still spinning, bursting with new thoughts, new ideas, the invitation to send material! And the first inkling that something might really come from all this. Bill Dana was a successful professional and he had liked our writing. This could be serious. Our big break was clearly right around the corner.

I've often wondered what I might've done had I known just how protracted a corner it was to be.

Thankfully, we always kept several pots on the stove at once. We never let one cool down without having another at full boil, a technique I heartily recommend. It helps keep the depression of rejection from the door.

Very few feelings in this life are as cold and lonely and destructive to enthusiasm as those bred by disapproval. They slither up your ego and attack the very core of your self esteem. Like a treacherous fog, thick and damp, that slowly envelopes hope, voiding perspective and blocking contact with things real and rational. A simple critique of a story or springboard can become, if allowed, an assault upon your entire person.

Of course, it never is, or *rarely* is. So there must be a design to keep the emotion in check because rejection and critique are necessary ingredients to the learning process, to growth and development. A way must be found to coexist with the rejection that will surely come more often than not. Only then will objectivity allow it to become part of the learning process. And for me, nothing has ever worked better than diversion, a new challenge, something else to be excited about, a separate but equal enthusiasm. It's an instinctive maneuver whenever emotional risk is involved. A reflex action. Even today, when we are pitching a new movie, or preparing a presentation for a network, a portion of my energy will be unconsciously but compulsively generating in another direction, that the bucket may never be empty.

Thus, we never dawdled, waiting for one project to bloom before planting new seeds. We would ride the momentum of a completed script or a meeting with Bill Dana right into new ideas and other possibilities. We never lingered by the phone to hear the response on one thing before beginning another. So whenever bad news came, the devastation was minimal. After all, the new project really had more going for it than the old one anyway, right?

We finished the *Green Acres* script, shipped it off to Tiger and immediately went to work on springboards for *Get Smart*. The series was only in its first year but was already a hit. A bumbling spy comedy created by laugh masters Mel Brooks and Buck Henry, it would capture the number twelve spot in the ratings that year, only one notch under *Green Acres*. We were certainly traveling in good company.

Dana was right about springboards. Trying to create good stories was strain enough, but condensing each one into a single short paragraph seemed like an interminable exercise in futility. It took us awhile to realize that this exercise was an enlightening and necessary part of the process because it pointed out story and structural weaknesses in flashing neon. If a story wasn't simple enough to condense, it was, more than likely, a candidate for the round file below the desk. Over the years, I've seen very few exceptions to this rule. The essence of the movie *Benji*, for example, can be told in one sentence.

We had barely begun to struggle with these new concepts when Erwin read that Jerry Van Dyke was coming to The Adolphus showroom. A pair of marvelously funny guest appearances on his brother's television series had catapulted him into mini-stardom. But he was strictly a comedian, not a writer. And his own first series—an awful thing called *My Mother The Car*—had been canceled a month earlier. Two perfectly good reasons why there was nothing to be gained by trying to meet him.

So, without further ado, we developed a full-fledged battle plan. First, he was to get the introductory note in his box. The next day, the *isolated writers* artwork would be left at the desk, then the script under the door, and, finally, a singing telegram.

On the day of his first appearance, about six in the evening, we tromped, in trio, over to the Adolphus and left Phase One in his box, then I drove straight home. As I turned the corner on to our street, panic suddenly gripped my throat. In the distance, Carolyn was in the middle of the driveway, leaping up and down and waving her arms at my approaching car. What could possibly be wrong?!

Joey had fallen out of a tree.

The dog had been run over by a truck.

I pressed the accelerator to the floor, wheeled into the driveway and slid to a stop.

"He called!" she screeched. "Jerry Van Dyke just called!"

"Absolutely not!" I bellowed at Erwin.

"It was just an idea," he said, retreating with a look that soaked me in shame for having yelled.

Erwin, like Tiger, is a *hard-shell* Southern Baptist. Orthodox to the core. The Bible verbatim. No drinking, even in the closet. He would, in time, be getting along famously with Tiger, but Harland and I were surely frustrations to him. We both considered ourselves believers, only I suppose, because we had been brought up to be. At that point, I had never really given it much thought. God was there, somewhere. Just not much of a factor in my life.

But I certainly didn't think it was appropriate for Erwin to use our meeting with Jerry Van Dyke to ask him to appear at the First Baptist Church. "He expects us to ask for advice," I admonished, "not free personal appearances!"

The wrangling was born of an event scheduled later in the week at First Baptist where Erwin was a deacon. Vonda Kay Van Dyke, the reigning Miss America, would be speaking to the Baptist youth and Erwin had conceived the idea of doubling the Van Dykes, having *two* instead of just one. "Think of the promotional value!" he said.

All I could think of was Jerry Van Dyke tossing us out of his room.

Erwin promised not to bring it up.

We moved on to strategy. An intelligent question or two was desperately needed. Our meeting was less than an hour away and I didn't think Harland's "What's it like being Dick Van Dyke's brother?" would get us off on quite the right foot.

It had been easy with Bill Dana. There were hundreds of questions about writing and scripts and selling, and each answer seemed to generate more questions. But Jerry wasn't a writer, he was the star of a show. And the show had been canceled. I feared it was going to be a short, if not embarrassing meeting.

It was a little of both. We prattled on excessively about his appearances on his brother's series, then fired our only real shot. What, we asked, were his perceptions of the mistakes that had been made on *My Mother The Car* leading to its cancellation. I think we struck a nerve. He rattled off a dozen or more. The most difficult to fathom, besides the title, was the fact that not one writer who had written for the series had ever seen Jerry perform. They hadn't seen his nightclub act, or the guest appearances on Dick's show, or anything!

I was amazed. How could anyone write comedy for someone else without having a working, if not intimate, knowledge of what that person does best? And what he *doesn't* do best! Delivery, personality, timing and pacing all had to be crucial ingredients for making comedy work. A joke written for Woody Allen wouldn't fit Bob Hope. A sight gag for Dick Van Dyke would fall flat with George Burns. I didn't understand. This was the big time! Network television! Professionals at work! How could they care so little about what they were doing?

"You *do* have a lot to learn," Jerry grinned. He sincerely wanted to be helpful, and tried to offer up several cogent bromides, but once we had sufficiently beaten up on the writers of *My Mother the Car*, the conversation began to evaporate. Soon we were all gazing silently out the windows. I decided we'd better go before E. Hearne—that's how he signs his paintings—was tempted to reach too far for conversation. We were standing in the doorway, saying our thank you's, when Erwin suddenly burst like a water balloon, pouring out the story of our argument over the Two-Van-Dyke promotion.

I wanted to crawl under the woodwork and was, in fact, looking for a crack large enough when I felt Jerry tug on my arm. "You guys aren't in a hurry are you?" he said. "This won't take long. Southern Baptist, huh?" He ushered the three of us back into the room saying how happy he would've been to appear with Vonda Kay had the timing not conflicted with his show at the Adolphus. He seated us side by side on the couch, walked a short distance away, then turned and gave himself a long moment, I suspect, to re-evaluate. Did we really look like the types to whom he should be giving away family secrets? Finally he said, "I'd like to toss something at you, just for a reaction."

Three hours later we left his room, our heads spinning, this time, out beyond the ionosphere.

He told us of a series idea he and brother Dick had been toying with. A situation comedy that Dick wanted to produce, in which Jerry would star. But they were questioning whether or not the series would make it in the Bible Belt. Especially among Southern Baptists! The concept, it seems, violated a long standing Hollywood rule because it involved a Protestant minister. A *young* Protestant minister, fresh out of seminary, in his first small town church. A young, *single,* Protestant minister, driving a beat up old sports car with a surfboard hanging out the back. Not what you might call down the middle. The church membership would skew heavily into the over-fifty ranks. The running conflict would be the old versus the new and the running solution would be the two gaining understanding, if not always appreciation, for each other.

I loved it! Harland loved it! Erwin loved it and was convinced other Baptists would too. And that's what Jerry wanted to hear.

The long standing Hollywood rule violation was that Protestant ministers don't do comedy. Whenever Hollywood found a member of the clergy in a funny film, they put a collar on him. Always! And they never asked *why,* believe it or not, because nobody ever had an answer.

"It's always been that way."

"Maybe Protestants don't laugh."

The reason for it all, I discovered later, was that, once upon a time, a director was afraid the audience wouldn't recognize his character as a man of the cloth, so he put a collar on him. The film was a comedy, so an axiom was born: if he wears a collar, you can laugh at him. If not, write him out.

Erwin was offering to arrange an audience for Jerry with a few lofty representatives of the Baptist hierarchy when I brushed him aside and leaped straight for the jugular.

"Has a pilot been written?"

"No, nothing's been written. It's just an idea."

"Would you like for a pilot to be written? Like, on speculation. Pay only if it sells."

"I can't ask you to write on spec," Jerry said. "Union rules."

"Oh." I slumped.

He strolled across the room to gaze out the window at the Dallas skyline.

"But if a script just happened to turn up on my doorstep..."

His finger traced a large circle in the fog on the window.

"...and if I just happened to like it..."

He dotted the center of the circle.

"I'm certain it would find its way into Dick's hands, and maybe Carl Reiner's."

Suddenly I was having trouble breathing again. Erwin began to stutter. Harland was in a coma.

A pilot for Dick and Jerry Van Dyke! *Series developed by Joe Camp, Erwin Hearne and Harland Wright!* Staff story consultants! More scripts!

I began to worry. How could I move to Los Angeles without a decent set of luggage?

Jerry's tour at the Adolphus was two weeks long. During that time, we saw his act three times, met him for lunch once at the hotel and once at the lovely Dallas Federal Savings Building Basement Cafeteria. The latter to flaunt him among those who were beginning to question our credibility, and our sanity.

Erwin scheduled meetings for Jerry to pitch the series to leadership representing the entire Southern Baptist Convention, the First Baptist Church of Dallas and the Campus Crusade for Christ. All to enthusiastically favorable response.

Erwin also roused Jerry out of bed at dawn on the last Sunday of his stay and dragged him to early church service. "Research!" he proclaimed. Harland, Carolyn and I joined them and we all sat on the back row of one of the most cavernous sanctuaries I had ever seen. Not exactly the kind of church we had in mind for the pilot. When collection time came, Jerry dug around in his pockets, then leaned over to me. "I'm really embarrassed," he said. "I don't have a dime on me."

I pulled out the only thing I had, a twenty dollar bill.

"Never mind," he said. "I'm not *that* embarrassed."

The next day he left town, wondering, I imagine, what in God's name he had gotten himself into. I doubt that he would ever again respond to strange notes in his hotel box.

Erwin, Harland and I were numb. In less than a three-week span, we had completed a *Green Acres* script which was being read by the producer of the series; we had been asked to submit springboards for *Get Smart*, which would be hand delivered to the star; and we were at work on a pilot script which, if good enough, would wind up in the hands of the crown princes of television comedy, Dick Van Dyke and Carl Reiner!

But there was something else.

Something nagging at my insides, and I couldn't shake it. I had been so harsh to Erwin, so adamant that he *not* talk about church to Jerry, yet it was only after he *did* that things began to happen. We had all agreed there was no valid reason to seek out Jerry Van Dyke, but for some inexplicable reason, we did. At the time, there were only three well-known Van Dyke's in the entire United States, and two of them were in Dallas; in contact with Erwin!

I had known Erwin for well over a year and during that time, any promise he had made had been as good as solid gold. And he had promised not to bring up the church thing to Jerry. Had he kept that promise, Jerry never would've discovered that Erwin was a Southern Baptist. And there would've been no incentive to get his reaction to the minister idea. And our empty thirty minute meeting would've never been transformed into three stimulating hours of rare opportunity that in a long and drawn out strange and wonderful sort of way... lead directly to Benji.

Jerry's attention was snatched by Erwin's proposition—which just happened to turn our meeting around, and, perhaps, my entire life—but, interestingly, the results had little to do with how good Erwin's idea might've been. It just happened to connect with something that was important to Jerry at the moment. Had Jerry not been toying with the minister show, or, let's say, had he recently been picketed by a crowd of Baptists because of a joke in his nightclub act, he might have tossed us out on our ears. And that, too, would have little bearing on the real value of Erwin's Van Dyke promotion. It wouldn't have suddenly become a terrible idea just because Jerry had a momentary distaste for Baptists. Understanding these concepts brings a healthy balance to perspective whenever you find yourself on the receiving end of either criticism *or* praise.

That particular day provided still one more illumination. It was the first time I had ever really *felt* the hand of God. He couldn't have painted a better picture for me if he had waltzed into Dallas, grabbed me by the throat and said, "Look stupid, I've gone to a lot of trouble to set all this up, now back off and let Erwin talk!" Erwin no longer had to worry about me. My differences with his Baptist dogma might endure, but, at last, I would begin a relationship with God, and my life would never be the same.

Through the years, I suspect that God has grown no less tired than Bill Dana, Jerry Van Dyke and all the others of my nagging questions and continual barrage of correspondence and phone calls.

After Jerry's departure, Carolyn and I began to tiptoe around the question of what we would do if something big happened. The very minute my writing would support her and Joey, I was ready to quit the advertising agency and move west. Carolyn wasn't quite so ready. The thought of living in Los Angeles didn't appeal much to her and she was concerned about the schools and the atmosphere in which our four-year-old Joey would be growing up. There were several lengthy discussions on the subject but never a conclusion. She never said yes. And she never said no.

Harland, also, was ready, but Erwin wasn't. His roots were too deep. He would have to be a distant consultant, he said. But that never mollified his enthusiasm.

We finished three springboards for *Get Smart,* wrote seven or eight pages of sample script for each, and shipped everything off to Bill Dana. Then, I shifted timetables to work out the story outline for Jerry's pilot. I had been in the *writing mode* for much of the last year. Up-at-four-in-the-morning, write for two hours, wake the family, eat breakfast, go to work. Discuss the writing with Erwin and Harland at lunch, go home after work, get to bed early so I could get up again at four. But whenever we needed more time for discussion, usually in the concept and outline stages, I would flip-flop my hours so we could meet at night. And once on the late-night schedule, there was no way back to the 4:00 a.m. wake-up without skipping over a day or two, sleeping late and turning in early. To say I looked forward to those in-between days is to eloquently understate.

There were occasions when the drain of those late nights and early mornings weighed heavy, but those moments were rare because the results of the effort were stimulating. For the first time in years, I didn't feel like I was standing still, or circling myself in a confused tangle. I was back in the race, stoking the fires of slumbering coals, long latent but still hot; and able, once stirred, to fuel upon themselves. The view toward the future was sprinkled with all sorts of fascinating wrinkles and warps. I wasn't sure where it would all lead, but now I *was* sure it would lead *somewhere.* I was finally in active pursuit of a dream that had haunted me for twenty years and it felt terrific!

6

RUDE AWAKENINGS

*"Our greatest glory is not in never falling,
but in rising every time we fall"*

Confucius

Messrs. J. S. Camp, Jr. and Erwin Hearne, Jr.
1600 Dallas Federal Savings Building
Elm & Akard
Dallas, Texas
Dear Messrs. Camp and Hearne:

*Tom Lester gave me your "Green Acres" script to read, and I am
returning it to you herewith. I'm sorry but we can't use it.*
*If it is any consolation to you, you have done amazingly well in
capturing our characters—in fact you have come closer to them
than some of the veteran tv writers who have attempted to
write for the show.*

*Unfortunately your script is woefully weak in story and con-
struction, which of course doesn't make the comedy come off at
all.*
I'm sorry but thanks for letting me read it.

Cordially,
Jay Sommers
Producer

It wouldn't be the last time we would hear criticism on story and
construction.

I read through the script again, searching its pages and between its lines, for some tiny glimmer of understanding, but was

blinded, I suspect, by how "amazingly well" we had captured the characters. It finally dawned on me that it was going to be difficult indeed to analyze the structure of a story when I didn't even know what one was.

I dug back through the books we had found on screenwriting but they were hopelessly entangled in form, and style. I ordered a volume entitled *How To Write Television Comedy*, but it never ventured beyond joke writing and technique. Carolyn found a book on how to develop characterization, but it ignored what to do with the characters once they were developed.

Finally, I unearthed a bright red opus entitled *Writing to Sell*. More than half its pages were devoted to story and structure. At last, I sighed. Answers! I devoured it twice, each time becoming more convinced that I must be missing something. It seemed to approach story writing like a spelling lesson. Memorize these words and sell your stories. Awfully cold and academic, I thought.

Still, it was a helpful primer, providing at least a skeletal idea of what story structure should look like. I re-read one of the scripts Tiger had sent us. It was there. A little fuzzy, and camouflaged with silliness, but I could see a ghostly image of a "plot skeleton" with a few appropriate "plot complications".

Begin with at least one *must*.

Toss in one or more good *can'ts*.

And, according to the bright red book, you now have a story. Again, it seemed cold and over-simplified, but the point was taken. We were beginning to learn why Jay Sommers had considered our story weak. At that, he was being kind because the red book said we didn't even *have* a story. It was non-existent. Story begins, it admonished, when the story's goal is important enough to make the reader, or viewer, want to know more.

In our *Green Acres* script, Oliver was notified that his new plow had arrived at the depot. He was excited beyond belief—quite literally, I'm afraid—and spent the entire script making desperate attempts, always in vain, to retrieve the plow before the depot closed for the weekend. A near perfect example of "Who cares?"

The structure of the script might've worked had the objective been meaningful. Like, maybe, Oliver's wife was going to leave him and return to the city if she didn't get a *real* stove by a certain deadline. Or running water for her bath. At least, then, he would have something to lose.

We were learning. A good story needed important goals, not easily accomplished; and dire consequences awaiting the hero should he fail. He should be caught between the absolute *must* that demands accomplishment and the absolute *can't* that prevents it. Young farmer Fred *must* get Nancy to the hospital because she's in labor. But he *can't* because he and Nancy are being held hostage by a group of escaped convicts laying low at Fred's farmhouse. Fred plots and plans and ultimately overcomes the guard assigned to watch them. He sneaks Nancy out to the old, dusty pickup truck. But the truck won't start. The bad guys have cut the fuel line. Fred and Nancy try to sneak away on foot, but she's in too much pain to walk. Time runs out. Fred will have to deliver the baby himself. But, historically, Fred faints at the first sight of blood. The solution, of course, is that Fred must gather his courage and deliver the baby himself, probably just as the police rush in.

One *must* and four *can'ts*, with each complicating *can't* making things a little bleaker.

It's interesting to note that, at the author's command, this structure could either become heavy drama or light comedy. As a drama, it would be a story of love, inner struggle and courage. As a comedy, the fun might come from Fred's insistence that the bad guys help with the delivery. Participating in the creation of life could even have a reforming effect on the convicts.

The red rule book worked. At least it provided physical guidelines, insight of a sort, but I was never very comfortable with it. I wasn't sure why because it *did* manage to locate the subject, and encircle it, but it never really seemed to venture close enough to find a pulse. The author saw, and reported, but never reached out to touch, and feel. It was difficult for me to believe that wonderful stories like Robert Louis Stevenson's *The Sire de Maletroit's Door* and de Maupassant's *The Piece of String* were born of cold, lifeless "lists of basic ingredients", "plot skeletons", and platitudes such as: "*(story) Complications are like sunbathes: they miss their purpose if each new one doesn't make things a little darker.*"

Still, we were learning, and I was anxious to put our new found wisdom to work.

Messrs. J. S. Camp, Jr., Erwin Hearne, Jr.,
and Harland Wright
1600 Dallas Federal Savings Bldg.
Elm and Akard
Dallas, Texas 75201

Dear Fellas:

Just got back to town and have belatedly gotten to your Get Smart story lines. Briefly, two out of three ain't bad. I liked the midget story and the snow machine, but thought story line three weak in comparison.

Don Adams is coming to dinner tonight, so I'll be feeding the horse's mouth. I definitely have a feeling you gentlemen have something to offer and have already discussed with my partners in California International Artists, which is my management company, that perhaps we can do something to further your careers.

However, don't go out and do any celebrating yet, because I'm known to be one of those Hollywood phonies that take great pleasure in building up people's hopes and then shattering them. Meanwhile, stand by for further instructions.

Sadistically,
Bill Dana

Green Acres was quickly forgotten and we worked harder on the minister pilot, hoping to finish it before Bill Dana's *further instructions*. I called Jerry to test our choice for a series name. The young minister would be Larry Masters and the series would be called *Lord and Masters*. Jerry was concerned about the word *Lord* in the title. "Actually, *I'm* not concerned," he said. "I'm concerned about *them* being concerned." I didn't ask who *them* might be. We changed Larry's last name to Host and the series became *Heavenly Host*.

Another month elapsed, then another. We finished the pilot and shipped it off to Jerry. But still nothing from Bill Dana. Almost three months in all since his letter. What, we wondered, had happened to our *Get Smart* springboards? And those discussions with his management company?

Maybe we should unpack.

It was 2:00 a.m.

I floundered through a boggy swamp of a mind, swiping at the fog, but it wouldn't clear. And the ringing in my ears grew louder.

I twisted and turned, struggling, reaching for something I couldn't quite see. My eyes blinked open. I had no idea where I was. The ringing was still louder, pummeling my eardrums with discord. I reached through the darkness and dragged the telephone receiver off its hook and, gloriously, the ringing stopped. I dropped it across my ear and mumbled something indistinguishable.

"Joe! It's Jerry!" bubbled a voice on the other end.

"Jerry." I tried to say intelligently, but I had no idea who Jerry was. I didn't even know who *I* was. I've heard doctors talk about the different levels of sleep and I must've been at the bottom of the deepest strata because I was still out cold!

"Joe, wake up! It's Jerry Van Dyke!"

A volcano exploded in my head and I shot to the surface, wide awake at the speed of light!

Jerry had never called any of us before, or even written! Every communication between us, *we* had initiated. And never at two o'clock in the morning.

He had just read *Heavenly Host* and was raving about it! He couldn't wait to call. He was in Seattle, had received the script just before show time and had read it immediately after. And Carol had phoned. She, too, was ecstatic.

"It's terrific!" he said. "I just can't tell you! I mean really terrific! Now, just sit tight. I talked to Dick. Carol is taking a copy over to him tomorrow. If he feels the same as we do, he'll show it to Carl Reiner, or maybe Sheldon Leonard. But it'll take time, so don't sit by the phone. Just relax. It's really good. You guys are on your way."

As it turned out, that wasn't a nice thing to say.

Messrs. Camp, Hearne & Wright
Norsworthy-Mercer, Inc.
1600 Dallas Federal Savings Bldg.
Elm and Akard
Dallas, Texas
Dear J.E.W.:

Geography is agin us. It just is impossible for me to be of any help to you long distance. As you know, I am now in pre-production as producer of the Milton Berle Show, and had you guys been in the area, there may have been a chance for you to get your feet wet in the prime time variety area. When you see the writing credits on the show, you will realize that if each of the writers' families watches the show, we should garner quite a rating. There are eight....count em...eight scriveners, not counting myself, who am not taking a writing credit (mainly because I didn't know whether to say is not or am not).

Even though the writing budget is 99% eaten up, I may be able to scrounge some money from time to time for outside sketch ideas and/or completed sketches. Please feel free to submit any of these directly to me at: 8418 Franklin Ave., Los Angeles 69, Calif.

Warmest personal regards,
Bill Dana

Mr. Bill Dana
8418 Franklin Avenue

Los Angeles, California 90069

Dear Bill:
Geography is not really agin us, merely between us.

We'll be sending along sketch ideas, blackouts and bits for the show and if there's anything that tickles your fancy, watch how short that "long distance" becomes.

When you get a minute, please check the appropriate boxes on the Attached Questionnaire and drop it in the mail.

Regards, regards and regards,
Joe Camp
Erwin Hearne
Harland Wright

It had been four and a half silent months since Bill had last mentioned the *Get Smart* material, saying he was giving it to Don Adams the same night. Our self-addressed card was finally returned two months after it was sent asking us to send the material again as Don Adams had lost it.

Reality was setting in. This wasn't going to be as fleet a rise to fame as we might've thought a few months back. *Green Acres* was off the list, the *Get Smart* springboards had never even made it to the producer, nothing we had sent to Dana for the Milton Berle Show had pushed his button, and *Heavenly Host* was now on the shelf. Jerry had informed us that even with Dick's enthusiasm, and strong evidence of Baptist support, producer and network types were still afraid of a situation comedy with a Protestant minister. Especially one as far out of the mainstream as Larry Host.

Our momentum was beginning to fizzle. We needed to stoke the fires; to multiply the efforts of our newfound friends; to meet producers and agents; to open new doors and spread some of our work around. And we couldn't do any of that in Dallas.

It would've been easy to just sit there and wait. We had been working long hours for many months, stretching ourselves and our families, and nothing substantive had happened. We were tired and disappointed, and not at all sure that a trip to Los Angeles would produce anything but debt? What if we spent the money, stole the time, and nothing came of it? Was this whole thing a silly fantasy? Were we kidding ourselves, trying to break in from Dallas?

There was really only one way to find out.

I discussed it with Carolyn. I could take a week of vacation from the agency, which would still leave a week for the family, but after the trip west there would be no money for the family to go anywhere. Six days in Los Angeles would consume all of our savings and probably melt our new American Express card.

"Go!" she said. "And do good. You still owe me a Hawaiian honeymoon."

My hands grew cold and clammy as the plane touched down. Pictures from eighteen years before were flooding through my sieve of a memory. The parades, the movie stars. I wondered if the backdrop for *Gone With The Wind* was still standing. Then I was driving away from Los Angeles, off into a snowstorm, tears spilling down my cheeks, vowing to return.

And here I was, returning.

Excitement throbbed through every vein, but butterflies were at war in the pit of my stomach. I was no less eager than I had been eighteen years before, but reality has a way of dilating focus, of mixing emotions. If all went as planned, the next five days would be spent dashing back and forth across Hollywood, in and out of network studios, producers' offices, and sound stages. Yet, a piece of me wanted to crawl back on the next plane and go home. I was an outsider here, an intruder. As much as I wanted to, I didn't belong. This wasn't fantasy land, it was hard-nosed Hollywood.

Carnivores at work. Busy, vicious, devourers of piddling little novices who aren't serious enough about their dreams to pack up and move to the only place where dreams can happen. Never mind about wives and kids and responsibility. Just pay up or move on.

Everyone had told us. If you guys really want to do this, you're going to have to live out here. "The producers want to know you're right across the street in case they need you at a moment's notice," Jerry had said. "They never will, but they want to know it just the same."

How to counter the Dallas factor had consumed my thoughts for days. Would they take us seriously? Would they see us at all?

Enough! I screeched quietly to myself as the plane turned into the gate area. I didn't need to be marinating my enthusiasm in more intimidation. Just being there, at last, right in the middle of working Hollywood, had already overflowed the limits of my audacity.

Thank goodness for Erwin. He was bubbling like a champagne fountain, gall in gear and primed for attack. I don't think he had once stopped talking since the plane had left Dallas. Harland, unhappily, wasn't with us. Somebody had to watch the studio. "And if only one can go," I had told them frankly, "it *has* to be Erwin." I had yet to see the time when Erwin was afraid to step up and speak out. He relished meeting new people and looked upon cold calls as merely new chances to make new friends.

I didn't. I've always been nervous and uncomfortable in first meetings. Particularly when I'm the seller instead of the sellee. I simply can't function until things warm up and the tempo is set. If that doesn't happen, I unravel into a stammering heap. Harland is much the same. So it wouldn't do for the two of us to go off together hunting bear.

Erwin and I, however, worked well together. He would bluster in like a North Atlantic ice-breaker, running off at the mouth and telling tales, then he'd dive into the pitch, knowing his garbled perception and lack of finesse would force me from the quiet comfort of my shell to prevent our quarry from throwing us bodily out of his office.

Today I remain the classic, textbook ambivert. *Extro* to a fault in familiar environs, with friends or acquaintances, or when dealing with a subject I know intimately; but introverted from bald spot to toenails when the situation reverses.

It took us only thirty minutes to find the cheapest rental car at LAX, then we consulted our complimentary map and struck out for Hollywood. Our home for the next week would be a tiny room with twin beds at the Travel Lodge on Sunset Boulevard. We had to change rooms to get the twin beds. The manager didn't understand, and we didn't try to explain. "Welcome to Hollywood," Erwin said.

We had prepared well for the trip. My suitcases were bulging with freshly produced copies of every single word we had written during the past year and my head was exploding with new thoughts and ideas. Our local contacts had promised to set up numerous meetings for us and Erwin had even discovered another friend who was a neighbor of a cousin of an executive at Twentieth Century Fox. The week promised to be a busy one and we wanted Harland to savor every nuance in the re-telling, so I penned a diary—of sorts—detailing the entire week's activities. That night we drove out to The Horn, a small club in Santa Monica, to see Guy Hovis perform. Guy was a fraternity brother from college days with a marvelous singing voice. He would soon marry a beautiful lass from Texas, also a singer, and they would spend the next fifteen or so years as headliners *Guy and Ralna* on *The Lawrence Welk Show*.

The next morning we met with Richard O. Linke, Jerry Van Dyke's manager. Also Andy Griffith's and Jim Neighbor's. He was the Associate Producer of *The Andy Griffith Show* and, according to

Jerry, could get our material delivered to the *Griffith* and *Gomer Pyle* shows, and probably open doors anywhere in town. But it was our first discouragement of the trip. Actually Richard O. Linke was more than discouraging, he was abrasive and rude. He told us, without the least hesitation or doubt, that we didn't have one chance in ten thousand to accomplish anything if we didn't live in L.A. Maybe one chance in five thousand if we did. And he wanted to know why we were taking up his time.

"Because Jerry is trying to help us and he thought..."

"Jerry can't even help *himself*, or his show would still be on the air!"

Our mouths gaped open in disbelief. I was incensed, and quite suddenly no longer afraid of this man. To speak like that to strangers about his own client was, to me, unforgivable. Why, I wondered, if he felt that way, did he continue to be Jerry's manager?

I relayed that it was our understanding that he might deliver some material to the producers of the *Andy Griffith* and *Gomer Pyle* shows for us, but if he didn't feel so inclined, we'd be happy to find other avenues. He agreed to deliver the material but told us we'd do best to stick to advertising. And we left.

Our week was to be filled, on the whole, with generous people and encouraging meetings, yet this was the incident that burned most indelibly into my memory. We were too much the fledglings, too inexperienced, to decipher whether his manner was merely an act for effect, or the real thing; whether he was trying to see what we were made of, or just showing his posterior. But I've never forgotten it. Of all the negatives I've been drenched with over the years, of all the people who have said "It's impossible. You can't. Forget it. Give up." there's only one person I really wanted to call after *Benji* sprinted to success. Richard O. Linke. I didn't, and I thrashed myself for the thought, but it didn't make me want to any less.

It was an empty way to begin the week.

After the Linke meeting, it was important that somebody like us, so went scampered back to the Hollywood Palace where Bill Dana was taping. His secretary spent half an hour telling us how much Bill thought of us and, afterward, we felt better. I imagine *anyone* would've sufficed, but the fact that it was Bill Dana helped balance the scales. His partner, Bill Lyon had been with MGM during its heyday, virtual father to Judy Garland and Mickey Rooney, and was now VP of Dana's production company. Arnie Rosen was the Producer of *Get Smart*. Bill Persky and Sam Denoff had written almost every episode of *The Dick Van Dyke Show* and were the show's Story Editors and Producers during its last year. And Dana had promised us meetings with all of the above.

Persky and Denoff had created and were currently Executive Producers of *That Girl*. I admired and emulated their work more than anyone else's in Hollywood, and this was the meeting I wanted above all others.

The next day was spent watching the filming of *Green Acres*. During a break, Smiley Burnette gave us our first lesson in production cost control. It came from one of those many westerns he made as Gene Autrey's sidekick. Late one afternoon, they were shooting a chase scene and running behind schedule. The director raced up to Autrey and said, "Now in this shot, Gene, you climb off your horse and say we'll go the rest of the way on foot. Then, everybody else will climb down and follow."

"But we're in the middle of a desert," Autrey exclaimed. "Why would we go on foot??"

"Because," the director barked, "tomorrow we can't afford the horses."

Later, Tom Lester arranged for us to meet with Paul Hen-

ning, the show's Executive Producer and creator and producer of
Beverly Hillbillies and *Petticoat Junction*. We were floored. He spent
over an hour with us and asked to read the minister pilot.

"Do you guys have any idea what you're accomplishing??" an
agent screeched at us the next day, slapping himself in the head.
"Writers all over this town, *working* writers, would cut off an arm
to spend an hour with Paul Henning! Jeez! Do you know what
that's worth?!" He slapped himself again and his eyes rolled back in
his head.

Actually we had already figured what it was worth. Paul Henning earned over a million dollars a year. During his conversation
with us, he cleared four hundred and eighty dollars! We probably
should've asked more important questions.

"Douglas Cramer??!" the agent shrieked. "You saw Douglas
Cramer too??!" He whacked his curly red head and his eyes rolled
away. A reaction, I was beginning to think, to the constant pounding he was giving his skull. But he was no more impressed than we
were. Our horizons were expanding considerably.

We even got in to see Persky and Dennoff. It was a short
meeting because they were two days behind on the week's schedule,
but they promised to read our material, and the carrot of *That Girl*
dangled enticingly.

Our plane was to leave at 9:30 Friday night and if it hadn't
been running late, we would've missed it. We turned in the rental
car and raced frantically, luggage in hand, down the endless marble
conduit to the gate. There were no seats left together so we
canvassed the plane for someone who might swap. It was important. We had a lot to talk about, decisions to make, new goals to
set. It had been a full week. Trading a middle seat for an aisle
wasn't easy, but things were still going our way. I scrunched in next
to a catfish farmer from Louisiana and Erwin settled into the aisle
seat. Now to review the week, to reflect upon what we had accom-

plished, calmly, objectively, without the hustle and bustle of the moment. The big jet roared down the runway, lifted effortlessly over the dark Pacific Ocean, then banked across the twinkling coastal lights of southern California. It felt good to relax. It was the first time in a week.

Ten minutes off the ground, we were both sound asleep.

7

CARPE DIEM

"The wise man in the storm prays God, not for safety
from danger, but for deliverance from fear."

Ralph Waldo Emerson

I paced nervously, and thumbed once again through the notes for
my presentation. This was an unusual assemblage of businessmen,
willing, so far, to step out, to take risks, to be as unique as the city
they wished to promote. Still, I was uneasy. This time I had only
ideas to work with. Intangible concepts. *Essence.* The visuals had all
been seen before. There were no new slides to show, no flashy new
ads, nothing but thin air in which to ignite the spark of imagination.

The Denton account had been dropped in my lap, more or
less, because I was low man on the agency totem pole. The City's
annual promotional budget was a mere $40,000, and almost
$12,000 of that was eaten up in agency fees. It didn't leave much to
work with, but by agency standards, the fees were negligible.
Therefore, the higher-paids couldn't justify spending much time in
Denton's behalf. That left only me. The account supervisor told me
it would be a good learning experience, but neither he, nor I, had
any idea just *how* good.

I studied the problems, the objectives, and the things Denton
had to offer. And, secretly, I began to smuggle a new philosophy
into my thinking; new, at least, for that particular agency. I had
brought it up before, curiously, questioningly, when some campaign

or promotion seemed to be heading down an uninspired *facts first* road to mediocre results. But I would get blank, often sympathetic, stares. No one on the entire sixteenth floor of the Dallas Federal Savings Building, save one, seemed to have the vaguest notion what I was talking about.

"Doesn't it need some emotion?"

"Emotion?"

"Yes, emotion."

"Meaning?"

"Meaning if you don't reach the emotion I think you're wasting your time. If your audience doesn't *feel* something about what you're trying to tell them, they won't retain your message, *nor* will they care about your product."

"Exactly what are you trying to say?"

And so it went. The business group wanted safe, conservative approaches to the intellect. "If you're selling a pencil, *show* it. A picture's worth a thousand words!" And—unsaid—it's also very safe. The client loves to see his product up big.

But clients, most of them, also want to sell something. And I couldn't remember ever buying *anything* that didn't have an emotional reason—or excuse—at it's core.

It seemed inconsistent to me to embark upon an intellectual approach to anything in which the desired response is some sort of emotional action, be it falling in love with a character in a story, buying a product, or reaching for a dream. The road to involvement was not, I theorized, through the intellect.

When a couple buys a house, it's usually the most important, most expensive item for which they'll ever obligate themselves, yet the decision on which house to buy is always based on emotional reasons. Intellectual considerations are certainly part of the process—we have thirteen kids so we need fourteen bedrooms—but, if we're honest with ourselves, it's the big stone fireplace, the view of the lake, the sunken tub, the color of the carpet, the size of the back yard, the trees on the lot, or the huge vaulted ceiling in the family room that swings the final decision. It's the same with cars, clothes, and even investments.

And in Denton's case, I reasoned, the same for corporate heads looking for mid-continental locations on which to build new facilities, or move old ones.

The agency padrones didn't share this pattern of logic, but I suppose they decided I could do little harm with such a small account so they pretty much left me alone with my bizarre new ideas.

Nobody seemed to understand except the people in Denton. The copy department didn't understand, so I shut the door to my office and wrote the ads myself. I found a composer in Denton— North Texas State University has one of the finest music schools in the country—and we wrote and produced a musical album about Denton, hiring the Shakespearean actor Hans Conreid for the short bits of talk, just the right touch to counter the prevailing yankee image of Texas. It was all about appealing to the emotion, trying to make people *feel* that Denton was actually as dynamic as it actually was.

I fought agency leanings toward smaller ads in more publications. They wanted to spread the media budget over a longer period of time, or a wider audience, or both; but I felt, given our message and our objective of lifting Denton out of the mangle of other communities seeking industrial growth, the impact of full pages in Fortune Magazine was critical.

I did battle with those who were certain that no high-ranking corporate official would ever order a *record album,* much less listen to it, no matter how good the copy in the ads, which, by the way, was too long. Not one person in five, I was told, would wade through it all. Maybe so, I reasoned, but that *one person* who reads it won't soon forget it. He or she will be well on the way to becoming a real friend of Denton and I felt it was better to have one good friend than five passing acquaintances.

In short, we were breaking all the rules. But rule-breaking wasn't the objective and I was frustrated with the controversy I was creating within the agency. I only wanted to do the job we had been hired to do, as well as it could be done. And make every dollar work like two. I believed in what I was trying to accomplish. I had done my homework, and I didn't feel that empty opinions and dusty, non-applicable traditions had any place within the program analysis. I tried to be open, but unless someone could give me a logical reason to re-evaluate, I stood firmly—okay, haltingly, nervously—by my guns.

The biggest flap came over the copy approach. Not only was it too long, it didn't have enough facts and figures. *Back to the intellect!* Months before, I had stressed to Denton city fathers that, all things being equal, Denton was a better place than most for those evaluating mid-continental locations because of the city's attitude, it's spirit. Everybody from the bank president to the young kid pumping gas was unabashedly enthusiastic about their city. And once taxes, land costs, labor costs, and the like had been evaluated as comparable to other communities, corporate decisions, I felt, would hang on such subjective, emotional criterion. "One community will be chosen over another because one is a more exciting place to be," I said, "a more dynamic place to be. The attitude is infectious. It can even improve productivity."

It wasn't the facts and figures, I pleaded, but that spirit we must project. Corporate heads respond to their emotions just like everybody else. And since most industrial development advertising looked the same, used the same tired words, appealed strictly to the intellect and was, on the whole, quite boring, the field appeared to be wide open for a bold, new approach to the problem.

But, traditionally, bold, new approaches carry with them the greater chance of failure. *New,* more often than not, is the sister word for *risk.* And therein, I think, lay the real concerns of the agency hierarchy. They would've preferred to play the cards a little closer to the chest; to linger further back in the crowd, out of the spotlight, where results, or lack of them, could not be tabulated so easily. Somewhere during the decades of balancing client problems against agency overhead, *safe* had become a way of life. They had forgotten—or chose to ignore—that protecting against a loss was also to protect against a win; that to eliminate the risk was to eliminate the *reach* that made winning possible; which, as David Mahoney once said, is to breed plodding mediocrity.

The album was offered up as a *Free Sample of Denton, Texas* and was definitely a risk and a reach. But, in the end, it received more responses than any industrial development advertisement ever to appear in Fortune magazine. Another of the Denton ads would capture one of the highest readership scores in the magazine—*Denton, Texas and Los Angeles, California could pass for twins... give or take six million people!* And over the next few years, Denton would make more corporate presentations than during any like period in their history and several would turn into new plants or distribution facilities.

The program was the coalescence of a number of philosophies I had wrangled with and nurtured for years but had said little about. I had so often puzzled my way through agency strategy sessions saying to myself: *that simply doesn't make sense; I would think this or that would work better.* But I was a novice. What did I know? Those in higher positions with more experience felt differently. So I would remain quiet. Then, later, when meager results would limp in, I'd wonder why I hadn't said something. In that way, I gradually began to forge a new confidence in my own thought processes, even when they struck discord among the experts of the moment. This would be an important lesson in years to come. The logical approach to problem solving, first learned from a jigsaw puzzle in a hotel room in Dayton, Ohio, worked even when thousands of dollars and presidents of huge corporations were involved.

But as I stood before the executive committee of the Denton Chamber of Commerce Study Group on that particular day, none of the results were in yet. The appearance of the first ad was still several weeks away. The committee had courageously approved the concept for the program months ago. Then, later, the ads and the musical album. Now, here I was, back selling a daring extension of the philosophy even before I knew whether or not it was really going to work.

It would be, as it turned out, one of the most important presentations I would ever make. I was recommending the production of a film.

It had been a year since our trip to Los Angeles, and we were beginning to notice a distressing trend. We were still unsold, uncredited writers.

But it was just around the corner! Any minute now!

I was becoming increasingly aware of how silly that was beginning to sound, even though I was the only one I was saying it to. The breakthrough had seemed so close so many times.

Paul Henning had written a pair of terrific letters complimenting our work and offering suggestions. He "enjoyed our Green Acres script immensely" and suggested that we submit some premises to Jay Sommers. "Jay has a new show going next fall and is going to need lots of help. Since he liked your dialogue, all you need to do is come up with some acceptable stories."

We followed his advice, but Jay Sommers' new show didn't get on the air. And neither did we.

Bill Dana's *Milton Burl Show* was off the air by January. He was immediately named producer of *The Las Vegas Show,* which had an even shorter life. And then he disappeared, I think, to Hawaii. Probably to question the sanity of his career decisions.

We wrote a script for *That Girl* and Bill Persky loved everything about it... except the story structure.

Story again.

"The basics are there," he had said, "it just needs strengthening. But don't do a thing until I get back to you. I want to discuss it with Danny Arnold." Arnold was the show's new producer.

We didn't wait for Persky to call. I completely revised the script and had it back to him within two weeks. He seemed to like it a lot, but still nothing happened. We eventually began to deduce that the problem was Danny Arnold. Apparently he neither liked the story nor the precocious kid around which the story revolved. We found out later that we had stumbled onto one of television's most story-conscious producers. A perfectionist who regularly drove writers to drink. He did not like the abnormal, unique, or unusual. He preferred emphasis on basic human qualities and readily identifiable emotional situations. And he appeared to wield the final say.

Once again, we had over-uniqued the premise and reached too far in efforts to generate interest and set up the comedy. The story line was shackled into an author-contrived situation rather than developing naturally from simple, basic emotions and character relationships. Looking back, it always seems so simple.

Persky tried to convince Danny Arnold to guide us in a revision, but by July, it seemed obvious that it wasn't going to happen. We decided to abandon the script and start from scratch with new story ideas. In early August, we shipped off two new treatments.

Meanwhile, Jerry Van Dyke had landed a new series, amidst squeals of joy from the Dallas Federal Savings Building Basement Cafeteria. Clearly this would be our best opportunity yet. By

January we had extracted a faithful promise from Jerry to work on the producer in our behalf. But in the months that followed, the series changed names three times and concepts twice, a pretty good indication that things weren't going too smoothly. Production began in July and by early August we still hadn't heard from Jerry, concluding that he probably had his share of internal strife without trying to sell the producer on a trio of untested writers.

We, of course, didn't *feel* untested. We'd been at it for two years. Old hopes had dissipated and new ones were in charge, but a single phone call could still send us on our way. Only the names had changed. No longer was the future hanging on *Green Acres* or *Get Smart* or *Heavenly Host,* but on *That Girl,* and Jerry's new series, *Accidental Family.*

There were moments when I chided myself, wondering how far along some corporate ladder I could've been if all the effort to crack Hollywood had been poured into advertising. I believed in the values of persistence and tenacity, but wondered for how long? At what point was I supposed to throw in the towel?

Only, I decided, when I no longer believed in myself.

"So what I'm proposing today is that we take the story of Denton, Texas on the road. That we schedule luncheons for industrial and business executives in major cities of the country, hosted by large numbers of Denton civic leaders. That we present, in person, Denton's dynamic story in an exciting, energetic program, anchored with a strong, emotionally impactful film."

There was a long silence.

Finally, Homer Bly spoke up. He was the banker in the group. "Don't films cost a lot of money?"

"This one would cost a ton if it weren't for two extraordinary circumstances."

I took a deep breath and flipped to the next note. The question had been anticipated.

"One. We've already got the soundtrack." I pointed with a flourish to the hot pink album cover, the free sample of Denton, Texas in sound and music. "It's a bit backward, I admit, producing the soundtrack first, but there it is. The perfect sound for the film, it's already paid for, and whenever the film is shown, each prospect will take home, as a free gift from Denton, *an original soundtrack recording!*"

Eyes twinkled; murmurs, smiles and nodding heads.

Then, from the banker again, "I heard Dallas spent fifty thousand dollars on a film last year. Our whole budget's only forty."

"The second extraordinary circumstance..." I tried to clear my throat, but a nerve troll had a stranglehold on my vocal chords, causing my words to sputter and crack. "The second extraordinary circumstance..." I repeated, wishing my heart wouldn't pound so hard... "is that Bill McGee and I will do the entire film ourselves, on weekends in our spare time, at no cost to Denton. You will only be billed for the actual cost of materials and equipment rental."

Silence.

Finally, from Roy Appleton, publisher of the Denton newspaper: "Extraordinary indeed."

They bought it!

As I drove back into Dallas, I was still in shock. And a little frightened at their blind trust. Over the past couple of years, the members of the executive committee and I had become very close, more so than the usual client-agency relationship. They knew I cared a lot about what they were trying to do and, in that, they seemed to find confidence. Probably to a fault. Their decision this day, however, bordered on insanity. They had just unanimously agreed that I should produce and direct a film for their city, knowing that I had no experience whatsoever in the field.

The realization was overwhelming! A film! I hadn't the foggiest idea where to begin. Yet the entire next phase of the Denton program would revolve around this film. If it failed, the whole program would fail.

I shuddered at the thought of breaking the news to my account supervisor and wondered if his coronary would occur before or after he relieved me of my job? New campaigns, even ideas for new campaigns, simply were not presented to clients until the agency had seen them first! It wasn't policy, just accepted procedure; sort of a dress rehearsal for the account executive and an opportunity for the agency to critique the presentation. But, over the past year, these rehearsals for Denton had become bloody battlefields. So I had concluded, a few months back, that a less volatile route through the process might help to preserve what was rapidly becoming a dangerously fragile relationship at the agency. My first option, of course, was to be less hard-headed. To give in and do it their way. At one point, I even tried. But I just couldn't make myself subordinate the process of analysis and simple logic to opinions admittedly forged from some ancient rule book that courted broad, general solutions for individually unique problems.

"Less copy is better than more copy."

"More ads are better than fewer ads."

"A picture is worth a thousand words."

Tell that to Shakespeare, or Dickens, or Hemingway, I wanted to say.

I seemed truly out of step, and it bothered me a lot. These people were older and supposed to be wiser. They had decades of experience. I had a few years. How could I believe, even for a moment, that they were wrong and I was right? Still, I couldn't let it go. I had to find out for myself whether I was making sense or silliness. To give in now, might be to never know. Would my kind of logic work out there in the real world? Or was most of the agency right? I was becoming desperate for the answer.

The Denton executive committee preferred to see all pitches before any full scale presentation was made to the entire study group. This flushed out weaknesses and placed the committee solidly behind the program when it was presented to the full group. After a few of those rousing knockabouts at the agency, it occurred to me that if I delayed agency presentations until after executive committee pitches, it might make for smoother sailing. Technically, I rationalized, there was nothing wrong with this decision. The agency still saw each campaign before the full blown study group presentation was made, but strategically, it put the executive committee solidly behind the program even before my account supervisor saw it.

That's the only thing that saved the film. After all, they bleated, film production was not my department. I was not experienced in film production and working on the weekends for free was very unprofessional! I could only agree on all points and mumble something about the end sometimes justifying the means. But what I said had nothing to do with their decision not to rock the boat. It all boiled down to the fact that the Denton executive committee was already enthusiastically behind the program, and without the film, there was no program.

I was accused, at least once, of orchestrating an elaborate con job, just to make a film. To begin, as it were, my demo reel. I suppose I'll always wonder if sub-consciously I was somehow arranging the pieces on the board to set up the need for a film, but it wasn't a con job. I cherish the trust of others too much to venture out on that kind of limb. Perhaps it was God fooling around in my life again. The coincidences are certainly striking in retrospect. Denton not only had to need a film, the need had to be for a caliber of film they couldn't afford any other way. The bid from a local film house was $35,000, more than Denton's entire annual budget after agency fees. But with everybody working for free, I was projecting costs at around $5,000.

We would have a total crew of three. Harland would be art director and one of six on-screen personalities. Bill McGee would be cameraman and editor, and together, the three of us would do whatever else needed to be done. Bill was the agency print production manager on the Denton account and knew little more than I did about film production, except he had once perched atop a press box with a Kodak K-100, filming football games for his high school coach. He had never even seen an Arriflex, the camera we'd be using in Denton. But, then, neither had I.

"Joe, I'd like to see you in my office."

The voice of the president. I wasn't thrilled. I knew I was going to get it, I just didn't know exactly what *it* was going to be. He lectured for nearly an hour, concluding straight to the point. "You will have to become more of a team player. You will stop shutting out the creative department. You will make *all* future client presentations to the agency first! Or I will have to make some changes."

His meaning was clear. I swallowed hard and promised to do better. As I reached for the closed door, he spoke again.

"This has been a very difficult conversation for me," he said. "A business must have form, and structure, and protocol. Everyone must pull together for the common goal of the company."

I wondered why he was repeating himself?

"A renegade, allowed to run without restraint, can be a very disruptive influence on order and morale..." There was a long pause, then the slightest hint of a smile. "No matter how good his work may be."

I'm certain my jaw must've hit the floor. He had never before indicated that he even knew what I was doing, much less that he liked any of it.

"What you've done for Denton is good," he said softly. "Very good. You can be proud of it. It's your methods we have to work on."

I was frozen in shock and it seemed like several minutes before I could muster something vaguely resembling a "yes sir". Then I scrambled for the door.

"Good luck with the film," he added.

I fairly sailed my way back through the narrow hallways to my office, shut the door and plopped against it for a long time with a very silly grin pasted across my face. I didn't know which felt better, his comments about my work or his blessing on the film. Finally, I dropped into the ancient squeak of a chair behind my desk and leaned back, feet on the frail little typewriter table across the way.

A film! I wanted to savor the moment. To swirl for a bit in the euphoria of realization that, at last, my childhood dream was about to come true. It wasn't *Song of the South*, but it would be *Directed by Joey Camp*, more or less.

I flipped on the portable tape recorder at my elbow and watched a series of images dance through my mind as I listened to the sounds and music of Denton, Texas.

But I wasn't the writer, or producer, or director of those images. I was a member of the audience, waiting to be moved, daring the images to reach into my emotions and cause me to *feel*. For that's where the film would win or lose, and I must never for a moment forget that. There was no time to dwell upon what it means to *be* a director, real or imagined. I must stay firmly seated as a member of the audience; every shot, every thought, every action, every decision dictated by the effect it would ultimately have upon those who would view it.

The phone rang.

I pushed the intercom button.

"Line two, Joe." There was a twinge of excitement pinching at her usual breathy whisper.

"It's Jerry Van Dyke. He says it's important."

8

THE BIG TIME

"Toil, says the proverb, is the sire of fame."
Euripides

The huge gray cavity seemed to dwarf the dozen or so people sitting around the long table. From somewhere high in the rigging, a lone spotlight encircled the group, bathing them in warm light, giving them color and life, painting them brightly against the gray, unlit television sets standing idle behind them.

Animated faces and waving arms tore at a helpless script, page by page, reading aloud, rewriting lines, arguing with each other over whether something was working or not.

"I just wouldn't say it that way!"

"This joke's not funny!"

"That bit doesn't play!"

They struggled and fought over an exchange of lines. Someone got up to pace—I think it was one of the writers—and he challenged the actor. The actor slammed the script onto the table, then someone else leaped to his feet and tried it a different way, new words, new inflection. The actor liked it. So did the writer.

"Can't do it," said another. "It gives away too much, too early."

"But it's funny!" said the writer.

Off in the shadows, well out of the spotlight, Erwin, Harland and I sat quietly in worn, faded director's chairs getting the education of a lifetime. We were discovering that writing was the same hair-pulling experience for professionals that it was for us. It was a revelation that flushed excitement through every vein. The best words were not coming instantaneously, magically, as I had suspected they would. These people were actually having to *work* at it.

It was a glorious feeling. Spread out before us was a table of highly-paid, mostly famous television artists and craftsman struggling with the same problems we struggled with and making the same ponderously slow progress through obstinate scripts.

"Drop the word 'coordinated'," I blurted out.

Erwin slapped his hand across my mouth. "You want to get us kicked outta here?!" he whispered through clinched teeth.

"It's true!" I hissed. "That's what's hanging them up. And the word's not even necessary."

"But it's not your position to say so!"

He was right of course, and I sank back in the chair, frustrated that I couldn't participate in the process, but delighted that my brain seemed to be working as well as theirs. It was an exciting, albeit biased, discovery. And quite unexpected.

"Nothing's guaranteed," Jerry had said on the phone, "but Sy likes your writing. If you come out for a few days, he'll screen some rough cuts for you to give you a feel of the series and let you sit in on a few sessions. Then if you can come up with a story he likes, you're on your way!"

We didn't even stop to count the number of times we had been on our way before. We simply climbed onto a plane two days later and flew west. Another week of vacation stolen from the family. Another six months in debt.

When we arrived, we were immediately ushered into the Monday morning read-through, where the director, the producer, the writers and the entire cast were gathered around a long table on the sound stage reading the script for the week, tearing it to pieces as they went. That afternoon, as the writers limped off with their shreds to make revisions, we were escorted into a plush, private screening room, just the three of us, to see several episodes of the series. Most of them were rough cuts, without music and laugh tracks, and with the editor's grease pencil marks all over the film. But we could tell it was going to be a good series. This was no *My Mother the Car*. Once the premise was set, the episodes seemed to work terrifically well. Only the pilot seemed weak, sort of silly and trivial by comparison, and distractingly complicated. Yet the pilot would be the first show to air, and it seemed to me the first should be the best of the batch, not the worst. We couldn't help but wonder why it hadn't been done as warmly and simply as the rest of the shows.

Jerry was introduced as a widowed Las Vegas entertainer attempting to further his career and take care of a young son at the same time. According to the script, he was actually doing a better than average job of fathering, but a hated in-law was suing for custody, maintaining that a Las Vegas hotel was not the proper atmosphere for child raising. The judge was ready to snatch the boy away unless Jerry immediately provided him with a more traditional family type environment. Through a maze of contrivances, Jerry met a divorced Lois Nettleton with a young daughter, bought a farm in the San Fernando Valley and convinced Lois to help him set up a phony home to fool the in-law and the judge. Lois and her daughter would live on the farm, in the same house, but at arm's length with Jerry and his son, all under the guise of being a family.

The object, of course, was to put two virtual strangers, both more or less traditional in their values, under the same roof playing husband and wife whenever anyone was around, but Iceberg and Frosty when the world wasn't watching. The kids, of course, were the same age and were prime prospects for all the problems that exist between brother and sister who aren't really brother and sister. And, as icing for the writers, there was a corn crib full of possibilities every time our hero, the urbane nightclub performer, stepped out of his element onto the farm.

Once over the initial hurdle, the scripts were being handled warmly and sensitively. The premise was not being played for shallow, cheap laughs, but rather to develop strong, character related humor, anchored with interesting and real problems among the players. All of which contributed to the mystery of the pilot. I was afraid it was going to be like trying out a new restaurant and finding a roach in your salad. The audience would all be gone before the main course was served.

I wanted to say something. To the producer, to Jerry, to anyone! But Erwin and Harland threatened to lock me in a trunk and ship me back to Dallas. It all seemed so simple! One tiny change could eliminate the contrivances and make the whole setup more believable, more natural.

"The pilot is already finished!" Erwin reminded me. "Shot! Cut! In the can!"

"But listen," I said. "What if they let Lois Nettleton be the pesky in-law?! Look how it simplifies things. She wants custody because she honestly believes the kid needs a better environment. And so does the judge. So, Jerry has no choice but to negotiate a deal. He'll agree to let his son reside on Lois' farm—the farm would be hers, not his—if she drops the custody battle and allows Jerry to live there between nightclub engagements.

"But, what would my principal say," Lois would ask. In this version, she's a teacher, at the local, small-town, conservative school."

"Tell 'em we're married." Jerry would answer.

"Not a chance!" Lois would say.

"Then Jerry would discover that Lois is having trouble paying the mortgage on the farm! New life for his plan! If she agrees to the deal, he'll take care of the mortgage. Reluctantly, she agrees, probably spelling out a trunk full of conditions.

"It's less complicated *and* more believable," I persisted. "And more interesting. Jerry and Lois are now adversaries living under the same roof, each with the other over the proverbial barrel, her with her custody threat and him with his mortgage payment. Yet both are basically warm and caring individuals. This is the kind of terrific, combustible stuff that great stories are made of!"

Erwin and Harland agreed. It might've been the best story analysis I had ever done. But it never escaped. They convinced me that one of the best ways to never be heard from again would be to tell Sy Gomberg that, in our terribly experienced opinions, the pilot he had already filmed which was to go on the air in less than a month, should be thrown away and remade from scratch.

They were right, of course, but it was excruciatingly frustrating. For Jerry's sake, I wanted to help. I also wanted to learn. If my seemingly simple solution wasn't any good, I wanted to know why. If it was, why hadn't someone else thought of it?

This question bothered me a lot, until the first time I was there myself, buried under the massive, blinding collage of kaleidoscopic pressures upon which every production seems to be constructed. Today, I remain amazed that anything ever gets produced at all, much less produced with some of the proper elements in their proper places.

We spent the next couple of days watching rehearsals and shooting. Then, later in the week, we were called into a private meeting with the producer, Sy Gomberg, and his story consultant, Jim Brooks. The same Jim Brooks who went on to create *The Mary Tyler Moore Show* and *The Lou Grant Show*, and, later, write, produce and direct the Academy Award winning *Terms of Endearment* and numerous other terrific films.

The meeting lasted for several hours. Actually, it was a dozen or so short meetings sandwiched between phone calls and production problems. We listened to their concepts of the characters and their visions for the series, then we tossed around several spring-boards we had developed during the week. They liked two of them a lot. One—Sy's favorite—was about an aging entertainer, once famous, once Jerry's idol, now terrified of performing before an audience. Jerry had to deal with his own disappointment before he could help the performer regain his confidence. The other story—my favorite—was about Jerry's beautiful cousin from Georgia who drops in unexpectedly for a visit, interrupting a trip to Disneyland for Jerry and son, Sandy. To make amends, she cooks up a big southern dinner, unwittingly serving as the main course, Sandy's pet chicken that he had raised from an egg.

Back in Dallas, we developed the two springboards into full outlines and shipped them off along with one more, a lighter one, we conceived on the plane flying home. The next week, Sy called to tell us the show was full for the first thirteen segments, but if the series was picked up for the rest of the year, he could promise us at least one script, maybe two. Meanwhile, he said he'd like to show our work around to other producers on the lot, and to his agent, Sylvia Hirsch, at William Morris.

"One script, maybe two!" I gurgled. "Other producers! William Morris!"

The suitcases came back off the shelf.

To Joe, Erwin, Harland

I think your outlines for "Accidental Family" are excellent—Hope for all concerned it gets picked up. I assume Sy has the original copies.

If you like I'll try to help you fellas along until you sell something, then we'll see.

Sylvia Hirsch

The word *excellent* leapt off the page and spun around me in a dizzying swirl. Sylvia Hirsch at William Morris, one of the most renowned talent agency in the world, had said our most recent writing was *excellent!* I supposed we had been naive before. We hadn't really been ready. We were still learning back then. But now, well, this time it was clearly different. Now, it was time for some serious packing.

Carolyn and I danced around the living room, thoroughly mystifying son Joey, now six. I never saw the anxiety that was tearing at her excitement, or, perhaps, I didn't want to. She had always known that this amusement of mine had been no simple diversion, but as long as it was unsuccessful, there was no cause for immediate concern. Now, however, looming close upon her horizon were wholesale changes in environment and lifestyle that she wanted no part of, like moving to Los Angeles. Still, she was my most enthusiastic cheerleader. With all of her energy and heart, she wanted to help me capture the dream I had chased for so long. Either way, for her, to win was to lose.

"What's going to happen?" she asked. "To us, I mean."

There was courage in the question that I couldn't match with an answer.

"No need to talk about problems that don't exist," I said. "In all probability, the series won't even be picked up."

I was stalling. Secretly, I was certain that it would be.

But it wasn't.

We were devastated, our hopes dashed like champagne glasses against a stone hearth.

I couldn't help but wonder what might have happened if I had passed my thoughts about the pilot along to Sy while there was still time to do something. How arrogant of me, I also thought. But the truth was the pilot drew a pretty good audience and they simply didn't come back for the *good* shows. How many times in your life have you absolutely believed something to be true, but said nothing because the experts should know better. For better or worse, I vowed to never let it happen to me again.

Before he left for the desert, Sy made one more contribution to our education that would become one of the keys, a corner--stone, to my entire future. He had a long talk with *That Girl* producer, Danny Arnold.

It must've been more than Danny could take—Bill Persky from one side, Sy Gomberg from the other—because he phoned the next day.

"Hi, this is Danny Arnold and I give up, surrender, holler uncle! Call off Persky and Gomberg and you guys come on out. I want you to do an assignment for *That Girl*. I don't know what it'll be yet, but whatever it is, it'll pay enough to at least cover your expenses. And, maybe get you that first screen credit. Then, you'll be on your way."

Real money?? A screen credit?? This *had* to be the one!

I pried our last week of vacation from Carolyn's clutching arms. Erwin cajoled his wife into manning the phone at the art studio. And off we went.

Danny Arnold's office at Paramount-Cahuenga, the old Desilu Studios, looked like a tornado had preceded us by only a matter of moments. Scripts, stories, outlines and other papers were scattered everywhere, on his desk, on shelves, even on the floor. We were ushered in and seated on a soft, overstuffed leather couch across from the desk. Danny was winding up a phone call. As I sank out of sight into the inner reaches of the couch, I remember feeling very ill at ease. It had something to do with inferior eye level, a manipulation discovered by certain types of businessmen to keep their quarry uncomfortable and on the defensive. I think it was Louie B. Mayer I had read about who actually ordered a sloped, virtually undetectable, platform added to the floor behind his desk so that he would always be looking ever-so-slightly down on those across from him.

I wondered if Danny Arnold was a Louie B. Mayer type. The answer came quickly, a definite no. He didn't need an eye level advantage. His manner was imposing enough. I imagine the couch was there, instead of chairs, so he'd have a place to grab a nap when working into the wee hours, which, I was discovering, people in this industry seem to do as a matter of course. But I've never forgotten that feeling, gazing helplessly up from the depths of that couch, and I've always remembered to arrange my offices over the years to keep eyes across the desk on the same level. Except, of course, during contract negotiations.

The phone plopped into its cradle, then Danny reached for a stack of material on the floor behind him, his huge frame twisting and struggling against a creaking chair that fit him like a glove. The material landed on the desk in front of us with a splat. On top was the script for *That Girl* we had submitted to Bill Persky. Next was the new story outline that had followed, then the minister script and our three story outlines for *Accidental Family*. He had read them all.

"You write terrific dialog," he said. "But your story structure sucks."

I wondered if he always had so much trouble coming to the

point.

We scraped ourselves off the floor and tried to react intelligently, but it wasn't easy. After our recent experiences with *Accidental Family*, we had thought we were beginning to find the handle. And I suppose we were, sort of, because before the week was out, he had made one, maybe two, virtually nice comments about the chicken story we had done for Sy. It was the stuff for *That Girl* he hated.

But, at last, this is where the dilemma on story structure would come to an end. In Danny Arnold's office, my torn and tattered red rule book would tumble from its lofty perch and crash to the floor. "The dynamics of feelings and emotions are not found in lists of rules and regulations," he would say. And I would finally learn, simply, that the best stories were born in the emotional conflicts within a character. Yes, even with comedy. It was something I had stumbled onto with the chicken story, but hadn't really focused upon. The conflict within the child is what made it work so well; his sorrow over the loss of his pet and his urge to blame, fighting an emotional tug-of-war with the need to understand and forgive.

During the next week, I would ingest every nuance Danny Arnold would offer and would learn more about the heart and soul of a good story than I ever had before, or probably since. He is a master story constructionist and whatever skills I've managed to develop in this area were planted and nurtured with his teachings.

But he had never really planned to hold class.

"Dialog and situation are your strong suits," he said, "Not story. So, I think the fastest way to a screen credit would be a rewrite." He summarized several scripts he had previously commissioned, all of sound story structure, but poorly written. "Rewriting any one of these will get you shared credit with the original writers, and that's all you need to be on your way."

That phrase again.

I swallowed hard, trying to dampen the sandpaper in my throat, sat up as high as the cushy couch would allow and said, "We'd rather start with a new story. If possible. We have several springboards. If none of them work for you, maybe, then, we could do the rewrite."

Find the most difficult, complicated way to approach anything and that's generally where I seem to put myself. I don't know why. Maybe winning too easily, or winning without merit, leaves nothing of value in the reward. But, for me, personally, the screen credit, and what it might do for us, was not as important as being able to start from scratch and do the entire job well. Particularly in the perfectionist eyes of someone like Danny Arnold.

Danny didn't care for any of our springboards, but one reminded him of another story idea that he had liked a lot. It was currently in the dead files. He had commissioned story development once before, but didn't like what came back. The springboard involved the plight of an aging janitor in Ann Marie's apartment building. He was about to be fired, which would render him homeless as well as jobless because he lived in the basement of the building. He had no family and nowhere to go. The story task was to involve Ann Marie (Marlo Thomas) in the old man's problem and build her concern into a way for her to help save his job and home.

The first writer had justified the firing by making the janitor a complete incompetent. Ann Marie wound up doing all the janitorial chores herself in an effort to make the old man appear capable of doing his job.

"It just doesn't work," Danny said. "You can't build a story around helping someone who can't help themselves."

He admitted it was a tricky problem. If the old man was really good, why would anyone want to fire him? If he wasn't, unfortunately, he deserved to be fired. But Danny loved the potential for relationship between Ann Marie and this old man and it was obvious that to solve this particular story problem would be to gain everlasting favor. It certainly seemed challenge enough to feed our uppity appetites, so off we went, sequestering ourselves in our ten-by-ten motel room where, by day, we paced and pounded the portable typewriter, and, by night, we slept in rotation, two on the beds and one on the floor. It was a frustrating, claustrophobic, hair-pulling week.

The first order of business was a new structural direction for the story. The moment we had it, or *thought* we had it, we raced the two blocks back to Danny's office for his reaction. An hour later, we were limping home, licking our wounds. This happened more times than I want to recall. Danny Arnold began to take on the likeness of a vicious, fire-breathing bridge troll, eyes and teeth flashing, hungrily awaiting each new effort and dining upon it with insatiable relish.

Then one morning I rolled over and gazed up from the musty motel room carpet at Harland's size-twelve feet dangling off the end of the bed, and suddenly all the pieces fell into place. I, at once, understood everything Danny Arnold had been trying to pound into our brains. It was like dropping the last piece of that now familiar jigsaw puzzle into place, at last revealing the total picture.

The mind is, indeed, a curious mechanism. I would think comprehension would come with absorption, as a direct relation-ship to study and effort; slowly, gradually, as each new piece is added to the puzzle. But it doesn't. At least it never has for me. It's always been a dawning light at the end of a persistent struggle. Back in the days of algebra and trigonometry, I can remember the same frustration. I would study some theorem or concept for days, memorizing the various steps and pieces, working out the assigned problems, but not really understanding what I was doing, or why. I could usually find the right answer, but was never satisfied in that alone. I wanted to know what made the whole thing work. The more I would study, the more frustrated I would become. Until one day, some insignificant scrap of information would slide surreptitiously into place and the fog would suddenly lift. The doggedness would pay off. I would, at last, understand. And the important point to remember here is that the continual struggle, the effort to uncover, the constant plowing of the soil was the engine that ultimately uncovered that last piece of the puzzle. Quitting in frustration leads nowhere. You don't give up. You keep on keepin' on.

That day was the day Danny Arnold became human again. The green wrinkly skin and flashing teeth were gone. It was also the day we would stop limping back to the motel room in scars and tatters. We would *race* back to finally begin the actual process of writing the story.

By the end of the week, we had finished a seven-page, single-spaced treatment. Danny loved most of it. There were some problems in the second act and he wanted those pages rewritten, but he was happy with the structure and thought the first act was near perfect.

The story solution had evolved by approaching the problem from a fresh direction. Mr. Plummer was now a recent replacement for the cold, all-business maintenance service that the building's owner had employed for years. The tenants loved their new janitor. He was wonderful. In addition to taking care of their maintenance problems, he taught new housewives how to cook, helped widows with their sewing, made decorating suggestions, and was truly a beloved jack of all trades.

So why would the building owner ask him to leave? The answer surfaces with a jolt in the following paragraphs that brought Act One of the treatment to a close.

"It wasn't Mr. Plummer's fault!" Ann screeches. "I'm the one who left the stopper in the sink!"

But she knows he'll get the blame, so she decides to beat Mrs. Hauptner to the punch. She calls the building owner herself and jabbers through a rapid-fire, virtually incomprehensible explanation of the tiny drip that turned into a bigger drip, that turned into a deluge, that flooded Mrs. Hauptner's apartment. But it wasn't the drip that caused the problem! It was the stopper she left in the sink! "The whole thing was my fault! So you can't blame anyone else! And what's more, things like this would never happen if you cheapskates would give your janitor the right kind of tools!!" She stops to grab a breath and suddenly a shock wave racks across her face.

"What did you say??!"

Ann is visibly stunned. "I see... yes, I suppose I was... No... that's all. Thank you. Goodbye."

She turns to Don and Ruth, blank-faced, groping for understanding. "He said they haven't had a janitor in this building for over two years."

FADE OUT.

The old man turned out to be a lonely, old Austrian immigrant, recently widowed, and very alone. All in the world he knew was building maintenance, but every attempt to work for the big services had ended in termination because he would spend too much time with the clients, getting to know them and helping them with other problems. His sinkside manner was terrific, but his company quota was never filled. When he discovered the vacant janitor's apartment in the basement of Ann's building, a building with such nice people, he simply decided to move in and take over. His physical needs were supplied by Social Security, and his emotional needs flourished with so many good friends. But he didn't belong and, in the second act, the building owner ordered him out.

Ann arranged a meeting between the two in which Mr. Plummer showed the owner how to turn his beef stroganoff recipe into an absolute masterpiece. The final outcome wasn't hurt any when the cheap owner discovered that Mr. Plummer would work for no more than room and board.

In November, after the second rewrite of Act Two, we shipped the final treatment to Danny Arnold, virtually assured that our first script assignment would be forthcoming. And, ironically, the prospect worried me. The film for Denton was only two months away and I wanted to see it through. Both for me, personally, and for the executive committee in Denton. They had placed a frighteningly large helping of faith in me and I was concerned about what would happen if suddenly I up and left.

It was a confusing time. I had worked hard to get to that first writing credit and I couldn't believe that, after all these years, I wasn't at all sure I wanted it to happen. Yet, if we were to write a script for a major network show, we had to capitalize then and there, or why bother?

Good story material, I thought. The struggle within. Whatever will he do?

"Hi Joe. Please hold for Danny Arnold."

My heart lurched upward and lodged in my throat. We hadn't heard from Danny in over a month when he had apologized for not yet reading the revised treatment. "But not to worry," he had said. "If it's like we discussed, it should work fine."

Then weeks of silence. Something had happened. I just felt it.

"Hi, Joe."

He sounded tired. "I've got bad news."

I knew it.

"They ASI'd a bunch of our shows over the holidays and I'm afraid the results have eliminated stories like the one we've been working on. It'll have to go on the shelf."

There seemed to be a trace of bitterness in his voice, but I might've imagined it. I certainly wanted it to be there. These near misses were becoming depressing.

"What's an ASI?" I asked.

"Audience Studies something-or-other. They test television shows with real audiences, statistical cross sections, to see what they like and don't like, and why. In our case, the big winners were the more sophisticated shows, so Danny wants all new scripts to go in that direction."

The Danny he mentioned was Danny Thomas, the star's father. He didn't have a credit on the show, but was apparently the real boss behind the scenes.

"What do you mean by *sophisticated?*" I asked.

"Sexy," he said flatly, an undisguised vexation confirming the earlier tone. "Shows that probe the relationship between Ann and her boyfriend. Like why aren't they married? How far do they go? And shows about sexy third parties creating triangles. Unfortunately, our Austrian janitor is a little too old for such nonsense."

He had just commissioned scripts on two such *sophisticated* stories that he had been holding for some time and these would finish him out for the year. He apologized, repeatedly. This was not the Danny Arnold we had come to know. I believe he really wanted to do the *Plummer* story and this new decree from the top, ordering him to bow before television's lowest common denominator, had exploded his personal vision for the series, and nettled his philosophy toward comedy. A distaste for exploiting sex and a true affection for his characters and their problems are certainly apparent in all of his work that followed *That Girl*. Work that he, himself, controlled.

He seemed genuinely upset that he hadn't been able to provide the nudge needed to produce our first writing credit. "Don't give up on me," he said. "I'll get you on the screen yet. It'll just have to wait until next season."

I don't doubt that he meant every word, but when next season came around, Danny's mind and time were consumed by the development of a new series entitled *My World and Welcome To It*; and Erwin, Harland and I were buried under the pages of our first full-length feature script.

My World and Welcome To It only ran for a year, but it won Danny an Emmy for Best Comedy Series, and he then went on to create and produce the hugely successful, long running *Barney Miller*.

We talked and corresponded for years. His commitment to excellence was a potion for the soul, an elixir for the spirit. He freely admitted that perfection was unattainable, "...but if you keep reaching for it," he would say, "the worst you're going to do is get close." Once when he was directing a show, I watched him go up against three technical *experts* who claimed that a particular shot was impossible. A cameraman, a camera operator and a dolly pusher were demanding that he simplify the scene because what he wanted to do just couldn't be done. He showed them otherwise and I never forgot it. It would've been easy for him to abort the fight, to simplify the shot, to give in to their harassment. But he stuck with what he believed and meticulously instructed the *experts* on how, with a little more thought and effort, mountains could indeed be moved. It was an inspiration to watch because I had already begun to conclude that accumulation of experience—*seniority*—was all too often, and all too automatically, translated into wisdom; that the longer someone had been around, the more awe he seemed to inspire, the more others would listen and nod unquestioningly, paying homage to the years, not to how wisely the owner had used them; that too many people in this world seemed to work the hardest to avoid working too hard; too many battles were fought to avoid efforts at excellence; and too few were fought to avoid mediocrity.

I never had the pleasure of working with Danny Arnold again but he left me with the raw materials, the conceptual seedlings that ultimately blossomed into the simple struggle of a fluffy, floppy-eared mutt trying to reach out and communicate without the benefits of language.

It had been three years since we had met Bill Dana. Nothing, directly, had come from that meeting, but had it not been for Dana, we might've never met Bill Persky, and would've never tried to meet Jerry Van Dyke. Had it not been for Jerry, we would've never met Sy Gomberg. Had it not been for Sy and Bill Persky, I doubt that we would've ever met Danny Arnold. And had it not been for Danny, well, there's so much I might never have found. The Lord works in mysterious ways. Thanks guys.

"Do it once more, please Phyllis. More sparkle in the eyes."

"I've got some glitter in the car," Harland said. Bill McGee chuckled and put his eye to the camera.

"Roll," I said.

The biting February wind cut into my face. It was near freezing with a chill factor, I imagine, well off the bottom of the scale. But the sun was shining, so I was hoping it wouldn't look so cold on film.

"Her nose is red," Bill whispered.

Shivering before the camera was a beautiful young junior from North Texas State University, one of three chosen to be in the film from more than two hundred college co-eds interviewed in Denton. Her only protection from the icy winds was a thin blue sweater and a pleated skirt. But she was still trying to find that magical sparkle for which she has since become famous. Her name was Phyllis George.

"Cut it," I said and motioned for Harland to jump in with her coat. "Phyllis, go warm up in the car for a minute, and maybe put some powder or something on your nose. The cold is showing."

She hurried over to join the others huddled in the warmth of a tiny red Volkswagen convertible donated by a local car dealer for use in the film. I turned to Bill who was breathing warm fog onto his cold, gloveless hands. "We need an early Spring," I said.

The initiation had begun. Blustery, February northers are not unusual in Texas. In fact, if anything, they're more normal than not. But I had overlooked northers in the planning of the schedule. I was trying to keep the easiest filming first. No tricky camera movements, no complicated blocking, no interiors with problem lighting. Just simple, short setups that would allow us, hopefully, to sneak up quietly on our inexperience.

But it was eleven o'clock on the first day of shooting and so far we only had one shot in the can. Our cast could stand maybe sixty seconds at a time without their coats before turning blue. The camera needed to be warmed between shots, but we couldn't rehearse without a camera, and every time it came out of the warm back into the cold, the lens would fog up. And I was afraid none of it mattered anyway because, come Monday, I would probably be without a job.

The morning had begun with a first class screaming match between Jim Gable and myself. Jim had recently become the agency's first Director of Broadcast Production. And since I knew nothing about production and Jim had experience, the agency president thought it would be helpful to ask Jim to sort of watch over the Denton effort. The problems began when Jim decided he wanted to direct it. Of course, looking back, I can't really blame him. If he felt this affair was going to be *his* responsibility, that is, if he was going to be blamed for it, what sense did it make to leave it in the hands of a marketing type, an account executive with no film background whatsoever?

I tried to put emotion aside and reason my way through it. He did have experience. But he had been at the agency less than a week and he didn't know the Denton program. He had seen the film script for the first time only a few days before. And this was my damn project and what the hell was he doing here anyway?!

I tried, again, to put emotion aside.

I backed off and let Jim direct the first shot of the morning. The script had been written and timed precisely to the existing soundtrack, something like a hundred and forty shots to fill a mere ten minutes of final film, the individual shots designed not to stand alone, but to weld themselves to those before and after creating a single, unified personality that, as a whole, would reach out and intoxicate the viewer with the very spirit of Denton. It was a precise blueprint for a film that had already been edited several times over in my head. It's the only way I knew to approach it. I had never directed a foot of professional film, I had never edited a frame, but I felt those were problems of minor importance. If I knew exactly what I was after, I could always find a way to get there. If the blueprint was good, if it was well thought out and complete enough, and if its objective, design and limits were followed closely enough, then the final film would work as a whole. Method could be discovered along the way.

To me, to veer from the script was to risk everything. But Jim didn't see it that way. Creativity, to him, was the offspring of spontaneity. Each shot should be a thing of beauty within itself. The script should conform to the results of the shoot.

It was reasonably clear that his approach differed from mine. Like night and day. So, we stood toe to toe in front of the cast and a handful of borrowed film students from North Texas State University and screamed at each other until Jim finally stalked off to his car and drove away to Dallas.

"Can't we do something inside?" Bill asked.

"Too late," I mumbled.

Setting up the schedule had been a bureaucratic nightmare for the Chamber of Commerce manager. I wouldn't have had the heart to ask him to change it on a Saturday, even if he could've.

Bill was dancing from one foot to the other trying to stir the circulation. I sighed and ushered everyone across the street to get some hot coffee. One shot a day would make for an awfully long schedule.

The trudge north to Denton continued for thirteen consecutive Saturdays and Sundays. Winter turned into spring and spring into the first waves of summer. The light wool sweaters the girls in the cast wore became walking saunas in the Texas heat. We were several weeks over our projected schedule, but managed to keep expenditures under budget. It's amazing how that can be accomplished when one simply has no choice.

Many of the excess days were consumed by the learning process, the school of trial and error. There were retakes by the dozens—shots re-filmed because they didn't look or work like they should have the first time around. There were scheduling mishaps when someone forgot, or somebody with keys or a permission slip failed to show up. And there were days of rain, and the morning one of the cast members simply decided to stay home.

One spring afternoon we were delayed three hours waiting for a custodian to come unlock the city's immense new civic center. It was a complicated but spectacular shot that could only be done on a Sunday, so, rather than reschedule, I decided to rouse whoever we could and wait the situation out. We were all sprawled around on the shiny, red Volkswagen—top down, for it was warm now—and someone decided that since this experience was going to be the starting point for many great careers, we should all confess what we wanted to do with our lives. Harland wanted to become an art director. Bill McGee would like to try out cinematography. One of the guys in the cast, a writer for the Denton paper, wanted to get into PR. Another wanted to become an actor. I wanted to write and direct *real* movies. Phyllis was last, and didn't have the foggiest notion what she wanted to do. Suggestions were abundant, but none to her liking. When the keys to the center finally arrived, I hopped off the car, and closed out the game. "Phyllis, there's nothing left. You'll just have to be Miss America."

It was with a bizarre mixture of feelings that I watched her walk down that long ramp in Atlantic City two and a half years later.

Each weekend, we shot as long as the sun would allow; trying, on week days, to be proper agency executives; editing at night; and I was still getting up at four in the mornings to work on a motion picture script that Sylvia Hirsch had encouraged us to write.

Little wonder that Carolyn threatened divorce when I told her we'd have to go a few extra weeks. That was after the agency president threatened murder when he heard about the Jim Gable affair. Thankfully, neither pressed the issues.

The film was edited in Bill McGee's living room, much to the dismay, I'm sure, of Bill's wife. For more weeks than I imagine they care to remember, editing equipment, assorted stacks of sixteen-millimeter reels and long, dangling tangles of celluloid were strung from one end of their house to the other. We had no moviola, didn't know what one was, and, in fact, knew no better than to edit the entire film on a hot splicer, which should bring a tittering of chuckles from those in the know. We had simply never heard of a *tape* splicer. Suffice to say, we encountered some interesting looks at the lab when the film went in for finishing.

Still, in the final analysis, it managed to work. Those who saw it, cheered, and became friends and supporters of the dynamic little city of Denton, Texas. And I had proven to myself that lack of knowledge and experience and an avalanche of embarrassing mistakes could be minimized and overcome by focusing continually on the final consumer. It didn't really matter to the people in the audience what shots were scheduled first and what type of splicer we used. What mattered to them was that emotional contact was made.

The words hung in the air like stars suspended in a midnight sky, twisting and turning, sparkling and twinkling.

"Would you mind repeating that?" I stammered into the phone.

The voice on the other end sounded puzzled, wondering, perhaps, if my hearing was bad. "I said, would you like to come to work for Jamieson Film Company as a producer-director of television commercials?"

It had simply never occurred to me that I could actually earn a living creating camera moves, provoking actors, and cutting little pieces of film together. At least not in Dallas. The two films I had done for the agency—the second one had been completed only a week before—were factored into my future as invaluable experience for the ultimate move west. Until then, the family had to be fed and that meant a legitimate occupation.

But now Tommy Terrell was on the phone asking if I would like to change all that. It was the most astonishing of surprises. The people at Jamieson knew everything there was to know about my second film. I had used their equipment, their crews, their editing rooms and one of their staff editors. And everybody there, from the generals to the janitors, knew, all too well, how seriously close this one had come to disaster.

It was a sales film for the John E. Mitchell Company, the agency's largest client and, surprisingly, was the brainchild of Tom Norsworthy, agency president. He had caught me—and several others—completely off guard with his immediate and unrestrained enthusiasm for the Denton film. I discovered that it can work to an advantage when bosses don't expect much. There's nowhere for them to go but up. No sooner had he seen the film, than he began talking about a similar project to kick off the Mitchell Company's upcoming national sales meeting for their ICEE distributors.

He didn't really spin into action, however, until after Denton's triumphant trip to California. The trek west had been successful beyond all hopes with the luncheons in Los Angeles and San Francisco all raves. Industry and big business turned out in quantity and quality to see just what this precocious little city was all about. They were barely in their seats when a bright, sparkling musical revue, starring the cast of the film, burst happily onto the stage, replete with tiny, but loud orchestra. The revue segued right into the film, stretching the dynamics of Denton dramatically from wall-to-wall on a huge screen; then there was a sumptuous lunch while questions were answered at the tables, one-on-one. We felt this break in tradition—usually the meal is first and the program last—would generate more meaningful conversation. Forty Denton business executives made the trip, each paying his own way, so there would be at least one Denton expert at every table for direct communication.

The Denton folks were ecstatic with the results and Tom Norsworthy wanted every detail of the program for presentation to the Mitchell Company. *Emotion* and *enthusiasm* became key words in his pitches. The ICEE sales meeting was to be the most exciting thing their distributors had ever seen!

I don't think the lower levels of Mitchell Company management understood much of what he was saying, but when it reached Don Mitchell, company president, he bought it immediately. The next day I was back on the phone to Jodie Lyons, the composer from Denton. We buried ourselves in manuscripts and lead sheets, emerging a few weeks later with a multi-media musical-comedy entitled *The Wizard of Ahhs*, combining three film projectors, six slide projectors, a live cast and a fifteen-piece orchestra. The response was so dramatic that, immediately afterward, we were asked to shoot the whole story on film so that it could be distributed around the country to generate enthusiasm among ICEE retailers.

The show was approximately half singing and half dialog and whereas the original cast could sing well enough to get by on stage surrounded by a brassy orchestra, most of them could not measure up to the demands of a studio-recorded film soundtrack. So we hired professional singers to pre-record the songs. That's not particularly unusual. What *is* a bit strange is that, for reasons I now find difficult to explain, we decided to pre-record the dialog too! The *entire* film would be shot to playback! That is, we would *not* record any sound on location; rather, the actors and actresses would sync their lips to the pre-recorded soundtrack being played back on a recorder as the film was being shot.

Again, shooting to playback is not a particularly unique process when singing is involved. But I've never heard of it being done, before or since, with dialog. Exactly why we did it that way is a complete—and possibly convenient—mystery. The memory banks are a blank. I can only suppose that the cost of shooting sound on location, with the inherent delays due to noisy traffic, airplanes and the like, was too expensive for the budget. At least, I hope it was something nearly rational like that.

Still, this decision, by itself, could not have created the embarrassing muddle that evolved, notwithstanding the fact that I had neglected the quantum leap in difficulty that would accompany trying to lip sync to dialog. A piece of music has a specific rhythm, a constant for those being filmed to line up on, to sync with. Dialog, on the other hand, does not. It's just talk, with random patterns that, once said, may squiggle off into the universe, never, again, to be recaptured.

Still, the opportunity for truly serious disaster didn't arise until I graduated from not knowing anything about tape splicers to not knowing anything about sync cameras and recorders. This is where my philosophy on methodology—*the mechanical part of the process can be discovered along the way*—exploded and splattered all over me. It seems that, to enhance the final production, it is advisable for the film traveling through the camera to always remain in sync with the sound tape on the recorder. But that doesn't happen by chance. Both the tape player and the camera must be controlled, or governed, by devices that make them run at exactly the same speed, relatively speaking.

Without these devices, the tiny variations in electrical current driving the machines can cause fluctuations in their relative speed and, thereby, throw the picture and sound completely out of sync. Irreparably.

I didn't know this.

Looking back, it's difficult to believe that somebody didn't grab me by the throat and say, "Hey, stupid! You can't do that!" Or maybe they did and, once again, I quickly erased the memory rather than deal with the mystery of why I didn't listen.

In any case, the entire fifty-eight minute film was shot on non-sync equipment. Scenes filmed using battery power were practically unusable, good for no longer than three or four seconds before the picture and sound would drift hopelessly out of sync. When we had access to electricity from a wall plug, things got better. Sync would last for six, maybe seven seconds.

Needless to say, the final film gave no one in the audience the opportunity to grow tired of any particular shot. Quick cuts, cutaways, reaction shots, head turns and long shots (where lips couldn't really be seen) were used to cover the drifting sync. The old editing plan was tossed out and a new one designed that relied more on continuity of feeling and energy than continuity of action. The film was in editing much longer than it should have been, and excuses had to be made to the client, but in the final analysis, it actually seemed to work. Again, focus upon the ultimate consumer, the audience, and the job the film was supposed to do, had saved the day and steamrollered the shortcomings. It was, astonishingly, a rousing success.

The folks at Jamieson Film Company were apparently amazed that any kind of film at all had risen from the ashes, much less a reasonably decent one. "God only knows what this idiot could do if he knew a few basics," someone reportedly said. And God must've smiled because this impressionable moment just happen to coincide with the resignation of one of their commercial directors.

I tugged at the phone cord, stretching to shut my office door. "I'm very interested," I tried to say casually.

"Can you come over after work and talk to David Orr?" Tommy asked. Orr was Dallas' premiere television commercial director and was head of production at Jamieson.

I promised to call him back after checking with Carolyn. I was buying time for my heart to slow down. It was about to pound its way out of my chest.

Had we been able to afford it, I would've taken a cut in salary to get the job. And certainly I would've gone for the same. But Carolyn and I decided I would ask for $14,000 a year! Two thousand more than I was currently making! So, I was a jangled wreck by the time I left for the meeting.

A year before, I had had no trouble asking for a fifty percent increase when offered a job at another agency. But I didn't *want* that job. It was across town and would've put an end to the noon sessions in the Dallas Federal Savings Building basement cafeteria. And it would've meant no ICEE film. Tom Norsworthy offered me half the increase and I stayed. But this was different, this offer from Jamieson. I *wanted* it!

It usually works that way. The ones you don't really care about are the easiest. Over the years, I've found this phenomenon to be very helpful in negotiating deals and contracts. The yield is always higher when my entire world is not hanging in the balance, perceptually or otherwise. When I can convince myself that it doesn't really matter whether we make the deal or not, confidence rises and fear subsides. What I *haven't* managed to discover, is exactly how to arrange such a mindset when I want the deal so badly I might consider killing for it.

Already, my thoughts were adrift, nurturing the tiniest of inklings that maybe a writing credit wasn't the only way to capture this aging dream of mine. And, even if it was, time spent learning production at a professional level would surely be valuable.

I was a frazzled, quivering bundle of nerves as I walked up to Jamieson's Stage East at 7:30. David would be shooting late into the night on a sales film for a toy company and it had been decided that we could talk between camera setups.

It was ten o'clock before David broke away, but I didn't mind. I was absorbed in what was going on. Compared to the films I had done, this was an extremely sophisticated production. Professional dancers, fancy costumes, colorful expensive sets, and a real camera dolly that boomed up and down! I had never been able to afford a dolly. When the camera had to move, we simply put our cameraman in a wheel chair.

David draped his arm over my shoulder and pulled me away from the set, "Walk to the john with me and we'll talk on the way."

I took a deep breath and steeled myself. This would be the dreaded salary discussion; if, of course, they hadn't changed their mind about offering me the job. He complimented me on the films I had done and said he understood that I was also a writer.

"I... write some," I said as we strolled into the men's room.

"That'll come in handy." He patted me on the shoulder. We each selected a urinal and went about our business.

"What's your salary requirement?"

I tried to keep my hand from shaking. He could've waited. "Fourteen thousand," I said, as casually as a blurt could sound.

"How much is that a week?" he asked flatly. "The film industry runs on a weekly basis."

I ran the division through my head calling off the numbers as they fell, "Two... six... nine... and something. Two hundred and sixty-nine dollars and some cents." I started to zip.

"No good," he said.

I froze.

"Too hard to keep up with. Let's make it an even three hundred dollars a week."

I was speechless. He had just added sixteen hundred dollars to the two thousand I was worried about!

"Let's get back to the set," he said. "When can you start?"

"I'd sort of like to wait until I've spoken with Tom Norsworthy before I give you a date... if that's all right."

"Just give me a call." He extended his hand. "Welcome aboard."

I thanked him. He reached for the door and I followed. Then, suddenly, he turned back, a tiny, knowing smile dancing at the corners of his mouth.

"You might want to zip up your fly."

Dear Joe, Erwin & Harland:

I just wanted you to know that I gave your pilot HEAVENLY HOST to Harry Ackerman at Screen Gems and he likes it! He will be talking to the New York people when they come out, about

*the 15ᵗʰ of this month, and if they agree with him
we may be able to work out some sort of a deal.*

*We are starting a new season, and if Harry doesn't
get the go ahead on it, I want to start submitting
it to other places. I have only one copy and if you
have a couple of other copies, please send them
along.*

*Harry said he would like to meet with you the next
time you are in Los Angeles. I don't think it is necessary for you to make a special trip; but if you are
planning to come out, let me know.*

Best regards.
Sylvia Hirsch

It felt strange, sort of degrading, sitting there like a salesman or
something. I glared across the familiar room at the unfamiliar face
behind the desk who had asked me to have a seat please and wait.
She obviously didn't understand. What, I wondered, had happened
to *breathy voice?*

The face glanced up and smiled. I swallowed my scowl and
looked away, straight up in the air. For four long years, I had
trudged through this underlit Danish modern reception area and
had never once realized there was a blotch on the ceiling. Like a
Rorschach splatter, in coffee stain yellow. I wondered if Norsworthy had tossed his cup at someone. Perhaps at the individual
who had purchased these chairs. They were definitely constructed
for looking, not sitting. But on this particular autumn morning, I
was sitting, quietly, meekly, crossing first one leg then the other,
doing my best to wait patiently. Tom Norsworthy, and the other
officers of the agency, were the only people I knew in the entire
world who had enough money to think about investments, and,

also, knew enough about Joe Camp to think that he might possibly be a good one.

In the short year-and-a-half since I had left the agency, I had managed to convince myself that the world was ready for one more film production company. The proposal I was paging through said, "...to produce television commercials and industrial films that would compete with Los Angeles and New York on a basis of quality, rather than with companies in Dallas on a basis of price... and, once successful, to, move into the production of family entertainment."

I was not the least bit nervous. The notion that anyone would place $50,000 into my hands for such a fantasy was so preposterous that it surely wasn't worth worrying about. This was merely an exercise, like throwing rings over Coke bottles at the fair. Besides, I had been down this road before, several times. During my tenure at the agency, I would parade into Helen's office at least once a week to expose her to some bizarre new idea. She would praise and applaud, my confidence would soar, and she would send me off to pitch Norsworthy, who, in turn, usually with dash, would disintegrate the bubble Helen had sculpted.

Helen was the Director of Media and Research, was an officer of the company, and one of my favorite people because she could usually induce Tom Norsworthy to listen when no one else could. A frustrated psychologist, she encouraged my exploration into the emotional-over-intellectual school of writing and production and would philosophize for hours about the nuances of some idea or piece of copy I had written. In the beginning, she was also my sole supporter on the Denton approach. This caused internal rifts of volcanic proportion because creative was not her area of responsibility.

But she seemed to understand what I was reaching for, and was certainly good for the ego, so I went to her a lot. She would prod me to stick with ideas that nobody else understood, and I've often wondered if I would've had the persistence or tenacity to accomplish the things I did at the agency had it not been for Helen's encouragement. Everyone should have a Helen.

She is precisely why I was sitting in the Norsworthy-Mercer reception lobby that November morning, watching all the new faces tromp back and forth to the rest rooms; their casual glances and polite smiles, assuming, I suppose, that I was selling advertising space in Progressive Farmer. I had had lunch with Helen the week before to get her reaction to this newest idea, which, like so many others, had been bred from frustration.

Dallas, I had discovered, was considered a discount market for television commercial production. When agencies wanted a commercial done *well*, they went to New York or Los Angeles, when they wanted it done *cheap*, they came to Dallas. And from what I had been able to discern in my year-and-a-half at Jamieson, precious few film people in Dallas even cared. The few at Jamieson who did, had long since given up the battle with management. There was token complaining about local agencies who tromped off to the west coast to produce their big budget spots, but nobody had indicated the least willingness to take any steps to change things, to crawl out on that proverbial risky limb. It's a good living, they said, so why rock the boat?

But I hated the whole idea of being hired simply because we had submitted the cheapest bid. I wanted people to come to us because we did good work! In the short time I had been at Jamieson, I had already managed to outrage management more than once by going to an outside lab because Jamieson's lab was an antique, sorely lacking in modern processes and equipment and, therefore, in capability. I had also been the one to suggest that directors and department heads gather after hours to formulate a report to management on how Jamieson could better compete in the national marketplace, to define the company's most pressing needs and to outline what we felt could be done about them. After weeks of discussions, the final report seemed to us like an intelligent, professional approach to the future of Dallas' oldest film production company. Many of the recommendations would've been expensive, like modernizing the lab, but many were simple, inexpensive suggestions, like a new bidding form. The current form was only one-page long, with virtually no detail, more of a guesstimate than an estimate, and it was not plugged into the accounting system so there was no way to compare original budget figures with actual expenditures.

But the entire report was ignored.

As I talked, Helen's eyes flashed with fire. She loved attacking apathy, anywhere, anytime, so the idea of forming a production company that would plow new ground in Dallas excited her.

"Take it to Tom," she said. "He heads our investment group. Whatever he says, we do, and I know he'll want to do this!"

But I wasn't about to walk into Tom Norsworthy's office and ask him for $50,000. At least, not without some indication that I wouldn't be thrown out a sixteenth story window.

"You've done it a hundred times before," Helen pressed.

"Not selling myself," I said.

That's always been a problem for me, and still is today. I tend to crumble like a fresh wafer when I'm the one trying to convince others they should invest their money in something Joe Camp wants to do. No matter how fiscally sound and well-thought-out it might be, if it's something I would *really like* to do, I can't escape the feeling that I'm asking people for money so I can go have fun. The alternative, of course, is ridiculous. Who in their right mind would invest in me doing something I hated?

I think we Americans tend to grow up with the concept that work must be painful or it's not really work. Never mind the labor and energy expended, if it's fun, if you enjoy it, it's simply not work, it's *play*. And, of course, it's not fair to earn your living at play. A notion rooted, I imagine, in the knowledge—or assumption—that most people don't really enjoy their work and anyone who does should at least feel guilty.

I also tend to muddle over why an investor would really believe anything I have to say. They know that people are always subjective about themselves. Isn't the truth more true if it comes from an objective third party? I dwell on such rationalizations, I suppose, because selling myself feels so much like begging. Yet, I've never been able to escape it. I've never found an effective alternative.

Helen, at least, agreed to run interference. She would discuss it with Norsworthy before I called him; sort of take his pulse, see if he giggled at the thought. And, much to my surprise, he didn't. He wanted to hear all about it. Or so she said. But I was not to be taken in. No expectations, no high hopes. Remember, I kept telling myself, this is merely an exercise, like all the others.

"Mr. Norsworthy will see you now," said the unfamiliar face without the breathy voice.

I stood up and tried to say thank you but nothing came out. The impact that the next few minutes could have upon the rest of my life was suddenly caught in my throat like a huge, knotted lump of dry yarn.

I had been an anointed, salaried film director for almost a year and a half, but there had been little time for realization, for reflection, no time to stand on a quiet soundstage and soak up the meaning of being there. My first day at Jamieson Film Company was like survival training in the jungle. I was tossed head over heels into a pool of gnashing crocodiles and told to swim for my life. My first commercial! I hadn't even been assigned an office. The spot was scheduled to shoot in less than a week, most of it was at night, and I had never directed a foot of film at night. The setting was on a ranch around a campfire and I knew nothing about specialty lighting. Dialog would be recorded as we filmed, another first. And it was a food commercial. Making food look good on film is difficult under the best of circumstances. Never mind in a pasture, around a campfire, in the middle of the night.

Topping things off, the clients would be in town for pre-production on the day the movers were coming to move Carolyn, Joey and myself into our new house! And, of course, the day—and night—of the actual shoot was Carolyn's and my ninth anniversary!

This, I kept telling myself, was what I'd been dreaming about for decades!

It was too late to change the moving day so Carolyn wound up handling the entire move herself while I, the shaking, petrified new director, scouted locations, plotted storyboards, worked with the client, and tried desperately to educate myself. On the day of the shoot, Carolyn came out to the ranch for dinner. The caterers produced a cake and the crew sang *Happy Anniversary*. Not exactly the quiet, romantic interlude she deserved after packing and unpacking an entire Bekins van!

We had a total of thirty-eight anniversaries and I long ago lost count of how many August-the-sevenths were foiled by shooting schedules, casting sessions, location scouting trips and promotional tours. Carolyn, I'm sure knew exactly, but she never complained. The only one she ever mentioned is the one I forgot. There was a note attached to my pillow when I got home after shooting late into the night. It said simply *Happy Anniversary to you too!* I never forgot another one.

Any remnant of routine and order that existed in our lives before the move to Jamieson quickly vanished thereafter. Hours were unpredictable and weekends became weekdays. I worked harder than I had ever worked before, but I also enjoyed it more. I was learning fast, but wanted to learn faster. I wanted each commercial to be as good as it could possibly be, and I found it very difficult to put a job out of mind until it was finished. Unlike any work I had done before, a film production could be continuously improved right up until the moment the prints were shipped. What wasn't thought of yesterday, might be uncovered today. There was always one last edit to more precisely hit a music beat, or once more through the lab to improve the color. And, as long as there was any possibility of making it better, I had trouble turning away.

The production process, I was discovering, can literally consume anyone who cares about their work. And for many, there is no way to effect a balance between work and play because the two are one in the same. My Dad hadn't warned me about this. I was suddenly quite close to attaining that state he had challenged me to seek, that elusive vocational utopia in which I would work even if earning a living was no longer an issue. But all was not bliss in paradise.

Work without passion, I had discovered in Houston, leaves empty, gaping holes in ones existence. Those holes tend to be filled with family and friends, camping, golf and stamp collecting. And for some, that's more than enough; those fortunate souls who work to live. But for those of us who live to work, when the work and the dreams and the goals are finally in sync, when the gaping holes are filled with great passions, these passions, like the plague, try to take over and squeeze out everything else. It demands an incredible will and discipline to fight against it. One that, frankly, I've never been able to grasp tightly enough to hang on to. The problems of production, unlike ordinary human problems, are alien to our atmosphere, extraterrestrial, unisexual! They multiply upon themselves, usually exponentially! And, of course, no matter how meticulously a budget is prepared, there's never enough money. So *time* is usually all that's left to solve the problems, to efface mediocrity, to make what lands up there on the screen a little better.

The only balance I've been able to find, and this took years, is to create more time *between* productions to make up for the time lost *during* production. But I had no control over this at Jamieson and, for the entire eighteen months I was there, the jobs seemed to pour in virtually back-to-back.

The time consumption began to tear at the family. And there was no reason to believe it would get any better unless I found another line of work, or discovered some new answers. Thankfully, it was the latter. I was glancing around the set one day when it hit me in the face like a huge, loaded powder puff.

Makeup!

Carolyn had been doing makeup most of her life! True, it was only on herself, but the results were always terrific, so I saw no logical reason why she couldn't apply that talent to others and do makeup for film.

We bought a few books, some makeup and supplies, a carrying case, and before the year was out, Carolyn was the makeup artist of record on every commercial I directed.

She was as nervous about her job as I was about mine and she approached it with the same meticulous drive to eliminate guess-work. She was constantly practicing, and when the cameras were idle, she was asking for tests, to compare her eye to the results on film. She even developed different approaches for negative and reversal lab processes. Soon, other directors at Jamieson began to ask for her, then other film companies began to call and, before long, she was having trouble finding time for *my* jobs. I had to remind her that the reason we started all this was to be able to see each other once in a while. Besides, no other makeup artist in town would work for me now because I had taken food off their table just to save a silly old marriage.

We put Joey to work on the other side of the camera. He was eight years old, blond, freckled, and cute, thankfully not taking after his father. And he was a natural ham. I distributed pictures among the directors at Jamieson, we found him an agent, and before long, he was the star of a commercial. He did several over the next few years, which, at least, involved and included him in what Carolyn and I were doing. And it helped, but not as much as I allowed myself to believe. Nothing could replace the time we were losing at home, together.

I rarely saw Erwin and Harland, until I talked Harland into designing sets for commercials. But our efforts to break into television and motion picture writing drifted quietly to the sidelines. I was working so late, so often, that I could never get home in time to go to bed in time to get up at 4:00 a.m. to write. Had I still been at the agency when Sylvia's letter arrived with the news of Harry Ackerman's interest in *Heavenly Host*, we would've been on the next plane to Los Angeles. But I wasn't, and we weren't. I simply couldn't spare the time. In fact, we didn't make a single trip to Los Angeles during my entire stay at Jamieson. In the end, Harry Ackerman's New York people didn't care for *Heavenly Host,* so we carved another notch into our log of near-misses. There was an occasional nibble on our feature script, but nothing serious. And there was no time to write anything new.

Spare hours were spent absorbing as much knowledge as I could in a programmed effort to leave as little of the commercial production process to chance as possible. I waned to know everything there was to know. About lighting, and labs, and lenses. About film and cameras.

Why did one laboratory produce prettier prints than another, and why did those prints look better on television? What were the limitations and tolerances of the various film stocks, and why use one over the other?

I quizzed cameramen about lighting, and ratios of dark areas to light. I learned about filters, and lens perspectives. I studied acting. And I learned that whenever I was told that something couldn't be done, chances were, the person doing the telling simply didn't care as much about doing it as I did, and thereby he or she didn't care as much about putting out the extra effort. I forged my way through new, unknown spaces, determined to grasp at least enough knowledge about each new subject to know when *I'm sorry, that's impossible* really meant *I don't know* or *It's too much trouble.*

I prickled management on improving cost controls, internal procedures, marketing and excellence of product.

In short, I suppose, I came out of the closet, convinced at last that a combination of knowledge and logic, even in my trembling hands, could work miracles. I confirmed a confidence in my ability to tackle new problems and effect positive solutions that began to overcome my natural shyness and introversion. Then, when management totally ignored our report, I asked Tommy Terrell and Jim Nicodemus if they would like to put together a company of our own.

Tommy was a producer-director and totally controlled the huge Holsum Bread account at Jamieson. Jim was the company production manager, five years my junior, a handsome, soft-spoken magician when it came to making impossible things happen. He was a practicing master of the jigsaw puzzle school of logic.

They both said yes. Then, two days later, Tommy changed his mind.

Jim and I discussed other candidates and decided we'd go it alone. He and I would make a good team. I could think it up and he could get it done. And his calm, collected nature would be a pleasant offset to my driving impatience. It would be rough trying to sell a quality product against the low prices of Dallas, but I was convinced that we could do it if we could capitalize a year of guaranteed operation to firmly establish our strange, new philosophies. Both of us were living virtually from paycheck to paycheck, so, clearly, capital would have to come from somewhere else. And, between us, we didn't have the faintest clue where to begin. That's when I picked up the phone and called Helen.

From the moment I stepped into Norsworthy's office, nothing went according to plan. I had carefully rehearsed leading him through the entire written presentation, right from the beginning. But he was already miles beyond that point. He had seen and studied Helen's copy. He didn't want to hear about our ability to run the company, or how we planned to obtain business, or the details of our salaries, projected expenses, advertising budgets or Jim's background. He only wanted to talk about one thing.

"Fifty-thousand is too much," he said. "I've been over the figures and you can do it in nine months for thirty-five."

There was a long moment of silence as I tried to orient myself. I mentally whisked through the presentation, searching for a rehearsed rebuttal, but there weren't any. Finally, I took a deep breath, looked him in the elbow and said, "I think we should budget for a year."

There was no statistical defense for the time span I was projecting. I simply felt that building our reputation as a quality house rather than a price house was going to be a delicate, fragile process. And it wouldn't happen overnight. We would be bidding higher prices than other production houses in Dallas, and, in the beginning, the only evidence of our capabilities would be the cheaper commercials we had done at Jamieson. Our philosophy was going to take time to establish.

"Won't take a year," Norsworthy said. "You'll know in nine months. Meanwhile, if you have to cut a few prices to keep the doors open, you do it."

My head was swimming. I was still back on page three: *Why does Dallas need another production company?* But he was already at the bottom line.

"We can't cut prices!" I blurted softly, trying to stay calm and find my place in the conversation. "A cut price means a cut production and that means a mediocre commercial and a client who's less than ecstatic about our work. A client who will only come back when price is the only object. To cut prices would undermine the very reason we want to form a company in the first place."

"You'll just have to sell faster," he said. "Thirty-five is all we feel we can put into it."

"Are you saying that if we feel we can do it for thirty-five thousand, your group is ready to go?"

"Ready to go."

I tried to cover the little squeak in my throat with a cough. Suddenly my temples were throbbing, my heart pounding, the blood racing through every vein spinning fears and concerns. No boss. No security. Nobody to fight but myself. No excuses. No job if it doesn't work. I was prepared to present our case, to debate, to argue. But I wasn't prepared to win.

"You and Jim will own half the company, our group will own half. I'll be chairman, you'll be president, Jim will be vice-president, Helen will be treasurer. You'll run the company as you see fit. And you'll promise to make us all lots of money."

Jim and I tried valiantly to convince ourselves that $35,000 wasn't enough. Maybe Norsworthy could be persuaded to raise the amount. Maybe he'd get mad, if pressed, and take it all back. We were playing games with ourselves. There was never a question in either of our minds what we would do. From the first moment we had discussed forming a company, we had never really given much chance to the possibility that it could actually become a reality. And, now, suddenly, it could live with the drop of a single "Yes." So, projections notwithstanding, we turned in our resignations, and Mulberry Square Productions was born.

The company name, we felt, should be unique enough to be

remembered but not so unique so as to be thought bizarre, or faddish; it should attempt to convey our somewhat old-fashioned philosophy about quality of workmanship; and it should conjure feelings of warmth and comfort, the very feelings we hoped each new client would carry away after a job. Slowly, gradually, we whittled away at a very long list until only one was left. Then it went to Harland for logo and letterhead design.

We departed Jamieson at the end of November and spent December finding offices, buying furniture, printing letterheads, writing promotional letters to agencies around the nation, designing announcement ads, making local sales calls, and phoning every contact we had ever made at Jamieson.

Jim surprised us by having his father, an artist of a metalsmith, create Harland's Mulberry Square logo in copper and stainless steel to hang by our front door. Jim and I had our picture taken raising the sign, and Mulberry Square Productions was officially open for business.

Carolyn held out the phone. "Somebody named Ronnie Jacobs." The pencil I was doodling with slipped from my fingers, careened off the kitchen table and dropped to the floor. A whole family of nerve trolls appeared out of nowhere, all clutching and grabbing at my throat. The name meant nothing to her, but I could see it pasted across the television screen at the end of every show Danny Thomas had ever produced. *Executive in Charge of Production: Ronald Jacobs.*

Why would he be calling me?? I hadn't heard a word from Sylvia in months. It must not be the same Ronald Jacobs. Carolyn wagged the phone in the air. "Earth to Joe."

I was at the kitchen table going over schedules for a week-long sales trip Jim and I were planning. A whirlwind tour of the frigid north calling on advertising agencies. We were in our sixth official week at Mulberry Square and so far, we hadn't bid on a single job. Panic hadn't set in yet but it was nibbling at our toes. Six weeks of writing sales letters, phoning agencies and mailing out demo reels had netted not one taker. We had processed over forty requests to see our reel. And almost as many guarded, polite responses. Unfortunately, there were only three commercials on the reel that were anywhere near terrific. Everything else we had done at Jamieson suffered, either in production value from low-bid budgeting, or conceptual weakness, usually the type of work low bidding attracts. We had considered having a sub-compact, three-spot reel, but felt showing only three commercials would scare away more prospects than a few bad concepts.

Not possible. According to the laws of mathematics, you can't exceed 100%. We were being introduced to one of the stranger phenomenons of the universe: the reaction gap. The inherent inability of most homo sapiens to respond emotionally in the precise way the intellect says it should. *"Oh, don't worry about concept. We're professionals. We can ignore concept and look only at execution."*

Seems simple enough.

I've said the same thing many times but it's virtually impossible to struggle through a perfectly awful concept or story to un-camouflage a piece of nice direction. It's like saying the painting is grotesque but the technique is nice. The director is a storyteller and a bad story, well told, is still a bad story. It's difficult to separate one from the other. If you hate it, you hate it! And no amount of intellectual dissection is going to make you like it any better. The emotion is simply born with a louder voice than the intellect. I knew that. But it's amazing how many times we put aside known truths to follow a path of lesser resistance. To take the easy way out. Having only three spots on our reel would've demanded explanation. Why, if indeed we were as good as we said we were, had we only reached the standards we had set for ourselves on three paltry occasions? When placed in that perspective, somehow the problems at Jamieson seemed more like excuses than real causes. So all those mediocre commercials began to look better. Not to mention that the world revolves on many different opinions. Who's to say ours was right?

Clever practitioners can rationalize just about anything, but fortunately, both Jim and I were also compulsively dependent upon results. If it's not working, swallow whatever must be swallowed, find out why, and make changes accordingly. Not so much because it's the smart thing to do. We just didn't care much for losing.

In any case, it was clear that we needed a shorter demo reel and some face-to-face conversation with our better prospects.

"Joe!" Carolyn pleaded. "This man is waiting!"

I was trying to re-orient. I hadn't thought much about television writing in months. We had been too busy with Mulberry. If this person dangling on the other end of the phone line was the same Ronnie Jacobs, what could he possibly want? Maybe he'd seen our work and was calling to offer us staff writing jobs! *The plot thickens. What does the young director do now? He's president of a company. He has responsibility to stockholders.* I stood up, eyes riveted on the receiver Carolyn was thrusting toward me. Breathing quickened. Tiny beads of perspiration popped out on my brow. Somewhere in the distance of my mind the London Philharmonic was swelling into something dramatic like Beethoven's Fifth. Slowly, I edged around the table and gathered in the receiver. Carolyn was beginning to wonder if the pressure had become too much for me. I covered the mouthpiece, cleared my throat and dug out the most casual "Hello" I could muster.

"It's Ronnie Jacobs, Joe. With Danny Thomas Productions."

The nerve trolls tied quick knots in my vocal chords and my heart leaped up to consume my adam's apple!

"Sylvia gave me your phone number. I hope you don't mind me calling you at home."

"Oh no," I squeaked. But it was a casual squeak.

"I've read *Heavenly Host*," he said, "and I love the character! Here's what I'd like to do if you guys are interested. The last segment of Danny's show *Make Room For Granddaddy* is still uncommitted. It goes into production in a couple of weeks. I have a script I can go with, but if you guys can come up with a good story to write Larry Host into the show, we'll go with it and try to spin it off next fall into a series of its own. Whaddaya think?"

There was a long silence.

"Joe?"

I was stunned.

"I know it's fast, but I don't have any choice. Production schedule, you know."

"When do you need the story?"

"By the end of the week. The script a week, maybe nine days later. And don't mail the story. Call me and we'll go over it by phone."

I hung up the receiver and collapsed, glassy-eyed, against the wall.

"What?!" Carolyn asked, coming at me whipping a large pot of potatoes with a beater. "What is it?!"

I told her, blow by blow, and we both began to giggle. This was a first! Someone was calling *us*, instead of vice versa! I twirled Carolyn and her potatoes around the kitchen. Then, suddenly, we looked at each other with the same question in our eyes, and I began to pace. Finally, she said it first.

"What about Mulberry Square?"

I didn't know. I certainly couldn't turn my back on Jim and the stockholders and go running off to Hollywood. But neither could I ignore this opportunity.

"It's only a problem when it becomes one," I said.

"I think I'll write that down," Carolyn quipped.

Erwin choked. "We have three whole days to come up with an interesting, believable story about a young Protestant minister who steps into the life of a Lebanese-converted Catholic star and makes a strong enough impression to get his own series while not stealing the show from the star??"

"A piece of cake," I chirped, defying the defeatists who preach that optimism ignores reality.

The deeper we got into it, however, the more convoluted our ideas became. If it were Larry's story, how could it also be Danny's story? And every idea was cross-examined by what Catholics might think. They weren't very ecumenical at the time and that distracted us. And how could anybody think clearly under such a panic deadline? And what would happen to Mulberry Square if we actually sold a series? Or if we didn't, because, at the moment, I should be off on a sales trip.

Whatever the reason, at the end of the week, I was forced to call Ronnie Jacobs and confess that we hadn't been able to come up with a single idea worth discussing. It was a difficult conversation. I had never faced a problem for which I was unable to generate at least a few fringe solutions, a decent suggestion or two, a trace of an idea. But the yield this time was zero. Nothing worked.

Months later, I was relating the incident to a friend and, without the pressure of necessity, a marvelously simple story idea congealed in a matter of moments! The famous Danny and preacher Larry find themselves alone together in an elevator that's stuck between floors. Danny is late for a performance and Larry is late for his final job interview with the pulpit committee of a local church. A committee who believes that bachelorhood is a synonym for irresponsibility. Both heroes are panicked about being late and they're both claustrophobic, a situation which alternately brings out the best and worst in each of them. They argue about whose appointment is more important. They snip at each other's theology. They take turns being practical and panicked, reassuring and scared, ecumenical and argumentative and, in the process, learn a great deal about each other's life, loves, hopes and dreams. After finally being freed from the elevator, Danny shows up unexpectedly at the pulpit committee meeting to confirm Larry's excuse for being an hour late and to tell them frankly how crazy they are if they let him get away. The committee is impressed and, of course, Larry is hired.

Had we been able to see through the entangled maze of complications, mostly of our own design, and discover so simple a story by the time I had to call Ronnie Jacobs, the career of a certain scruffy, floppy-eared mutt might have been in jeopardy. But it wasn't to be and, once again, the door to Hollywood slammed shut.

"It was a long shot," Ronnie had said. "We really didn't have enough time. But keep thinking about it. If the show is picked up, we'll write Larry into several episodes, then spin off the new series in the spring."

We were in Minneapolis on our sales trip when I read that *Make Room For Granddaddy* had not lived up to network expectations and would not be renewed in the fall.

9

CAVE CANEM

"Great works are performed not by strength, but perseverance."
Samuel Johnson

I remember the rage.

Everything good I had ever fancied about Tom Norsworthy and his cronies had been cast aside, flung to the floor, and stomped upon.

I sat in the car, cheeks streaked with salty tears—there wasn't a closet nearby, but it didn't matter. I felt empty and very confused, and wanted nothing more than to get away from the meeting the quickest way possible.

Mulberry Square Productions' tenth month of operation was apparently going to be its last, and the realization stung like a viper bite. It had been a lot rougher than I had expected. A lot slower coming together. Seven months, almost to the day, before we had our first job! And it was a stretch to call it a real job. A bunch of oranges rolling around on a piece of back-lit white plastic. But we made it the prettiest, best directed bunch of oranges ever filmed and, to our own amazement, it helped. With the new spot on our reel, and the accumulation of seven months of sales efforts, the pot had finally begun to boil. Additional jobs came tumbling through the doorway. Maybe it was simply that nobody wanted to be first.

Unfortunately, it was too late. We were over-extended on our original capital and trying to play catch up. The bill drawer was stacked high with debts, including a $450 lump to the IRS, which, at the time, could just as easily have been four-hundred-and-fifty-*thousand*.

The week before the meeting, we had completed a large package of spots for The Bloom Agency, and the dangling hope was that this group of commercials would finally thrust our demo reel into the big leagues. The spots were well written, well-designed, expensive commercials using recognizable Hollywood faces and the entire package would've been taken to Los Angeles for production, except for two extenuating circumstances. One, our reel, at last, had been scraped clean of all Jamieson spots and boasted exclusively Mulberry Square produced commercials. At the time, a certain lighting technique was in vogue on both coasts utilizing heavy fog filters in front of the lens so that light sources would blossom and bloom like the halos around street lights in a London fog. Glowing windows were especially the rage, simply achieved by hanging several thicknesses of sheer, translucent curtains, then lighting heavily from the rear so that, with a fog filter on the lens, the windows actually seemed to incandesce. Art directors across the country were in love with this *look,* so this is the look we wanted on our reel. We discussed the approach with Dallas' top cameraman and much to our surprise, he balked at the idea of *lowering himself* to do *New York* lighting. He would stick with Dallas lighting, thank you, whatever that was. No glowing windows for him.

I tried to explain that gaining the confidence of others is not an automatic process. First, show them that you can do what *they* think is good, then, maybe they'll listen to what *you* think is good. But he wouldn't budge. I finally had to advise him that we would make other arrangements for our camera work. After he left, Jim exploded like a water balloon. "You shouldn't've let him walk out mad! There's nobody else in town we can trust with a job this big!"

"Yes, there is," I said, leaning back in my chair and propping my feet on the desk.

"Who?!" he yelped, pacing back and forth. "Just who?!"

"You," I said.

The color drained from his face. Then an uncertain smile crept across his lips.

"Yeah?"

"Yeah," I said.

I knew exactly how I wanted the lighting to look and I knew we had the knowledge, ability and good sense to be able to work it out. Overnight, Jim became the best New York cameraman in Dallas, and our reel finally began to resemble the quality and philosophy we had been selling.

Don Bellisario, The Bloom Agency creative director, liked it a lot. "It looks like Los Angeles," he said.

"I thought it was New York." I said.

"No, no. Definitely Los Angeles."

As long as he liked it, he could call it Spokane. But the reel wasn't the only reason he offered the job to Mulberry Square. He wanted to try his hand at film directing and the more established companies in Los Angeles and New York would probably say no to such a condition. The package was ours if we'd let him direct the spots.

There was no question how valuable this job could be to Mulberry's future, so I attached only one condition to the deal. We would jointly discuss the directorial plan for each commercial, then he could direct, with me watching over his shoulder. If, at any time, I disagreed with what he was doing, we'd shoot it two ways. Once for him and once for our demo reel.

He accepted the terms and we went to work. There were very few disagreements, none which had to be shot two ways. A few months later, Don quit his job, packed up and moved to Los Angeles to become a full-time commercial director. Soon he began to write for Universal and ultimately created and produced the hit television series *Magnum PI, Airwolf*, *Quantum Leap, JAG and others.*

The new spots not only gave Don his Hollywood connection, they opened eyes and ears for us that were heretofore tightly closed. Agencies we had only dreamed of working with were calling and sending storyboards for bids. The future couldn't have looked brighter.

Except for one thing. We were broke.

Overextended. Stretched beyond all limits. The new reel, after only a few weeks, had brought in two new jobs and more possibilities than we had ever had before. But they were all too far in the future to help. We had enough money for six weeks of salaries *if* we didn't pay the rent, and if we didn't pay IRS, who had already sent us their *final notice before search and seizure.* They were threatening to padlock the doors.

I prepared a detailed report to the stockholders. It showed that we were poised to turn the corner. Cash flow projections, if we could make it through January—month thirteen—put us on the way to achieving our every objective. By the time I finished the report, we had been awarded jobs totaling more than $30,000, all to shoot after the first of the year. They were itemized. And I listed the outstanding bids which we felt were better-than-even possibilities. I included letters of praise for our reel, our work, everything I could get my hands on to give the stockholders confidence that what we had worked and struggled for was about to happen. But we needed $15,000 to pay overdue bills and make it to February—which, ironically, would bring the total capitalization to the $50,000 figure projected in the original proposal to Tom Norsworthy. We set up a luncheon for all the stockholders at a nearby Holiday Inn and I presented the report.

Norsworthy said, "No."

Flatly. Unequivocally. And each of the six other stockholders, except Erwin, followed his lead. Their purpose was set, their minds made up before they ever walked in the door. They neither saw, nor listened. Or chose not to believe, because it was all there. The $15,000 would be returned in February from jobs already awarded! Their entire investment would be returned by June! But Norsworthy would only dwell upon his insistence that we had abandoned reality and were chasing an unattainable dream.

"Cut prices and cut expenses," he said. "Cut salaries!"

There were only three of us. Jim, myself and a secretary and none of us could afford to miss a single paycheck, much less several.

I pointed again to the facts. The new jobs on the books. The difference the new reel had made. The quality of commercials we had bid over the past few weeks, and the quantity. More than four times as many as any like period during our first ten months. It was convincing. In addition to the commercial jobs, Erwin had even wrangled a film out of the Baptist Annuity Board, on the books for December. But it all fell on deaf ears.

"Work for nothing until these *projected* sales come in or find yourself some other stockholders!" Norsworthy said.

I wanted to scream, Where the hell do we work when the IRS padlocks the door??

I was furious. At him. And at myself! It would've never come to this if I had had the courage to hold out for the projected fifty-thousand on the original investment. Still, with such positive news before him, why was he being such a frustrating, impenetrable block of stone? It was like he felt I was trying to steal from him. The report was treated as if I had made it all up! There wasn't the slightest glimmer of comprehension or belief in any of the material I presented, from any of them, including Helen. I was astounded, baffled, at a complete loss. I remember just staring at them for the longest time, not speaking, just staring, mouth, and mind, agape. I had never dreamed the meeting could end this way. Thoughts careened through my head like pinballs off a flashing bumper. Brandon Andrew Camp had arrived four months earlier and now there were four mouths to feed. A week without a paycheck was out of the question. But I couldn't let the company survive if only to be another Jamieson? I knew I would rather be working at a job for which I had no passion, than enduring a spent dream that I had *allowed* to go sour.

I finally closed the report and said quietly that I would shut the doors before I would take food away from my family or undercut the philosophy upon which the company was founded.

"Whatever," Norsworthy said. And we left.

Jim cranked the car. "If it'll buy some time," he said, "you can have my salary for the next couple of weeks. I've got a big jar of peanut butter at home." *Real* men didn't hug back then, so I simply smiled and said thanks.

I didn't understand how Norsworthy's group could simply refuse to see.

"I think it's an ego thing between you and Tom. He told the others you could do it for $35,000, but you didn't. Now the only way he can save face is to tell them that he was right and you're wrong. He let you play it your way and the money ran out, now it's going to be his way, or else."

We drove for several minutes in silence, each wrapped in our own thoughts. Erwin's, alone, were constructive. He finally said, "Monday, I'll go down to the IRS office and see if I can find a Baptist brother with a big heart. And I'll make a few phone calls. Maybe we can find somebody to buy out the Norsworthy group."

Finding someone to put up $50,000 before we ran out of money was wishful thinking. Even with an extension from the IRS, and a hold on all the other bills, we only had enough cash to last a month or so. The attorneys could take that long just brushing their teeth. I had never felt such despair. How could we have gotten so close and still be so far?

To me, Mulberry Square was much more than just a corporate framework for the production of television commercials. It was a breathing, living philosophy that had become part and parcel of my dream. From the moment the company had become a reality, I had never doubted that, as we became successful, as we gained knowledge and perfected our craft, we would be able to use our accomplishments to pry our way into family entertainment. For months, I had kept copies of *Tom Sawyer* and *Huckleberry Finn* on my desk with a concept for turning them into film musicals in the style of *Oliver*, one of my all-time favorites. And during the summer, with everybody working for free, a little money from an outside partner, and Carolyn exactly nine months pregnant, we had produced a television pilot entitled *Treehouse*, an all-kid version of the *Tonight Show* with a twelve-year-old host, a thirteen-year-old announcer, and a seventeen-piece orchestra with kids averaging only fifteen years of age. The night we taped the show, Carolyn did makeup for all twenty-two kids, by herself, then, the next morning, went to the hospital to give birth to Brandon.

Executives at all three networks seemed to like the show but none of them could figure out what to do with it. We came close at CBS, but in the final analysis it was "too expensive for Saturday morning, and not adult enough for prime time." I took that to mean that in prime time kids couldn't act like adults, only vice versa—*notice how quickly the cynicism sets in*. At least, we were spreading our wings, reaching out, at last, into the mysterious, amorphous nebulae of entertainment production. But, at the moment, none of that mattered. The walls were caving in around me.

I could only wonder why God was such a tease? Time and time again, I had scrambled to the threshold, only to be turned away. This time, I imagined, I would be starting over. Back to advertising, if I was lucky. Surely no production company in Dallas would be interested. I had spent the last eleven months reminding the nation that they were all, in effect, discount houses. Maybe there was a message here. Maybe I was never supposed to follow this silly dream. Maybe I should've stayed with advertising, safely chugging down the tracks of least resistance. I was thirty-two years old. It was about time for me to settle down, be responsible, build security.

I should've spent the weekend calling friends, searching for job possibilities. The handwriting was clearly on the wall. Mulberry Square, barely nine months old, would soon have to shut its doors. But, instead, I spent the weekend re-writing our unsold feature script. Carolyn was understandably distressed. She felt I was burying my head, closing my eyes to the inevitable, ignoring the bleak horizon in hopes that it would go away. I'm sure it looked that way. But I've learned, over the years, to defer problems when I'm down because, in those dark moments, I'm absolutely worthless. Decisions made when depressed almost invariably compound the problem. Dejection breeds self-pity which cries for more justification, which tends to spawn decisions that are exactly opposite what they should be. So I simply divert. It's like refusing to drive under the influence of alcohol. When vision is blurred and perspective is warped, it's not the time to be making important decisions. I depend heavily upon this protective antibody—built up during the years of trying to break into television writing—to arrest the lows and clear the sightlines. It kicks in whenever the despair level reaches the saturation point. When enthusiasm bottoms out. Like a determined little gremlin, it scurries around and finds something else for me to be enthusiastic about. Something to keep the juices flowing, to help banish the grays and blacks for a while, to give rest to the heart and head, and to, hopefully, return balance to perspective.

But this time the gremlin was coming up blank.

I spent the weekend at the typewriter in a spiritless effort to re-write our feature script. It was more a disciplined diversion than a source of enthusiasm. My thoughts kept drifting away to the disintegrating Mulberry Square. By Sunday night, I had made little progress on the script, or my attitude, so I joined the family around the television set to eat supper and watch *The Wonderful World of Disney*. This particular evening, the program was built around a celebration of the animated classics. We were showered with the warm memories of *Snow White, Cinderella, Bambi, Dumbo,* and *Pinocchio*. But the one in particular that had completely captured my heart as a kid was *Lady and the Tramp*.

Tramp, a wiry, scoundrel of a mutt from the wrong side of the tracks comes to the rescue of the sheltered Lady, a bashful, beautiful, pedigreed spaniel from a proper home, and true love blooms. I've never forgotten the scene in the alley behind Tony's Italian Ristorante when Tony himself sings *Bella Notte* to Tramp and Lady as they unknowingly nibble up the same noodle from a plate of spaghetti and find themselves, blushingly, nose to nose.

I sat, totally entranced, gazing at the television set as if it were a living, breathing thing, feeling quite silly because I couldn't control the emotions welling within me. The same emotions I had felt as a kid, sitting in a theater, a slave to the magical web that Mr. Disney was weaving. But something else was beginning to stir, like a baby chick pecking and poking its way out of an egg. And quite suddenly I found myself toying with a curious idea.

As we ferried the dinner plates into the kitchen, I asked Carolyn if she thought it would be possible to film a story as strong and emotionally involving as *Lady and the Tramp*, told completely from a dog's point-of-view... but with *real* dogs instead of animation.

She looked at me as if I was nuts. And that's where it all began.

We tossed it around as we loaded the dishwasher. Disney's dogs could talk and real dogs, of course, couldn't. Or *shouldn't.* That's the mysterious difference between animation and live-action. Animation somehow lifts us across the threshold into the animals' own world. When we hear them speak, it's not really English, as we know it. It's some sort of magical translation that allows us to eavesdrop and understand what they're saying without suspending our belief in them as real creatures. Even today, with all the special effects available, a *Finding Nemo* works, but animating the mouth of a real dog or cat as in *Cats and Dogs* or *Good Boy* doesn't. It's neither fish nor fowl. Neither magical animation nor real animals. Believability goes right out the window. In the old days, if Lassie had talked, we would have no longer accepted her as a real dog, but rather as something manufactured by the movie people. Cute, sometimes, maybe good for a laugh, but *not* the stuff for creating romantic adventure as emotionally satisfying as *Lady and the Tramp.*

For this type of story to work, the audience must care a great deal for the central characters, and such emotional attachments evolve only when the story is told believably through the eyes and feelings of those characters; dogs in this case, *real* dogs who cannot talk. "But how in the world," I puzzled, "do you get the story across when your lead characters never utter a word?"

"A narrator might work," Carolyn said.

Gross. I reached deep into the diaphragm for a facsimile of Rex-Allen-mellow. "And then Spot, thinking that Dick and Jane must surely be in perilous trouble, decided to risk the mighty leap from the top of the Sears Tower."

That dealt me a dripping dishrag right to the face.

We continued to paint the idea into a corner. The very concept of a story from a dog's point-of-view meant that it could not be told through the eyes of people. Lassie stories, for example, were not really dog stories, but *human* stories, *about* a dog, from a *human's* point-of-view. Even animal stories without people, when told on film by a narrator, are unavoidably locked to the narrator's point-of-view. To create a story as wonderful, and as centered within a dogs' world as *Lady and the Tramp*, with real dogs, and with no acceptable way for them to communicate to an audience, I finally decided, was probably impossible.

We finished in the kitchen and returned to an evening of television, but I wasn't fully in attendance. Dogs were still scratching around in my head. Even if the communication barrier could be breached, there was still the problem of story. Could a well-structured story be written, purely from a dog's point-of-view, that didn't violate a dog's ability to understand and react? Not allowed: the old scam where clever Rover appears out of nowhere and grabs clever guy by the pants leg causing clever guy to instantly shriek, "Great balls of fire! Rover wants us to follow him!"

When the late news was over, Carolyn wandered off to bed, but I sat with a book for the better part of an hour, mostly chatting with our dog. I watched him prowl around the room, and studied his responses to my changing moods; his spinning reaction to squealing brakes or a siren down the street, his playful tracking of a moth flitting across the carpet, his curious concern for his master's feigned frightened huddle in the corner. By the time I turned out the lights, I was no longer certain that it couldn't be done. Dogs, I was discovering, do talk. They speak quite loudly with their faces, their bodies, their ears, and especially their eyes. Like a human, a dog will radiate with happiness, or wilt like a flower in sadness. When angry, the sparks are unmistakable; when afraid, the fear indisputable. Anxious, they'll flit about nervously, tightly strung, eyes darting from one thing to another. Content, they'll settle like a reflective sigh, relaxed and calm, with the mood always reading like an open book.

Or so it was with Sir Benjamin of Courtney, our little Yorkshire Terrier. He had never really known his registered name, of course. He answered, simply, to Benji.

I could usually generate two-and-a-half to three pages, four at the most, during the two hours before waking the family at six each morning. Three or four pages in screenplay format, double-spaced for re-writing, is *not* very many words, which is why the events of the next morning were so unusual.

The night before, my errant gremlin had finally swung into action. All the talk, and thought, about a movie from a dog's point-of-view, with real dogs, had ignited new fires. Mulberry's troubles were, at least temporarily, off my mind. I had slept like a baby and felt fresh and alive as I poured my first cup of coffee and settled in behind the typewriter. But the moment I sat down, something happened. I stared at the half-written page of the feature script before me and my mind suddenly erupted like a volcano. I ripped the sheet out of the typewriter, shoved in a fresh one and started to type. But my six intelligent fingers and occasional thumb couldn't keep up. Words were spewing out of my head faster than the keys would record it. I had never experienced such before. Finally I shoved the typewriter aside and began to scribble on a legal pad.

It was quite literally as if someone else had control of the pen. I wasn't stopping to think, I wasn't plotting structure, I wasn't doing any of the things I had disciplined myself to do when working on a new story. I was just writing, as absolutely fast as I could.

By a little after six, I had amassed over twenty hand-scrawled pages, a complete story outline, from beginning to end! I took a few moments to glance back through it, then raced into the bedroom and woke Carolyn from a sound sleep.

"I have to read this to you!" I babbled.

She struggled into a state of consciousness as I shoved a pillow behind her back.

"What time is it?"

"A little after six," I lied. It was really *twenty* after.

"You're late," she yawned.

"A bit. But you've gotta hear this! Are you awake?"

"I suppose. But I'd rather read it myself. You go start the kids."

"I can't," I said. "It's in scribble, and shorthand, and you couldn't possibly decipher it. I'll have to read it to you."

She sighed and settled back against her pillow.

"It's a story outline for a movie," I said. "It's called *Benji*."

She smiled. The name was her's. She had attached it to our Yorkie the first time his tiny, brown, six-week-old eyes had blinked up at her.

I took a deep breath and began to read.

Benji is a story-in-film about a dog... but not like any that has gone before it. Not a story about people and dogs... or even a story about dogs as told by people. Benji is a story revealed entirely from the dog's level and viewpoint...

Twenty pages later, I looked up at Carolyn and waited. Her eyes seemed moist, but I could've imagined it.

"It's really nice," she finally said. "It made me cry."

"Serious?"

"I love it."

What a rush!

It didn't seem right, somehow, that I should feel so good when Mulberry Square was on its way to extinction.

My first college girlfriend was a petite blonde. Quiet and demure. I treated her with steadfast respect, like a lady, keeping my hands strictly to myself. All the while, she was making it with half the football team, and I was the only one on campus who didn't know.

An embarrassing miscalculation of the human spirit. My life abounds with them. Given a choice, I simply prefer to believe, rather than doubt, what people tell me. I prefer faith to suspicion. So I tend to thwart what little intuition I might have with an assumption that people are basically honest, caring, intelligent, understanding, and benevolent, until proven otherwise.

That, of course, is a dangerous way to approach the wonderful world of commerce. It tends to create too large a target. So, after being spun around a few times, I began to compensate, to forge a shield for my vulnerable intuitive skills by bundling all my dealings with people into a structured package of specific objectives that can be seen and measured. I forced myself to stand alone, to minimize dependence upon any outsider, to double check every aspect of every decision, to attempt to know as much about any subject as those I was depending upon, and to base judgments only upon clearly identifiable benchmarks, never on feelings or intuitive opinions.

The values and the pitfalls of such a philosophy are, unfortunately, one and the same. When achievement of specific objectives is the only trusted yardstick, there is little room for compromise. Like an SAT test, it's all cut and dried, black and white. Six incorrect answers knocks off twelve points. No arguments.

I tried to never rely on gut feeling or the advice of others without thorough inquiry and evaluation. I was perceived by many as cold, hard and unyielding, but it was a box from which I could see no escape. Whenever I relented, and bypassed the homework, disaster was the invariable result. And the pressure to relent, at times, seemed overwhelming.

Which brings me to that certain January, the thirteenth month of Mulberry Square's existence, fourteen weeks after *Benji's* conception. A month—mentioned earlier—that I'll never fully understand, but will never forget. Within a matter of days, the original stockholders said *no*, legally and finally, to Mulberry Square. And Hollywood said *no* to *Benji*.

It had never occurred to me to reserve the *Benji* treatment for ourselves. Mulberry, after all, was gasping its last dying breath. So, back in October, I had sent it to Sylvia. She called in January to say that she had passed it around to the major studios and a few independent producers... to unanimous rejection. *It's cute, but would be impossible with real dogs. Animation is the only way, and Disney's already done it.* And the inevitable: *Dog stories are too old fashioned. They simply won't sell.*

Less than a week later, the stockholders of Mulberry Square Productions, all except Erwin, signed their stock back to the company in return for a promised payment of fifty cents on the dollar. In *notes*, not cash! Payable over a three year period, with no payments to begin for six months!

Our billings for that thirteenth month were greater than our cumulative gross income for the entire first year of operation! We were actually in the black before the papers were signed!

I've never understood it. Why, if I could see these things, couldn't they? Why, in the face of virtual guaranteed return of their entire investment, would these people with far more business experience than I, accept a long term note for half of what they invested?

And why didn't at least some of the people in Hollywood who had read the *Benji* treatment see what I saw in it? Why would so many years of entertainment experience say *no* to a project that would soon be stealing the hearts of millions throughout the free world?

I suppose this can happen anytime one person is trying to decide what another person will like. I've heard that when *Star Wars* was first screened for the Board of Directors of Twentieth Century-Fox, they were convinced they had a disaster on their hands and they voted to put it on the shelf. Alan Ladd, Jr. had to threaten resignation just to get it released. And then they only allowed it to open in fifty theaters around the country. So I can understand about Benji. Sort of.

But I've never been able to understand why the stockholders left Mulberry. To this day, I remain completely baffled.

The vestige, however, has borne a value beyond measure. That particular January is like a curative fountain of bubbling energy and dedication, a spring of rejuvenating waters. I go back whenever I begin to lose faith in myself and feel intimidated by the experience of others, whenever I consider casting aside a logical answer in response to the sheer weight of negative numbers. And, too, whenever I find that I've gone too far and stopped listening. Because, during this memorable month, I learned, for all its worth, that experienced, intelligent, successful people can be very, very wrong.

"Ed Vanston," Erwin said.

"I don't remember," I said.

"He ate lunch with us a couple of times in the cafeteria."

"The insurance guy?"

"That's the one. He was at the taping of *Treehouse*, remember?"

I didn't.

Erwin had spent hours on the phone with his well-to-do Baptist brethren, trying to find a savior for Mulberry Square. To no avail. Next, he went after neighbors and friends, then, finally, his client list. He and Harland had designed some literature for one of Ed Vanston's insurance companies.

"Does he have that kind of money from just selling insurance?" I asked.

"It doesn't really matter," Erwin said. "He's the only person I could find who'd even listen. Everybody else hung up when I said film company!"

That was early November, right after Erwin had burrowed through the IRS and uncovered a compassionate Baptist willing to give us a thirty-day reprieve on the *Search and Seizure Notice*. If Mulberry were to survive, it would clearly be Erwin's fault. It had been eight years since we had first gathered around the lunch table in the Dallas Federal Savings Building Basement Cafeteria and I'm sure, at times, he was asking himself why he hadn't gone for a piece of pie instead of opening his mouth about writing. Why, indeed, had he invited Joe Camp to lunch in the first place??

Ed Vanston appeared at Mulberry the same day Erwin spoke with him and spent an entire afternoon examining our books, screening commercials, wading through our debts, and asking questions about the jobs we had on the schedule for January and February. We made him a proposal for the acquisition of fifty-percent of Mulberry Square that not only included the needed infusion of capital and the cash to buy out the original stockholders, but a dollar commitment to the production of a feature-length motion picture about a certain scruffy little dog. A sane person might think I would focus simply upon saving the company but, apparently, the creation of *Benji* had completely sprung my central emotional mechanism, banishing pessimism and rational judgment as if they were one and the same.

Ed was interested. He liked what he saw. And I was certain I sensed a flickering acquiescence to that inexplicable allure of the silver screen that can seduce and entrap even the most prudent.

His offices were in the Dallas Federal Savings Building, and during my years there he had more or less kept up with our Hollywood exploits by joining us for lunch every once in a while. His original concern that we were all a bit loony had mollified somewhat over the years, but he wasn't at all sure that we belonged in the real world of dollars and cents. Still, he liked the numbers, particularly the projections for Mulberry's immediate future. So, it was like catching a driving fist in the stomach when he called the next day and said he wasn't interested.

Even with my proclivity for misjudging people, I couldn't believe I had been that wrong about Ed Vanston. The day before, I had made a conscious effort to get a handle on this feisty little bantam who had the guts—or lacked the good sense—to take a serious look at our situation. He was short and fiery, and attacked anything that captured his interest with a zeal that reminded me a bit of myself. He bounced into our offices in a knit shirt, no jacket, and loafers with no socks; his usual business attire, Erwin told us later. Certainly not your standard-issue insurance man. He described himself as an alley cat who sees something he likes and goes for it, who prefers the unorthodox to the norm. In short, I thought, a good match for Mulberry. He seemed bright, logical and perceptive. The chemistry seemed to work. But, the next day, on the phone, he was a different person, cold and evasive. It didn't make any sense.

"I just don't know anything about the film business," he said with a finality that tried to eclipse any further discussion.

I swallowed my usual reticence and pressed hard. His lack of knowledge hadn't kept him from spending half a day going over Mulberry with a fine tooth comb. And leaving with a smile. Something had changed. I scratched and dug for a clue, but his armor was up. Either I had made another classic misjudgment of character, or he was lying through his teeth.

The feeling wouldn't go away, and there was really nothing to lose so I asked Erwin to take a shot at him. If we could sneak behind his protective shield and shake out the real problem, maybe we could deal with it. Ed finally told Erwin what he wouldn't tell me, that, after mulling it over, he simply didn't believe all he had seen and heard. There had to be a fly in the ointment somewhere. The whole thing looked too good. Joe and Jim must be hiding something. Why else would the stockholders, to a person except for Erwin, want out? Erwin suggested that Ed pose that question to Tom Norsworthy himself, because it didn't make any sense to us either.

Two days later Ed met with Norsworthy and came away scratching his head, no less confused than he was before. "He wants out," he told Erwin, "but I'm not even sure *he* knows why. In fact, the *only* thing I'm sure of is that he and Joe have a well-cultivated personality conflict."

"Joe has very strong views on what he's trying to accomplish," Erwin told him. "It would be an understatement to say that he can be difficult to work with."

"Difficult is only a problem when it's not profitable," Ed said. "Nobody bails out just when the money begins to flow. Why suffer through all the pains of pregnancy and then give the baby away?"

"It's a mystery," Erwin said.

"It's stupid is what it is," Ed said. "But if they want out that bad, I've got a plan. If you guys like it, I'm in."

Ed proposed that the company buy back all the outstanding stock, except Erwin's, and, in effect, start over. The Norsworthy group would be offered a total buyout price equal to one-half their investment, in installment notes, not cash. Payment on the notes wouldn't begin for six months and would extend for three years thereafter, *without interest*. With all the stock back in the treasury, Ed would purchase fifty-six percent of the company for $10,000.

Erwin's four percent would remain unaltered and Jim and I would go to Ed's bank and borrow $5,000 apiece to each purchase twenty percent of the company—we had paid nothing and would receive nothing for our original shares.

Nobody even blinked. The Norsworthy group accepted the offer without change. They felt they had little choice. So did we. I wasn't happy about an outsider having clear-cut control, but it was the only game in town. The papers were signed in January, tying the knot on a masterfully woven piece of handiwork by Ed Vanston. He had orchestrated the elimination of the dissident stockholders with no drain whatsoever on himself or Mulberry, he had infused the company with more cash than it needed to turn the corner, Mulberry had agreed to provide him with an office and pay half his secretary's salary, and he had wound up with almost sixty-percent of the corporate stock, all for $10,000. Less than a third of what the original group had invested.

He also placed himself on the payroll for $1,500 a month in consulting fees, which, alone, would recoup his entire cash outlay in seven months and virtually double it by the end of the year.

This was my first lesson in negotiation and it would prove to be an expensive one.

The only point I had dallied with was the movie. Ed wanted it to go away, to be discussed at a later date. I wanted assurance that he intended to help us move into entertainment as quickly as possible. Finally, he offered a compromise. "Show me twelve consecutive months in the black," he promised, "and I'll put you face-to-face with the people who can finance your motion picture."

In late November, with twelve months of profits assured, I strolled into Ed's office and informed him that it was time to finance a movie. That's when I discovered that he never really intended to fulfill his promise. Or, rather, he had never expected that he'd *have* to. It had been a year, almost to the day, since our first meeting and even after he was in, and the old stockholders were out, Ed still wasn't convinced that Mulberry's future was as bright as we had portrayed it. His interest had pivoted on how badly the Norsworthy group wanted out and, thereby, how inexpensively he could put the deal together. Whether Joe was right or wrong was conjecture, and not terribly material. What mattered was how little Ed would have at risk. For $10,000, he'd gamble. He could save that much in rent alone. But he hadn't, in his wildest dreams, expected to have more than twice his money back by the end of the year. And he certainly hadn't anticipated twelve consecutive months in the black when he promised to turn me loose on his rich friends. These were his tennis buddies for God's sake! And motion picture investments were even riskier than oil! With fewer tax advantages! Surely I could understand that.

I couldn't.

"Even so,"—he didn't miss a beat—"is it really wise to withdraw yourself from the commercial area right now, just when things are going so well?"

I looked him in the eyes and said that there was no question about it.

He squirmed, and I squirmed. I was trying to keep a lid on the anger that was boiling up inside me. Jim and I had done our part, now he was trying to renege. I talked about how well Ben Vaughn, our new producer-director, was doing, and what a terrific handle Jim had on things, and, potentially, how much more valuable I could be to the company making motion pictures instead of commercials. But it was like talking to a stump.

"We can't even think about approaching investors until we've done our homework," he lectured in a fatherly, patronizing tone. "We don't even know what movie we want to do. We'll need a budget, and some income projections, and a presentation of some kind." He leaned back in his chair and smiled, confident that he had just delayed any further discussion for weeks, if not months.

I dropped the treatment for *Benji* on his desk.

Plop.

"This is the picture."

Plop.

"This is the budget."

Plop. Plop.

"These are income projections, and a rough draft of a presentation."

He gazed at the stack of papers in front of him and the color slowly drained from his face. He was in the soup and he knew it. The homework was done, and a promise was, after all, a promise. "Every friend I have," he groaned, "right down the tubes."

I tried to pinch back the silly grin that was inching across my face. "On the contrary," I said. "You're about to become a world-class hero."

Carolyn and I had decided that a home in the country, or a small town, a few acres, a barn, some horses, and a white rail fence would surely solve most of our problems. We didn't, of course, realize that the new ones we were creating would make the old ones seem insignificant by comparison.

For a while, we looked at old houses that needed restoration, which led us on a tour of McKinney, Texas, a treasure trove of ancient, Victorian homes nestled among huge, sprawling oaks on narrow, shady streets; many restored, many in need. One in particular captured our fancy, a huge, old, graying two-story, once an impressive mansion, now weathered and paintless for years and completely overgrown with weeds and vines that seemed to shroud the place in crawling shadows. It was the real-life manifestation of every kid's vision of a creaky, old haunted house. And it was for sale.

We went straight to a pay phone and called the number on the sign, but the twelve acres and the house together were well beyond our means. We moped reluctantly away, but the next weekend, our drive through the countryside somehow wound up back in McKinney, to look again, and wish. We were driving home, cloaked in the tired silence that comes from an entire day in the car, when an idea struck Carolyn. "It'd be a wonderful place for Benji to live."

"What would?!" I snapped with a sting that startled me even more than it did Carolyn.

"The old gray house in McKinney. It has so much character. It's eerie and spooky. More interesting, I think, than some old basement." In the original story treatment, read to Carolyn in bed that morning almost two years before, Benji was a big-city dog living in the cellar of a crumbling, abandoned, big-city building.

What happened next reveals a facet of the human psyche that I've never really understood, never liked, but is a frequent antagonist. The hair prickled on the back of my neck, I became defensive, and the tone of my voice seemed to scoff, almost mockingly.

"I don't think so," I said flatly. "It would change the whole character and feeling of the story. This is a center-city story. The setting is urban, not rural. You wouldn't find a house like that in center-city. No, it wouldn't work at all."

How stupid, I thought. *Benji* isn't a center-city story. None of what I had said made any sense whatsoever. It was simply a reaction, like a cat's growl when a dog barks.

Carolyn was visibly hurt. She shriveled in her seat and stared out the window, surely wondering what in the world she had done to provoke such a sharp reaction.

This was my wife, simply offering what she thought might be a helpful suggestion. She certainly wasn't trying to steal my idea and redesign it to suit her own purposes. What was I afraid of? Why was I so possessive? I still wonder where such ugly, cruel emotions are born, and why? I find myself fighting them even today, hopefully a little better than I did on that Sunday afternoon.

I wanted to apologize, but I just couldn't squeeze it out. Not as such. But the more I thought about the old house, about how much I liked it, and how much character it had, the more I realized that Carolyn had not made such a bad suggestion after all. It was, in fact, a pretty good idea. Actually, a terrific idea!

I took the next exit and wheeled over the bridge to head north again. A little town like McKinney would actually give the film a better texture than center-city, I thought.

"Where are you going?" Carolyn asked.

"It's early yet," I said. "I don't suppose it would hurt to take another look at the old house."

"You said it wouldn't work."

"What I meant was, it wouldn't be easy."

What I actually meant was, it was a wonderful idea. As we wandered through the cobwebs and climbed the dusty, creaking stairs, I could visualize it all. The soft, north light pouring in through the high windows cast an eerie, yet warm spell through the old house. I loved it! It was a succulent visual anchor for the film. Finally, when I could no longer keep the studied look pasted across my face, when my enthusiasm was fairly ripping it's way through the thin outer shell of forged concentration, I turned to Carolyn and said calmly, "I think it has possibilities."

She nodded.

Then, like a busted water main, I erupted, "I think it's *great!* It's not only more visually exciting, it could actually become an element in the story, like another character. With a personality, and a background."

She smiled happily, coyly, but refrained from saying what was surely on the tip of her tongue. I threw my arms around her and kissed her long and hard on the lips. I wanted to say how sorry I was for the way I had spoken to her; what a terrific suggestion it had been; how much I loved and appreciated her.

"Thanks," I finally whispered, and the rest clogged up somewhere in the line. I hoped desperately that she knew.

I had never been more certain of anything in my life than I was of *Benji's* potential for success. There wasn't a single doubt in my mind that I could make the picture work conceptually, that I could tell the story sensitively, that I could involve and entertain all ages, or that we could promote the picture well enough to have major distributors calling *us*—instead of vice-versa—by time the film was ready to screen.

And somewhere within the honesty of this absolute conviction can be found a key, I believe, to everything that followed. The value and power of such strong belief can be a potent force. With it, the impossible becomes possible. The fires and passions and persistence needed to overcome the myriad obstacles and gremlins blocking every route to the rainbow's end burn ever brightly when stoked by the surety of genuine, unimpeachable confidence. Not so when I try to talk myself into something I don't really believe. Then confidence becomes synthetic. Doubts, questions and uncertainties dot the horizon from the very beginning, and I might just as well stay home. Of course, I haven't been successful every time I was sure I would be. Far from it. But I've never had *any*thing succeed that I haven't fully believed in from the very start, that hasn't totally captured my imagination and commitment. Back to *passion*. And the dedication passion provides to ensure the energy, the courage, the perseverance, and the accumulation of knowledge necessary to reach the final destination.

But with all that unabashed confidence running loose, it still took six weeks to get Ed Vanston to read the material I had given him. He put it off, and made excuses, and dragged his feet, until, finally, in early January, I pitched a squealing conniption about obligations, and profits to date, and promises, and who had lived up to theirs and who hadn't. It was a spontaneous and childish approach to the problem, but effective. Ed came in the next day ready to talk.

"I think the dog picture is a mistake," he began. "How many people in this day and time are going to put out cash money to see a G-rated dog movie?"

"It's not a dog movie," I said. "It's a motion picture *first!* Our star will have to turn in an acting performance every bit as good as any human's. He'll have to convey his every feeling and emotion. No dog star has ever done that. And because it's a first, the picture will have a strong promotional hook. A curiosity factor. Can a dog really act? And the answer will be yes!" I exclaimed, with a punctuating slap of the desk. "A dog can *really* act, and while he's doing it, he'll be reaching out and holding those audiences every bit as close as those wonderful old Disney classics."

I paused for a moment, for emphasis, and settled back in my chair.

"And grossing every bit as much at the boxoffice."

"How much is that?"

I was learning how to get Ed's attention.

"In a minute," I said, "there's still one more reason why I want to do this kind of picture."

"What could be more important than boxoffice?" Ed asked innocently.

"I've thought a lot about the future during the past few months," I said, "and this is really what it's all about for me." I read him a letter addressed to one of the country's leading film critics.

Dear Mr. Champlin:

*With the following pages, I enthusiastically intro-
duce you to Mulberry Square Productions, a sincere
little outfit with an incredibly big goal:*

*To follow in the footsteps of Walt Disney. To be
one of the very few entities in the entertainment
world that philosophically stands for something.
To exert all efforts to bring clean and wholesome
excitement, inspiration, laughter and joy to young
people of all ages. To combine the proper elements
in the proper mixtures to create that level of fantasy that almost all children and adults like to experience. And, like Mr. Disney, to do it as well as
it can be done.*

*Our background and our philosophies are high-
lighted in the enclosed material. We're honest...
we're real... we believe we're talented... and we
know we're going to be doing some pretty great
things in the field of family entertainment. We
hope you'll be a part of it.*

Ed sat quietly for a long moment. "That's really powerful," he
finally said. "I like what it says a lot." He was serious. Ed's concept
of God certainly doesn't follow traditional denominational lines,
but his family values and personal philosophies read like the
hardest-shell Southern Baptist. "I'm proud to be part of such an effort," he said. "We should send that letter to every important critic
in the country."

"It's going out tomorrow to 818 motion picture and entertainment writers at newspapers and magazines in each of the top 260
U.S. markets," I said.

Ed chuckled. "I'm glad I liked it." Then the chuckle was gone.
"Now how much can this picture make? Realistically."

I reached for the presentation draft on the desk before him.

"I've read the projections," he said. "But I found no basis for your figures. Where'd you get the numbers?"

I handed him a chart of Disney grosses and his eyes virtually spun in their sockets as he scanned the list. *That Darn Cat, Lady and the Tramp, The Jungle Book,* And *Mary Poppins.*

"These should be in the presentation," he tried to say calmly. "And you're quite certain you can make *Benji* for $365,000??"

"Plus or minus," I said. "It's difficult to budget exactly until the script is finished."

"The script!!" he exclaimed. "How can we sell investors without a script??" Was this another excuse for delay?

"We'll have to sell it on the treatment," I said. "I don't think I should take a month or two away from the company to write a script until we know for sure we're going to make the movie."

Ed would never argue with logic like that.

"Okay," he said. "Last test. Before I try to sell *them,* you sell *me.*"

I spent the next hour trying to convince Ed that there was little chance of anyone losing money on *Benji* and at least a reasonable chance of making a lot. The budget was tiny by Hollywood standards, so there was less to recoup, a shorter road to profits. I talked about low-budget pictures and listed recent successes. I went over an analysis of the marketplace and why I felt the time was right for a picture like *Benji*—a recent article in *Daily Variety* had revealed that, over the past forty years, Disney's family films had topped all other major studios by more than six to one in percentages of films that were profitable.

I emphasized Mulberry's proven track record in setting and attaining goals, and running a profitable business. I pointed out that advertising and public relations would continue throughout the production and post-production processes, constantly dripping, hitting, pounding—*ever so softly*—until we had a better attention quotient than any ever achieved by first-timers.

Then I underscored that the *real* potential would come from the picture itself. The key to Disney classics is the heart. They take their audiences through an emotional experience, let them feel, and laugh, and cry, and leave the theater with smiles spread across their faces.

"If I do my job right, *Benji* will get those exact results,"

I said, "so there's no logical reason why it shouldn't do at least nearly as well at the box office." Then, to drive home the point, I found myself racing through the story, pacing the office, waving my arms, darting from one emotional point to another, squeezing out every ounce of feeling, as if I were Benji himself, pulling Ed inside the dog's own heart as he saw the children mistreated, as he recoiled from the kick that landed in Tiffany's side, as he raced, eyes overflowing, toward the people who would understand the wadded note clenched between his teeth.

"Stop!" Ed finally pleaded. We were both sniffing back tears. "Here's the plan! I'm going to bring 'em in here and you're going to jump around the room waving your arms and telling that story exactly as you just told it to me. We'll have the money raised by the first of April!"

"He's here."

I looked up with a gulp. Nerves were scrambling now; mouth dry, heart pounding. This was *not* a drill, this was an actual alert, the real thing.

Ed's face was poking through my doorway and he was grinning from ear to ear. "Hollywood here we come," he said, "Let's go sell dogs." And he was gone.

Our first potential investor, a close friend of Ed's, had arrived at our offices, and eighteen years of mental preparation were about to go on the line. The rules had been defined. We were the hunters and he was the quarry, the prey. He knew what we were after we knew he could deliver. We planned to lock him in our conference room where there was only one door, well-guarded, and ask him to invest $25,000 in our first ever honest-to-God motion picture. And he could do it out of pocket change if he believed we could accomplish what we were about to say we could.

Earlier, Ed had explored the idea of organizing one large meeting with fifteen or twenty potential investors, but I had asked to meet them one at a time, in *our* offices, not theirs, away from distracting phones, secretaries and associates; requesting, if at all possible, at least a couple of hours with each. I felt more comfortable one-on-one than I would standing before a crowd, and I wanted each prospect to have the time and opportunity to tear us apart, if necessary, in order to form thoughtful, trusted conclusions about Mulberry Square, Joe Camp, and our financial proposal. Especially Joe Camp, because I knew the proposal would never sell on its merits alone. As an investment, it really had no merits beyond whatever belief and confidence we could generate in favor of that guy who would be writing, producing, directing and promoting the picture. With few exceptions, that's all *any* movie deal has to offer. There are those who believe that if the last movie about horses did well, then horse movies must surely be good investments; but there is usually no correlation whatsoever between what the last horse movie did at the box office and what the next one will do. People don't go to see *horse* movies, they go to see *good* movies. So a good story is a nice place to start, but it certainly carries no guarantee. A story can be demolished by direction and acting. Conversely, a good director can't save a terrible script. A star with a string of successes can be torpedoed by bad writing or an inept director. And misspent promotion can destroy them all. The bottom line inevitably revolves around who's in control, and evaluation of a project's potential depends upon how much one believes in that particular person. I've never been able to find a better way to approach something as elusive as a movie deal. It's the riskiest of all investments even when the most experienced people are brought together. And those of us involved with *Benji* had no direct experience at all.

We could draw upon the fact that we were running a successful, profitable business. Success, after all, is supposed to breed success. We could flash examples on the screen of our film production and direction prowess and hope prospects believed the hypothesis that a commercial is just a very short movie. We could talk about my experience writing screenplays, and, of course, the fact that I had never sold one. And we could point to my years in advertising, marketing and promotion, but I would have to admit that I had never tried to appeal to an audience quite as fickle as motion picture distributors.

All good support, but alone, not the stuff serious investors clamor to be part of. What I really had to sell was myself. And the only way I knew to do that was not to sell at all, but to merely present, and then lay what was presented open for scrutiny. Encourage the prospect to poke around, to dig out answers that were meaningful to him. *Is this guy for real, or just a talker? Can he accomplish difficult goals? Do I believe he can put something on the screen that will make me cry? Does he know enough about business to control a production? Can he really promote it effectively? Can he make things happen?*

Private meetings, I felt, would encourage such exploration with open, uninhibited conversation. A potential investor could ask questions that might seem stupid to him—or her—without feeling stupid about asking them. He could ask prickly, pointed questions that might never come up if surrounded by those whose esteem was cherished, or coveted, or loathed, as the case may be. Ed agreed.

The pages of our formal presentation, fresh from the Xerox machine, were still scattered across my desk the morning our first prospect arrived. I was hurriedly threading them into a thin, black, *not*-very-formal, loose-leaf notebook. There were almost as many subject dividers as there were pages of information which, of course, was something else for me to worry about.

"It's concise," Ed had said. "To the point."

We had never seen a *real* presentation, so we had no guide. Thankfully.

I've seen dozens since, and they do run on, but I don't think any one of them ever said any more, and they were all much more expensive. Ours was all typing and Xerox, but I had worked hard to keep it looking professional, and I had almost succeeded.

The first page was a letter, similar to the one we had sent to entertainment writers across the country, followed by a short background piece on Mulberry along with complimentary editorial from various advertising trade publications. We included copies of ads we had placed in Daily Variety and Hollywood Reporter, a few articles on family-type movie successes and several pages of grosses on related pictures, either low-budget or G-rated. Based upon those grosses, there was a chart projecting what we felt *Benji* could do, both minimum and maximum, a copy of the story treatment, and a delineation of the proposed investment—which, in a nutshell, was a limited partnership seeking a total of $300,000 in return for 100% of the profits until the $300,000 was recouped, and 50% thereafter.

Ed was back in the doorway. "Let's go!" he said. "We're all set up in the screening room."

"I'll be right there," I said, fumbling frantically with a three-hole puncher that for some reason was only punching *two* holes. My secretary raced in with the last page, a series of notes on major story revisions which established with reasonable accuracy the degree of importance we placed upon the contents of the black notebook. The *Benji* story treatment *should've* been rewritten to incorporate the changes, but that would've taken time. And once Ed's fire was lit, he was ready to go. Right now.

"Besides," he had said, "the selling will be done and the questions answered face-to-face. That's where the game will be won or lost, not in the presentation book."

The revisions, at least most of them, had occurred almost automatically when I began telling the tale out loud, principally because the first quarter of the story simply wasn't very interesting. There was no conflict, too much repetition, and very little story progression. Just happy dogs and happy people. It didn't take long for me to stumble upon this discovery—or admit it—when I was pleading for response from a warm body across the room.

The more I told Benji's story to others, the more it improved. I began to use those times to explore new regions of the tale, to search for holes, and try out new ideas. I found, for example, that it helped story momentum to delay revealing the father's negative attitude toward stray dogs until later in the film, only hinting at the problem with early references. The reason why was left unanswered to dangle as a point of curiosity before the audience until almost halfway through the picture. Also, it seemed to strengthen the picture's emotional conflict to put Daddy's rejection of Benji closer to the kidnapping.

One villain's name was changed from Kevin to Mitch because Ed insisted that a *Kevin* simply wouldn't kick a poor, helpless dog, but a *Mitch* would. Decisions get made for sillier reasons. I seem to recall a movie that was set in Texas but filmed in Mississippi because the towns in Texas just didn't look like Texas. Of course, we once filmed the River Seine in Paris to represent the Thames in London, but we can thank British quarantine laws for that. The latest film, *Benji Off the Leash*, was set in Mississippi, but filmed in

Utah.

I shuddered as I snapped the revisions into the black note-book. I could imagine pitching a story this way in Hollywood. But, of course, this wasn't Hollywood. I slapped the book shut, swallowed the lump in my throat, took a deep breath, and headed for the conference room.

Happily, our first investor prospect was like a data sponge. He had a ravenous appetite for information and seemed to enjoy learning about our business. The meeting lasted almost three hours. Ed opened with a short discourse on his involvement with Mulberry. We showed the demo reel, I spoke about Mulberry's background and philosophies, then about family films, and Disney, and finally I worked my way into the concept of a dog acting and the marketing value of such a unique proposition.

"How are you going to accomplish that?" he asked. "How do you get a dog to act?"

I knew this would come and I was prepared, sort of, but the truth was, there was no quick, pat answer. The handling of every shot would be different. A good actor allows the audience to read his thoughts and feelings by the emotion mirrored on his face, so the logical place to start was with the actual emotion. If we wanted Benji to look happy, we would attempt to supply him with a stimulus that would get a natural, happy reaction. Many human actors use this technique. If, for example, a script calls for an actor to feel sad because his best friend was lost at sea, he might dig back into his childhood to the time his dog was hit by a car to help stimulate the feeling called for in the script. By contrast, in animal movies of old, when a bobcat would squeal in a tree above Rin Tin Tin, the dog's reaction would usually be nothing more than a quick look, called by a trainer, with none of the emotion that would normally accompany such an encounter. A dog actually surprised by the squeal of a bobcat would spin violently and leap into a crouch, every hair on his body responding to the action! If that's the response we needed, we'd look for the stimulus that would make it happen naturally. If it simply wasn't possible without risking mistreatment of the star, then we'd tighten the shot to eliminate any portions of the body that were not "acting" in character. If we needed a nasty snap, for example, and if Benji had a great nasty snap—which he did—except that, perhaps, his wagging tail gave away the fact that it was a trained action—which it did—then we would simply move the camera closer to exclude his tail, focusing exclusively on the snap itself. Or, going the other way, if we wanted a *lost and alone* feeling, we might make the shot very high and wide, with Benji a mere dot in the middle of an otherwise bleak and desolate frame.

I'm not sure our investor prospect understood everything I was saying but, after twenty minutes on the subject, there was no doubt in his mind that I had a plan. I saved telling the story itself until our various wave-lengths were sorted out, until my inhibitions—at least most of them—were buried under the momentum of the presentation; until I felt the man sitting across from me was as receptive as he was going to get; until the stage had been set and lit with talk of Walt Disney's ability to reach into an audience's emotions and lift them away into one of his fantasies. And how that ability translated into dollars and cents at the box office. Then, I dove headlong into the story that I passionately believed could become a new classic in the genre of family films.

Inching up in the chair, little by little, I *became* Benji, waking with a yawn, happily sniffing the morning air. I dug around in the trash can. I leaned across to whisper a thought reflected in Benji's eyes. I was up, moping across the room when Benji was sad, I leaped into a run, I cowered in a corner, and I sank back into the chair when all was lost.

Our first $25,000 check was delivered the next day, with a

promise to consider another one just like it if we came up a little short.

We didn't. That same week, our favorite client, an executive with an El Paso advertising agency, sent us another $25,000, his agency took $25,000 more, one of Erwin's clients—possibly the highest paid woman in the country—took a $25,000 share, and before we could blink, we were a third of the way home. The remaining two-thirds took a bit longer but, on the final tally, one out of every two prospects who agreed to meet with us wound up investing in the picture. The last one didn't even wait to hear our presentation. He was another very wealthy friend of Ed's. Introductions had no sooner been made and the presentation turned over to me when the man said, rather impatiently, "No offense, but I really don't want to hear this." He turned to Ed. "You've got your twenty-five. Let's go have lunch." And he was up and out of the room.

I wanted to yell after him, "Bring it back in here and listen to our pitch or we won't take your stupid money!"

I wanted to, but I didn't.

I had suspected that raising money would be the hardest part of the process, but it was far and away the easiest. The hard stuff had not even begun.

10

ROLL 'EM

*"It is not the going out of port,
but the coming in, that determines
the success of the voyage."*

Henry Ward Beecher
*Proverbs from a
Plymouth Pulpit*

A single Indian Paintbrush shuddered in the first warm, breathless shimmer of morning, shedding the gray of night from its orange and gold tresses. It was a lonely remnant from the swarm of wildflowers that had danced here a few short weeks ago. Crystal droplets of dew began to sparkle on the tall grasses around the old house as dawn crept over the horizon behind me. The still morning air was moist, and layered with the fresh, sweet smells of country summer.

The seat of my pants was soaked. I had been sitting there on the damp ground for almost an hour watching the shadowy pieces come together for the initial scene of our first sit-in-a-theater-and-laugh-and-cry-as-you-eat-popcorn kind of movie. There would never be another morning quite like this one, and, for once, I had planned ahead to savor it. My homework was done. Each of the 443 shots in the script had been plotted, most of them diagrammed, casting was finished, the crew hired, locations selected, props and set dressings were approved, the arbor behind the house that Benji would climb to reach the broken window on the second floor had been constructed and aged and looked for the world like it had been part of the house for half a century; the opening shot had been described to all, and I had had nothing to do for the past hour but sit, and absorb, and reflect. I was drifting in and out of the present, from the clanging of metal dolly track and the questions of the crew, back to a certain neighborhood theater where I had first shared Mr. Disney's dreams. At long, long last it was happening. I was finally getting my chance to change places with the dream makers, to leave my seat in the theater and become the one reaching out to move, and entertain. To stir in others those wonderful feelings others had stirred in me. And I was anxious to get at it. I had been given a unique opportunity for a first picture. I was director, producer, writer, and president of the production company. No one could ruin it but me, at least, not without my permission.

A light breeze rippled the tall grasses around the gray mansion. The Indian Paintbrush danced a bit and then, again, grew still. I knew how it must feel, out there by itself. This was going to be a lonely vigil. The risk and responsibility were all mine and the weight of it scared me a little, but I wouldn't have it any other way. This was *my* time! I had worked and waited forever, it seemed, for this moment, and I had promised myself that I would not allow the intimidation, confusion and frustration that I knew would be forthcoming to intercept or interfere with whatever I believed was right. The entire future was at stake, but I felt I was up to the task. The lessons of the jigsaw puzzle, pieced together in that dismal hotel room in Dayton, Ohio, so many years before had never let me down. One step at a time. No hasty decisions. No short cuts. Deal with each problem as it comes up, give it full attention, solve it, then move on. I felt like I was in the Notre Dame locker room listening to The Gipper. *Whatever it takes*, I thought.

"The other way, Tony!" I screeched above the clatter of equipment coming off the van. I was also the official yard guard, protecting the tall grasses that would be in the first shot from being trampled by a stray crew member looking for a shortcut. Tony had been lugging sections of steel dolly track into place for almost an hour.

"If I had known you wanted to dolly all the way to Waco, I would've called the Southern Pacific," Tony grumbled. "Their track's already in place."

I hoped he was grinning. In the wisps of early morning light, I couldn't tell for sure.

"You better hold it down out there if you want this dog to stay asleep!" It was the soon to be familiar bark of Frank Inn, dog trainer extraordinaire. Higgins, the dog playing Benji, was napping inside the old house. He had rehearsed the afternoon before and wouldn't be awakened until the last minute because the shot called for natural sniffs, stretches and yawns, like he had just risen to greet the morning.

The search for Benji had begun back in April. The money for the picture was no sooner in the bank than I was on a plane headed west with several copies of the treatment-cum-revision-notes tucked under my arm. I spent a full week interviewing virtually every dog and dog trainer Hollywood had to offer and, by the end of the fourth day, things were looking awfully bleak.

Efforts to convince those weathered old trainers that *Benji* might be the toughest job they had ever encountered only evoked polite chuckles. A few expressed genuine sympathy when they discovered I was from Dallas and had never directed a motion picture before. I would explain the *Benji* concept, about it being from a dog's point-of-view; about the dog *acting*, and how his ability to show emotion would have to carry the movie; and I would tell the story, just like I had told it to every one of our prospective investors, only where some of Dallas' richest eyes would begin to moisten, these crunchy old trainers would merely wrinkle their brows and leap, with no emotion whatsoever, straight to the next "dog stunt."

"Where's the camera going to be when he does that? How many cuts in that scene? Strike that one, it can't be done. I think you'd better build a phony foot for that."

"Nevermind all that right now," I would plead. "Just listen to the story and try to get a feel for what we're trying to do."

"Feeling is your job, son. Dog tricks are mine."

"That's just the point," I would say. "This is not a picture of tricks. It's a picture of emotion."

Nothing. Zero. I was speaking Greek.

I would ask to see their best dogs go through some paces. Then, I would attempt to duplicate a few difficult situations that might occur in the picture to see how the trainer would handle them. I suppose, in a roundabout way, I was trying to scare off anyone whose inner fires hadn't been lit by the challenge. And it was working. I've never encountered such a negative bunch of people in my life. I *would*, later, when it was time to talk to distributors, but for now, these guys had a firm grasp on the trophy.

One absolute necessity was that, on occasions, the dog playing Benji would need to be trained into a specific action, then *turned loose* by the trainer, to do the action, more or less, on his own. That is, the trainer might be asked to back away so the dog wouldn't constantly be looking at him. If, for example, we wanted Benji to trot down a path, pausing here and there to sniff, naturally, doggie-like, we wouldn't want him popping looks up at the trainer every few seconds with one of those *Am I doing good?* expressions.

An uncontrolled, duck-like screech was usually the response to this. It showed, I was told, how very little I knew about making movies!

"If I turn my dog loose in the middle of a movie set," said one, "with hundreds of people, and noise, and distractions, you'll never get a shot and I'll lose a dog!!"

Army dogs work in the midst of raging battle. Police dogs work in riot conditions. It seemed logical to me that a dog could be trained to trot down a country path without looking up at his trainer. I sensed, however, that this was not the particular trainer with whom to debate the issue.

"I'll tell you how you can bring this thing off," proclaimed another. "You film the dog chewing on food, and then dub in a voice, you know, like he was talking! It works great! Real Cute."

I was striking out at every turn. And it wasn't just the trainers. Many of the dogs I saw displayed personality traits that would never work for *Benji*. Dogs, like people, have vastly differing personalities. They can be arrogant, aloof, near cat-like at one extreme, and meek, submissive and dependent at the other. The latter group is probably the easier to train, but the result, enhanced, possibly, by the trainer's methods, is a dog whose pleading, compliant expression is a constant reminder of how desperately he wants to please his master. His ears lie prostrate against his head, his tail wags feverishly, and his eyes are usually saying *Oh God, please let me do good this time so I'll get a pat on the head.* To ask this type of personality to project character traits like independence and self-reliance from a huge motion picture screen would be pointless. And the flow of looks from dog to trainer would continually interrupt any hopes for a believable character that could generate a true, emotional rapport with the audience.

Cute, sweet, monochromatic dogs and parochial, dogmatic trainers were keeping me up every night pacing the hotel room floor. I was beginning to panic. Every one I met with was saying the same thing, that what I was trying to do was simply impossible. Couldn't be done. On the afternoon of the fourth day I drove over to Universal Studios to meet with the next-to-last name on my list. A young bird trainer named Ray Berwick. He had trained the flocks in Alfred Hitchcock's *The Birds* and *The Birdman of Alcatraz*, and the cat in *Eye of the Cat.* Dogs, suffice to say, were not his specialty. But he was my first real glimmer of hope. He seemed to truly understand what I was trying to accomplish. He was excited about the concept, and the challenge. But he didn't have a dog. Or, rather, he didn't have one he felt was up to the task. His only dog was too young, and not fully trained. I asked to see the dog anyway. This man's attitude was too wonderful to lose.

He was right, of course. His dog was a toddler, a mere puppy that would eventually grow up to play the title role on the NBC television series *Here's Boomer,* but for now, for *Benji,* he wasn't the right choice.

"What about other dogs?" I begged. "Couldn't you find one, grow one, build one from scratch?"

Thankfully, he had the integrity to say that he couldn't. He asked if I had seen Frank Inn and Higgins. My appointment was for the next morning. Frank was the last name on my list. If I drew another blank, I really didn't know which way I would turn. I spent another sleepless night.

The next morning I told the *Benji* story to a huge, balloon of a man, who sat across from me without saying a word for the longest time. He must've weighed at least three-hundred pounds, maybe four. I had no way of knowing. I had never been that close to anyone that large before. His eyes twinkled as he gazed off into space, twisting and twirling on a thick, walrus mustache with waxed, looping, curls on the ends.

He likes it, I thought. It's funny how you can sometimes tell. So why didn't he say so? A white sea captain's hat was perched at a jaunty angle atop his head, trying unsuccessfully to corral a bushy, salt-flecked thatch of hair. I would learn that the hat never came off except at bedtime and then it hung only two feet away on the bedpost. I tried to picture this man with a beard. He'd be every kid's image of jolly ol' St. Nick. Despite his weight and his age, he looked remarkably fit and healthy. I guessed he was around fifty. I was wrong. He was fifty-seven.

I learned quickly to allow plenty of time whenever I asked him a question because his answers were usually woven into a loom full of fascinating yarns and anecdotes. A simple query about his background had yielded an hour's worth of incredible tales, all marvelously told. This man would be wonderful with the press, I thought.

Frank Inn had lead a full and charmed life, beginning his animal training career in the mid-thirties after being pronounced dead at the morgue, the result of an automobile accident. Fortunately, a second opinion sent him to the hospital, and, ultimately, home in a wheelchair with the news that he might never walk again. He lived alone, two thousand miles from any family, so a friend gave him a dog to lift his spirits and keep him company. Frank saw the dog as an extra pair of hands and a working set of legs and he began to train his new friend to do things for him that he had trouble doing for himself. It was a classic case of something wonderful and magical emerging from something tragic. Sitting there in that wheelchair, Frank fell in love, and he developed an understanding, a rapport, and a compassionate ability to communicate with an animal that few trainers have the opportunity to discover when training purely for money with specific tricks and structured routines.

The experience lifted his spirits, and the physical followed. He was soon walking again; but not quite well enough to return to his job as a rodeo clown, so he took whatever he could get. Fortunately for all of us, it turned out to be a job sweeping the streets and sound stages on the MGM studio lot.

One day, he paused to watch trainer Henry East on the set of *The Thin Man*—the original, with Myrna Loy and William Powell. East was trying to get the dog Asta to do a particular routine. It wasn't working so the crew finally broke for lunch. Frank slipped over to East and told him that he had a dog who could do the sequence. "Show me and I'll put you to work," East said. But Frank's boss forbade it, promising that he'd be fired if he brought his dog on the lot. At lunchtime the next day, Frank instructed his dog to dig under the back lot fence and follow him at a safe distance to the stage where East was working.

"The dog is supposed to run up the stairs," East explained, "jump in the bed, dive under the covers, scratch around a bit, then poke his head out and bark. All in one shot. No cuts."

Frank borrowed a ball from East and went to work. He took his dog up the stairs and placed him on the bed. He showed him the ball, tossed it under the covers, and let the dog dive in after it. Then he repeated the process, this time placing the dog on the floor before turning him loose. Next, he took the dog halfway down the stairs before sending him after the ball, then, once more from the bottom of the stairs, each time showing him that the ball was on the bed under the covers before letting him go.

He picked up his dog and climbed the stairs one last time, but he only *pretended* to place the ball under the covers, actually hiding it in his pocket. He carried the dog to the bottom of the stairs and told East he was ready.

The dog raced up the stairs, jumped onto the bed, dived under the covers and scratched around feverishly looking for the ball. Frank called his name, the dog's head poked out from under the covers, Frank showed him the ball and said "Here it is. Speak!"

The dog barked, and Frank had a new job.

Since that day, in one way or another, Frank Inn had touched virtually every famous animal whose face had appeared on a motion picture or television screen. He assisted with Daisy and the pups in the original Dagwood and Blondie pictures. He assisted with Rin Tin Tin, and was with Rudd Weatherwax and Lassie for thirteen years. He broke out on his own with Rhubarb the cat who starred in the movie of the same name. He trained the cats in *Breakfast at Tiffany's* and *Bell, Book and Candle*. He owned Cleo, the talking basset hound on the long-running television series *People's Choice*. He trained Arnold the Pig on *Green Acres,* Tramp on *My Three Sons*, all of Ellie Mae's critters on *The Beverly Hillbillies*, and most of the cats and dogs seen in pet food commercials during the sixties and seventies.

Of the several hundred dogs Frank owned, the one I had come to see—the one Ray Berwick had mentioned—was apparently light years ahead of his peers. His name was Higgins and he was in retirement, more or less, after seven years of playing Dog on the hit television series *Petticoat Junction*. Higgins had learned to do something new every week, thirty-six weeks a year, for the entire run of the series.

"And now," Frank said, "he's a little tired. He's thirteen years old and getting a much deserved rest. I'm a little tired myself," he added.

There it is, I thought. That's the problem. That's what Frank is mulling over as he twirls and twists on that magnificent mustache. *Benji* was going to be a long and difficult shoot at best. Was the challenge and the accomplishment really worth the labor for a trainer and his dog whose sights were already set on retirement? Was the picture even possible with this first-time nobody from Texas? Could he really pull it off? Or was he all talk? And the bills. Would they get paid, or, like so many independent productions, would this one end up as a bankrupt disaster?

Frank hadn't responded emotionally to the story like Ray Berwick had, but he had listened intently and I felt that he understood what I was after. I also felt, as he continued to toy with the ends of his mustache, that the excitement of the challenge was winning.

"You know," he finally said, "what you're trying to do has never been done before..."

A huge lump lodged in my throat. I hoped he wasn't going to join those who proclaimed the whole thing an impossible mess. No, I thought, he might *think* it. He might even say it. But this man will never truly believe that *anything* is out of his reach. We had, it seemed to me, at least that much in common.

"I don't know exactly how we'll go about getting it done," he said, "but if you really like me and my dog, we'll surely give it everything we've got."

I tried to contain myself. We hadn't talked money yet. I should smile quietly and speak softly, be an exhibit of control.

"Fantastic!" I blurted, leaping into the air and pounding the table with joy! I couldn't have asked for a better attitude!

Moments later, I was outside, snapping pictures as fast as the wind lever would crank, talking all the time to Frank. "Too curious," I said. "A strong, alert look. More intent. Even more. Now happy. Now sad. Try angry... determined."

The big, golden-brown eyes in my view finder were incredible! Frank was scuffling around behind me generating some astounding looks on the face of this veteran floppy-eared star with the big reputation. Finally, I couldn't stand it any longer. I stopped clicking the shutter and turned back to see exactly what Frank was doing to achieve the looks I was photographing. At that moment, he was waving a huge, white, flapping chicken around with one hand, while the other held a wreathing, wriggling snake behind his back, thankfully made of rubber.

Higgins was fascinated with the chicken. His eyes were wide with anticipation, clearly wondering what was going to happen next. Then, when he saw the snake, he recoiled with a snap, ready to dodge a strike. He had obviously encountered a snake before.

Frank understood! What a wonderful feeling of relief after a week of mounting fear! And he seemed to be having a good time finding ways to cue the looks I was asking for. It was going to work after all. The concept, the picture, everything!

Higgins was not exactly the portrait of Benji I had painted in my mind—colored, I'm sure, by memories of *Lady and the Tramp*—but that portrait would simply have to change. This dog actually looked more like Lady than Tramp, but those marvelous, expressive eyes easily devoured any perceived shortcomings. I was already his subject. And his personality was perfect. He was independent, curious, and interested in the world around him. He never failed to respond to Frank's instructions but, almost always, it was with casual nonchalance, as if to say *I hear you and I'll do what you ask, but it's because we know and love and understand each other, not because I'm begging for a pat on the head. And don't you forget it, Mister.*

I rewound my fifth roll of film, put away the 35mm and pulled out the Polaroid. So casual and matter of fact was Higgins' attitude that I would often catch myself thinking that he hadn't heard a particular instruction from Frank. But he would always surprise me and respond exactly as requested.

I was in love! For the first time I was seeing the words I had written and told so many times actually coming to life before my eyes. This dog was Benji. This man could make it happen. We spent the rest of the morning wandering through Frank's kennels looking for Benji's girlfriend, Tiffany.

In just a few short hours, the dogs had been cast, the deals made, and once again the future looked rosy. That night, I would be flying home on the red-eye, on top of the world, after a terrific day, and a delightful dinner with Tom Lester talking old times. It was while waiting to meet Tom that things got a little strange. I've rarely talked about it, because even good friends start backing away and looking for the door. I was sitting alone at a table in the bar of the Hollywood Holiday Inn, browsing over the dozen or so Polaroids I had taken of Higgins, mentally beginning to write the script, visualizing that wonderful face in first one scene, then another, when somebody put a quarter in the jukebox and punched up the love theme from *The Godfather*. Its haunting, soulful melody melted through my emotions. I found myself drifting deep into Benji's story to see him cast out of the doctor's house, sent into the streets, lost and alone. His friends were in trouble, but he was helpless to make anyone understand. I felt his despair, his spirit crushed, as he moped from one familiar haunt to another, looking for an ally, but finding only empty streets and closed doors. The music on the jukebox swelled, the strains of its minor chords wrenching at my insides as the camera in my mind drifted up, high above the ground, leaving Benji a mere lonely speck in an otherwise empty and desolate frame.

Suddenly I realized that tears were dribbling down my cheeks, and the men at the next table had stopped talking and were staring at me, mouths agape. I quickly gathered up the pictures, dropped too much money on the table for the beer I hadn't finished, and disappeared out the door. But in those few moments, an entire sequence of the movie was written, and the importance of the role music would play in the final product was engraved upon my emotions in a manner I wouldn't soon forget.

The next morning, back in Dallas, Frank was already calling. He wanted pages of the script sent to him as they were written. And he wanted them written *immediately!* I think panic was setting in. He must have re-read the treatment after I left and now he was desperate for specifics so he could get a head start on training.

But I couldn't begin the script until we had our key location nailed down. The old house in McKinney had just been purchased by a metal sculptor from Dallas who planned to move in right away and begin restoration work, which would ruin it for our purposes; and there wasn't another house like it anywhere in the area. It was perfect. Old, rundown, neglected, haunted-looking, two story—*all* haunted houses are two story—and, it was *au naturelle*. It fit our story needs exactly as it sat, which was important because we had no money to make a house over. If we couldn't use this particular old house, then the entire location concept would probably have to change. I supposed back to center-city and the old, abandoned warehouse. In any case, I couldn't start writing until I knew.

Wherever Benji was to live, we had to virtually *own* that location for the duration of the production schedule. There would be several weeks of shooting in and around it, and it would be our only cover set for weather—a set that could stand, ready to shoot at any time in case the rains came. And, of course, we needed it cheap.

After a few days of unabashed begging and pitiful crying, the sculptor finally, graciously agreed to postpone his move for a few months and rent us the entire house for the duration of the shoot. Normally I would never recommend to anyone that they let a film crew anywhere near their home, much less into it. No matter how much care is taken, when that many people wielding that much equipment descend upon small rooms and delicate furniture, something terrible is bound to happen. But, in this case, the house was in such bad shape—it had been vacant for quite some time—I felt that our plans might even enhance its worth.

The old house became our headquarters. Production offices, dressing rooms, an editing room and the like were assigned to rooms that wouldn't be used for filming. I spent several days walking through the house, studying its every nook and cranny, absorbing its feel, and working with Harland—who would be Art Director on the film—designing the arbor out back that would allow Benji climbing access to the broken window on the second floor. We decided on a second floor entry to point up Benji's ingenuity, to subtly begin the process of letting the audience know that Benji could solve simple problems. A restricted access would also enhance one of the chase scenes, and a second floor entry would allow Benji and the audience a dramatic overview of the happenings on the first floor.

With the logistics of the location all clearly in mind, I finally sat down at the kitchen table and started to write. Carolyn and I had just sold our former dream home in town—the one with a small but private study—so we could build our future dream home in the country—the one with a slightly larger, private study—and in the interim, coinciding perfectly with the time I would spend writing the most important script I had ever written, the four of us would be crammed into a tiny two bedroom apartment with a small and very public kitchen table. I tried writing at the office, but the telephones and general chaos eliminated any possibility of a moment's peace. At least at home, for a few hours a day, Joe III was in school and Brandon took naps.

Frank was calling daily, screaming bloody murder for script pages. But those first few didn't come easily. I must've started fifty times. That first page seemed so important, and I wanted every word to be perfect. The only way I finally got to page two was to force myself to stop re-reading page one. Apparently, I haven't changed much over the years. Writing this book, I begin each morning reading from the first word of the chapter in progress and often spend so much time making changes, I never get back to wherever I left off the day before. It's even worse today because word processing has eliminated the hated need to retype those scratched-up, illegible rewrites.

I finally amassed three, maybe four pages and rushed them off to Frank, thankful that, at last, his phone calls would stop.

But they didn't.

"I can't train that dog to go to the bathroom on cue!" he bellowed over the phone. The scene was part of the opening title sequence. Benji would be trotting happily through town, doing doggie-like things and I thought it would help the audience get into the character and forget they were watching a dog acting if Benji were to pause along his route and lift his leg behind a tree—with only his head and shoulders poking out, just enough to tastefully convey what was happening.

"I suppose I could make him just *stop* behind a tree," Frank said, "and it might *look like* he was going."

"No," I sighed, "It wouldn't look natural. The shoulder wouldn't roll, he wouldn't scratch the ground like dogs do. And his expression would be different."

"His expression???"

Frank thought I was nuts. But I'd rather not do it at all than do it wrong. So I wrote it out. Higgins must've stumbled onto Frank's original draft, however, because when the scene was filmed, he trotted jauntily through the grass and—completely on his own—paused behind the perfect tree and performed the desired action exactly as it had been originally written! On the first take!

As the script progressed, every evening we sent copies of the day's pages to Frank, and before long I was able to predict his calls. I began to schedule lunch accordingly, around two in the afternoon, any day after I had sent pages in which Benji did something a little out of the ordinary. Like when he opens the pudding cup for Tiffany.

"Can we take the lid off and just lay it back on top of the can," Frank pleaded, "then shoot it from a low angle and let Higgins just pick it up."

"No, Frank. We can't get the lens lower than a pudding cup without cutting a hole in the floor. And if there's no struggle when he pulls it open, it won't *look like* he's really pulling it open, and there goes the believability quotient."

If there's one thing Frank got sick of hearing about it was my *believability quotients.*

"It can't be done," he said. "How's he going to hold it down and pull it up at the same time? It's impossible!"

If there's one thing I got sick of hearing about it was Frank's *impossibilities*.

These little tiffs were a precursor of what was to come when we started shooting. Our screaming matches on the set became legendary, but I've never seen two people who fought each other so hard, understand each other any better, care for each other any more, and when it was all said and done, be able to sit next to one another in a theater shedding tears and asking each other how the hell we ever pulled it off.

Like all of the other impossible things he couldn't do, Frank worked out the pudding cup beautifully. It wasn't actually pulling the lid off that worried him, it was Higgins' lack of hands and fingers to hold the can down as the lid was pulled up. A single paw holding the cup from the top would be unstable and would get in the way of the top coming off. Frank and Harland worked out the ultimate solution by bolting an insert sleeve to a board. The sleeve was just slightly smaller than the pudding cup, but a tight fit. The board was nailed to the floor and a hole cut in the carpet. Then, for each take, it was a simple matter to cut the bottom out of a fresh pudding cup and slide it over the sleeve, which, of course, was filled with pudding. The cup, then, was held solid. It couldn't slip and slide. Benji could put a foot on it, grab the ring with his teeth and pull till his heart's content and the cup itself would never move. Thus, I've always provided honest answers to those faithless who keep asking if Benji really pulled the top off that pudding cup all by himself. Happily, no one's ever asked if he held it down all by himself.

"Time to tense up. We'll have full sun in five minutes."

It was Neil Roach, our production manager. The butterflies began their cycle in the pit of my stomach. This was it. The first shot.

I glanced around at the crew. Most of them, like me, were experiencing this for the first time, many in jobs they had never performed before. The only person on the set, besides Frank Inn, who had ever worked on a full-length motion picture was the gaffer. He was from Hollywood and was Don Reddy's price for signing on as Director of Photography.

The gaffer would be Don's right hand, interpreting his wishes, directing the placement of lights, and overseeing the work of the electrical crew. He was supposed to be a luxury that Dallas had never experienced because the need never existed on the sparsely-crewed, short, commercial type productions on which the Dallas industry had cut its teeth. Our gaffer had been making pictures at Disney for something like twenty years and his depth of experience was a *comfort factor* for a camera operator who would be making his debut as a full-fledged lighting cameraman.

Don Reddy was, at a mere twenty-five years old, in my opinion, one of the best camera operators in the country. But he had never performed officially as a lighting cameraman—a Director of Photography—on *anything*, even a commercial. He had substituted for Jim Nicodemus on a couple of occasions when conflicting schedules arose and those few times had been enough for me. I was convinced that his eye for lighting was every bit as wonderful as his eye for composition.

The problem was that Don Reddy wasn't convinced. He didn't seem to trust his own ideas, wanting to place more importance on experience than potential—*not unlike a junior ad guy I once knew*—and he doubted his ability to handle two jobs at once. Usually, at least on motion pictures, the director of photography and the camera operator are two separate people. One lights the scene and the other runs the camera. Don had agreed to the latter but had contrived enough rhetoric to win political office in his efforts to convince me to hire an *experienced* director of photography. I countered with lengthy, logical arguments, built around perceptions and potential, designed to inspire and motivate. I was convinced he could do it better than anyone I knew and I didn't want to lose him to his own insecurities.

Lighting can play an important emotional role in the final look and feel of a film. I learned this the hard way, screening dailies from my first commercial at Jamieson, that fateful night-shoot around the campfire. After excusing myself from the screening room to go throw up, I had decided that there was no logical reason for lighting to detract from a scene when it could—and should—be enhancing it, nourishing mood and amplifying dramatic impact. The logical place to start—except for the obvious exceptions—was to design lighting that looked *undesigned*, natural to the situation being filmed; real, unlit. Lights in real life don't have harsh, focusing lenses, for example, but most movie lights do. Consequently, when nothing is done to counteract the effect, lights on a movie set tend to be more severe, shadows sharper and deeper, and contrast heavier than the eye sees in real life. There's a time and place for such lighting—like *Halloween* or *The Vampire's Dentist*—but these aren't the norm.

Another pre-emptive manifestation of movie lighting—and this one drives me crazy—is an actor casting five or six shadows up a wall as he strolls across the room, the result of having to walk through the beams of as many lights. This simply doesn't happen in real life and, for me, is a reminder to the audience that they're watching a movie; one more dent, however tiny, in the fragile outer shell of the film's *believability quotient*.

That term again.

Marginally esoteric, I admit. The director speaks and because nobody has the vaguest idea what he said, shoulders are shrugged and heads nod quietly in agreement. Not once in my entire life has anyone looked me in the eye and said "What in the bleeping hell is a believability quotient?!" Most people merely ignore it, Frank Inn at the top of the list. But nobody ever asks what it means.

I usually explain anyway, even to those who don't want to know, so paranoid am I about being categorized in that group of artistic frauds who use such obscurity to befuddle and get their way. A commercial director I once knew always kept his clients at a distance by embarrassing them on the set with pure nonsensical double-talk. One day, a client asked him a legitimate question about lighting. He turned to the poor soul and barked for all to hear, "What do you want to do, de-polarize the film?!"

Pure nonsense, but the client didn't know enough, or wasn't sure enough to want to risk further embarrassment, so he slithered quietly back into a corner. I've heard that director is now selling oil field equipment somewhere in Louisiana.

To fully understand believability quotients requires a willingness to separate *believability* from *reality*. To work solely within the audience's level of *belief* in a particular story or movie, reality notwithstanding. Does the story and its execution so envelop you that, within its own context, if only for the moment, you can accept everything that happens? In *Star Wars,* did you believe in the power of *The Force?* Did you believe that Han Solo's spaceship could shift into warp speed? Millions did, and loved it. But when Solo and Luke stumble upon the death star, would you have bought it if Luke had suddenly reached far beyond his established limitations and invoked the full power of *The Force* to save himself and his friends? Not likely. He hadn't yet learned enough.

Did you sit on the edge of your seat in *Jaws?* Did you believe in the characters and their trauma without regard for the fact that Great White Sharks never get as far north as Martha's Vineyard? I did! Absolutely! I was even the first one in the theater to scream when that grotesque head dropped down. But how would you have felt if Roy Scheider had suddenly produced a laser pistol to kill the shark? Or invoked the power of The Force?

Did you believe the birds singing in *Cinderella?* The animals talking in *Jungle Book?* The monster in *Frankenstein?* The loving relationship between Elliot and E.T., even though, to our knowledge, such creatures don't exist?

There you have it. Given the context of the film, the characters and the story unfolding on the screen before you are able to capture your belief and hold it hostage until you are once again back out on the streets of reality. And anything that disrupts that belief, that raises questions about the validity of a scene or a character's action, that slaps you in the face with a reminder that you're merely watching a movie rather than experiencing a story, however fantastical, dilutes the believability quotient and, in turn, diminishes the overall effect of the film.

Bad or inappropriate lighting, among myriad others things, has such an effect on me. Don Reddy felt the same way and I knew he could translate his feelings about lighting to the screen. He was also a *known.* I had already begun to learn that credits on a picture are not always the definitive answer as to who was responsible for what. Writers get credited when directors or producers or other writers completely rewrite their scripts; editors run the gamut from autonomous creative geniuses to merely being the robotic hands of the director; some directors totally control the lighting on a film, while others have little or nothing to do with it. So, there's often no way to really know who's good at what until you've actually worked with them, which made Don Reddy the only logical answer for me. He shared my philosophy on lighting. I had worked compatibly with him for years. And, in my opinion if not his, he was thoroughly capable of accomplishing the look I wanted for the film.

But I also wanted him to operate. The operator is the only one who sees exactly what the camera sees, and that job could only be filled by someone I could fully trust. Following a dog around, at dog's eye level, was not going to be an easy task, and I had learned through years of working with Don that whatever I described to him would be exactly what came back on film, virtually every time! There's always video assist, a tiny tube in the camera viewfinder, that allows the director and others to see what the operator is seeing, but I don't use it. My place is by the camera, with the operator, the trainer, and the actors; not standing off somewhere in front of a video monitor. Don finally agreed to do both jobs, *if* I would let him hire a top notch Hollywood gaffer. He was on the next plane to California.

The first shot on our production schedule was also the first shot in the script. This was not a result of prudent production scheduling procedures, but rather because I found it symbolic and simply couldn't resist. Normally, on the first day, simple shots are scheduled to get everyone off on the right foot, primed with accomplishment. Me, I wheel out the toughest, most complicated shot in the script, laden to the brim with variables and timing problems.

FADE IN:

1 *EXT. OLD HOUSE - DAY*

ESTABLISHING SHOT of an old graying two-story house, once an impressive mansion, but now up to its porches in weeds. Bushes and shrubs grown out of control for years seem to shroud the house in shadows. The glass in a pair of upstairs windows has been broken out; a shutter hangs ajar from its bottom hinge and even on this bright summer morning, the old house stirs an unsettling feeling. It's the kind of place that causes local kids to cross to the other side of the street. WE HEAR MORNING SOUNDS (BIRDS CHIRPING, A ROOSTER CROW-ING, A DOG BARKING OFF IN THE DISTANCE) and we BEGIN TO MOVE SLOWLY, DIAGONALLY,

ACROSS THE YARD, TOWARD THE HOUSE, studying it more closely, finally picking out an upstairs window that opens onto a side porch and WE ZOOM SLOWLY to an EXTREME CLOSE-UP of a broken-out pane in the window. At exactly that moment, BENJI'S head pops into the window. He's a mixed breed, un-groomed mutt of a dog but somehow still projects a lot of class. At our first sight of Benji, bright, happy THEME MUSIC begins. Our hero sniffs the morning air, yawns, stretches and climbs out through the broken window pane.

The shot would start with the camera virtually in the street on a wide shot of the house, then it would dolly slowly in toward one side, eventually rounding a corner to find the second-story window where Benji would appear. The zoom would begin, almost imperceptibly, tracking slowly toward a very tight shot of the single pane where the glass had been broken out. The dolly and the zoom would stop at precisely the same moment, exactly one beat ahead of Benji's face popping through the broken pane, yawning and sniffing the morning air as if he had just awakened for the day. The precision was necessary because the downbeat for the opening music would punctuate that exact moment and thrust us happily off into our story. It was all *one shot.* No cuts. And it had to be filmed just as the sun crept over the horizon to capture the *feel* of early morning light.

There were a hundred places for things to go wrong. But none of them could be allowed to show. This was the opening shot of an unknown film about an unknown dog, made by a tiny, unknown company, with unknown filmmakers. We had to snatch the audience away from their daily muddle the moment the film began to roll. There could be no technical distractions. Also, my paranoia assured me that certain segments of the industry would be lying in wait for us, anxious for flaws and imperfections to expose our backwoods inexperience. I was determined they wouldn't find any. *Benji* was going to look like the best of Hollywood, which meant rejecting the shot if the dolly wasn't smooth, if the zoom didn't begin just right, if the focus changes weren't on the money, if the zoom and dolly didn't end together just as Benji popped into the window, if the final composition wasn't right, or if Benji's attitude didn't project that he had just awakened to greet a brand new morning.

Tony pushing the dolly, Jim, the focus-puller, Donnie on camera, Frank Inn outside the house, Juanita Inn releasing Benji inside, and Benji himself all had to coordinate perfectly for everything to work. We had spent three hours rehearsing the afternoon before because to rehearse now, immediately prior to shooting, would take the fresh, morning edge off Benji's attitude.

Carolyn slipped up next to me and entwined her fingers in mine. "Good luck," she said.

"I wonder where it'll all lead," I said. "I wonder where we'll be a year from now, ten years from now."

She squeezed my hand and I felt her tremble. I sensed that she was once again torn between the wish for success and concern over the changes it might bring. But, outwardly, it didn't show. She was working as hard as anyone on the set. She had signed on to do makeup, but weeks ago she had been handed hairdressing and wardrobe. She was also helping the script girl with continuity and Harland with props, and, in her spare time, she was magically handling the multitude of odd jobs I tossed at her when I felt I could trust no one else to do them. She was, in effect, the producer, but it was years later before I finally realized it and gave up to her the unencumbered responsibility, and the title.

Joey, now twelve and insisting that everyone call him Joe, or, at least, Joe III, worked the entire summer on the set, assisting

Frank and Juanita with the dogs and helping the grips and electricians tote lights and equipment. It lead to a career. Primarily as a first assistant director of huge movies, but he has also written and directed a picture of his own entitled Abilene. Brandon, who would become one of Hollywood's highest paid writers at a very young age, was at home with a baby sitter,

"If nothing else," I said to Carolyn, "at least we're starting out well prepared."

Of course, I shouldn't have said that. At least, not out loud. The opening shot was the first shot we filmed and, eleven weeks later, it was the last shot we filmed. In all, we photographed the opening scene of *Benji* eighty-four times. It became a weekly event, something everyone could count on, like inflation.

On the very first take, the camera was perfect, the timings were right and Benji's actions and attitude were exactly what I had hoped for. He looked for the world like he had just awakened for the day, because, in fact, he had. But the lighting on the house was wrong. The aging mansion faced east, bathing its old, graying visage in the direct rays of the early morning sun, shining deep orange through the haze of our metropolitan atmosphere. It looked like we had filmed at sunset! I wanted to kick myself. I should've known better. I was so sure everything had been thought out.

Too late, the solution was obvious. We'd have to shoot the scene back-lit, in the afternoon when the sun was setting *behind* the house. This would overexpose the orange out of the sky and leave the house seemingly veiled in a softer, cooler, morning-type light. We set it up for a week later. Benji's "portable" one-ton air conditioner had to go back upstairs. The scaffolding outside the window had to be re-erected for Frank, and the dolly track had to be re-laid across the front yard. Needless to say, the crew was less than tickled. Nobody likes to do the same work a second time. A job finished should stay finished. To do it again is to halt progress and start going backwards. And, I suppose, it's worse when the reason for this rearward motion is someone else's mistake. The roar of the whispered grumblings rumbled across my senses trying to flatten the bulwarks I had erected. I dug the trenches deeper, repeating the admonitions I had preached to myself. No short cuts. Deal with each problem as it comes up. Give it full attention, solve it, then— and *only* then—move on.

This time the house looked terrific! But when Benji pulled himself into the window he looked like he had been hit by a truck. He had been slaving in the melting Texas summer heat for almost twelve hours and he was completely done in, tongue hanging out a foot.

The next week, we tried again, this time letting Higgins take a long nap in an air-conditioned room before shooting. He was better, but, to him, it still wasn't morning so there were no sniffs. By now we had decided to take the yawn in a close-up right after the sniffs. But the sniffs had to be there. It *had* to feel that real. Editing can solve a lot of problems, but it can't make a bored dog appear fresh and alert. Dogs love mornings like humans love Spring. Each one is filled with the anticipation of marvelous new discoveries. This is how I wanted the audience to see Benji for the first time, wrapped in his own environment, doing his own thing, not a trick dog doing stunts for a movie.

We *had* to have sniffs!

"He's over the edge," I heard Juanita say one afternoon as we prepared to shoot the opening shot for the fifth or sixth time. And by now, the crew was seriously considering mutiny. Others in the industry around Dallas who were not working the picture were hearing the tales and beginning to needle those who were.

"Camp obviously doesn't have the vaguest idea what he's doing," they were saying. "The picture will never get finished."

What they failed to understand is that whatever the level of truth that was attached to the first statement, it had no bearing on that of the second. But, the words didn't set well with a crew who, for the most part, had deferred some of their wages for shares of the profits. Morale began to sink.

It would've been very easy to give up and simply make do with whatever we had. I dreaded facing the crew each time I wasn't satisfied. Finally, one morning I gathered everyone into the living room of the old house and stumbled my way through a pep talk. The problem had become very personal, but also very important, I felt, to the outcome of the picture.

"I don't believe that being good at something is predicated upon being an *expert*, or being *perfect*," I stammered. "Or being above mistakes. What I *do* believe is that being good demands a willingness to recognize those mistakes and correct them. To look beyond the criticism of the moment to make decisions that are hopefully best for the project in the long run, when, for example, a year or so from now an audience is sitting in a theater daring us to entertain them."

When we left the room we had lost almost an hour of shooting time but the dividends were readily apparent. The crew was back on the offensive and aggressive in their work, even with Scene *RRRR1*.

Whenever a scene is re-shot, an *R* is placed before the scene number to distinguish it from the original. If it's re-shot twice, two *R's* precede the scene number, and so on. By the time we were finished with Scene #1, the *R's* were running off the slate. Each time there would be some new idea, but nothing seemed to work until the last week of production. We let Higgins sleep for almost six hours before the shot. We put six strips of bacon into an electric skillet, upwind, out of sight so Benji wouldn't look at it, let it come to full sizzle, the aroma wafted along by a small electric fan to land right under his nose. When he popped his head through the window, he sniffed the air like it was a fresh new day.

"Cut and print!" I shrieked happily. It was the seventy-ninth time the scene had been filmed.

A week into the shoot, we fired the gaffer.

A week after that, Don Reddy quit.

Record rainfall -- 9.38 inches, four times the July norm! -- buffeted and sank our schedule.

When it wasn't raining, it was so hot we had to trade in Benji's one-ton air conditioner for a three-ton unit to keep his tongue from dragging the ground. It was a standard home compressor, huge, heavy and not very portable, yet it had to follow him everywhere, gobbling up unscheduled time and money.

The actress we flew in to play the neighborhood lady with the cat persuaded—*intimidated*—me into letting her play the scene a bit tipsy. It wasn't right. I knew it at the time. And the dailies confirmed it. Every night for a week I would go upstairs to the editing room and ask Leon to put the film up again, hoping each time that the scenes would look better. They never did. We had to throw the film away, fly in another actress and shoot the scenes again.

Which meant Frank had to fly the cats back into town to start their training over from scratch.

The Dallas Parks Department decided to spray the grasses of Samuels Park with a highly toxic insecticide, dangerous to dogs, on the very day they had given us permission to shoot the slow motion love montage.

The actor playing the kids' father was commuting by car to Austin every night to star in a dinner theater production of *The Rainmaker*. He had promised, of course, that the play would have no effect on our schedule or his ability to perform in *Benji*. And, of course, he was late to the set most mornings, missed several calls completely and was generally incoherent when he showed up.

He fell asleep at the wheel one night on his way back to Dallas, hit a tree and wound up in the hospital.

Actors Christopher Connelly and Mark Slade had decided before arriving in McKinney that *real* movies couldn't possibly be made this far from Hollywood. To them it was a joke, and their attitude was undermining the morale of the cast and the crew.

We discovered that Tiffany was typecast. A dumb blonde. Couldn't act a lick.

Our second try at the scenes in Samuels Park found huge sprinklers exactly where we wanted to shoot. 9.38 inches of rain wasn't enough for the Dallas Parks Department. The sprinklers could not be shut down for a day, nor could they be moved. We had to wait.

The hundreds of butterflies collected for the end of the love montage all died.

Twice.

My seven-week schedule stretched to eleven and Ed had to raise more money to cover the extra time, only to find, once the picture was edited, that it was too short. Still more money had to be raised, I had to write another ten minutes into the script, fly Higgins, Frank, Juanita, Patsy Garrett—the wonderful actress playing the housekeeper—and Terry Carter, the actor playing Benji's policeman friend, back to Dallas, rehire the kids and the crew and shoot another full week, trying to match winter for Summer and avoid the Christmas decorations now hanging from every streetlamp and store window in McKinney.

Seven-year-old Cindy had lost two front teeth in the interim. And the trees that had shadowed the back porch during the Summer had lost all their leaves.

Higgins began the picture with a full, thick coat of hair, but by the hot Summer's end, he had shed so much of it that the nub of his tail was actually showing. The change was barely noticeable as we progressed through the eleven weeks of shooting, but when scenes shot out of sequence, weeks apart, were cut together, our fat, fluffy, full-coated dog, in the blinking of an eye, would lose all his hair, then miraculously get it all back again. Not unlike Cindy's teeth.

But through all the mistakes, mishaps, detours and delays, the most important element of the picture was working. The point-of-view and the emotional heart of the story were leaping off the screen with more fidelity than I had hoped for. Even screening raw dailies, with scenes out of context, out of sequence, with slates, and crew noise, and Frank's voice on the track, when Benji's face filled the screen and those big brown eyes went to work, truly magical things were happening! Benji *was* acting!

The crew laughed and joked as they feasted upon gravy-smothered chicken-fried steak and swilled down huge glasses of iced tea. Several tables had been gathered end-to-end over near the window so they could all sit together. None of them knew that Don Reddy had quit. Nor that Shaw's Cafe had been selected for a summit meeting that could—as it turned out—affect the names of thousands of dogs for years to come.

Away from the window, four yellowing plaster walls, chipped and marred by time, supported a tired, buckling metal ceiling. Good food was the only long suit here at Shaw's. Down-home cooking at its best. A pair of ceiling fans turned lazily overhead. This was back before ceiling fans were the thing. Or after, depending upon your age. A dozen or so square wooden tables, covered in faded red and white checkered oil cloth, were overflowing with the usual collage of McKinney locals—farmers, bankers, store clerks, mechanics, lawyers—each working on, or waiting for a country scrumptious meal. We didn't eat here often because the inevitable overindulgence would usually slow the afternoon pace down to a crawl.

But today was different. I had cleverly called an early lunch to avoid having to figure out how to film a movie without a cameraman. And I needed time to talk to Donnie, alone.

We sat across the noisy cafe at a small table, two grown men mostly whimpering and blubbering our way through the meal. More than employer and employee, we were good friends. He treasured what I was trying to accomplish and he agonized over wanting to be part of it. But he was scared to death of stepping out on the end of the diving board, of exposing his mistakes for all to see, and he was thoroughly confused with the messages I was sending; critical and complaining on the one hand, yet, on the other, begging him to stay and trust in his own ideas.

"Listen to *yourself!*" I pleaded. "Stop listening to everyone else!"

"Does that include you?"

"Almost everyone else."

I grinned. So did he.

I was certain beyond doubt that his eye, his judgment, if allowed to escape the confines of his fears, would result in stunning pictures on the screen.

Not exactly the way things had begun. It was 5:00 a.m. the morning of Day #4. We were worn out from work and short nights getting shorter, but still flying high under the exhilaration of at last being off on the venture of making real movies. Our bubble was about to burst, however, and we would hit the ground with a thud. We were sitting in the Westgate Theater in McKinney, sleepy but wide-eyed with anticipation at seeing our first batch of dailies, which, in our case, were almost weeklies because the film had to make its way from McKinney to CFI's lab in Los Angeles and back again before we could see it.

None of us had ever seen any of our work on a screen larger than maybe four feet by six feet. And, heretofore, I had only worked with sixteen millimeter film. This was my first experience with four-times-as-large thirty-five millimeter. The anticipation of seeing the first day's shoot on a full-sized theater screen was exciting. I'm at a loss to explain why. I'm usually not one of those who believe that bigger is better. More often than not, I preach the opposite. But there's something about seeing your work spreading from wall-to-wall and floor-to-ceiling that is truly thrilling.

That is, if the work you're seeing is any good. Unfortunately, this time, the anticipated thrill was quickly punctured by the first picture on the screen, our miscalculated sunrise, Scene #1.

The following morning made it two for two. Our first effort at interior lighting, a day scene inside the old house. It was supposed to be low-key and spooky looking, with the only obvious light coming from two huge windows, creating long, soft shadows amongst the dust and cobwebs. Instead, the house resembled the inside of a neon arcade, with bright, harsh light careening from every corner.

I was sick. It looked terrible. And it was my fault. I had known from the beginning that Don was insecure and I had suspected that his quest for a gaffer was really a search for someone to lean on, not someone to direct and instruct, so I should've gone to Los Angeles with him to speak with the gaffer myself and to look at lighting in films he had gaffed. I imagine they all resembled the scenes he lit for us, and that's probably what the cameramen and directors of those pictures wanted. But we didn't. Don had chosen him because of his twenty years of experience, and I went along blindly ignoring past lessons, specifically that *volume* of experience, isolated from other considerations, is meaningless. The precise type of experience and the results of that experience are so much more important. But this particular gaffer truly believed that his accumulation of years, alone, was the answer to all of our problems. And this became a real obstacle when the gaffer realized that no one else on the crew had ever worked on a feature before. He couldn't resist setting himself up as the expert. He had his list of things that worked, accumulated over those twenty years, and if what we wanted to try wasn't on the list, too bad. I think he was actually trying to be helpful but it became a plight of seniority intimidation. How could any first-timer possibly know enough to direct an old pro of twenty years? When someone's been around that long, he's got to know what he's doing, right? How well I understood. Donnie was not likely to rise to the task of being this crusty old veteran's boss. So, for me, there was only one choice. The crusty old veteran went home.

We hired Bill Roper, an ex-Jamieson cameraman. He was actually to be the gaffer, but in deference to his experience as a full-fledged cameraman, he would be credited as Lighting Consultant. He and Don had worked together for years and had always gotten along well. And Bill shared our philosophy of simple, soft, uncomplicated lighting. I had a long talk with Bill to make sure he understood that Don would be calling the shots. He did, and he was excited about being part of the production. And none too soon, because the rains came and forced us back inside the old house.

The lights were soon up and in place for another try at the same scene lit by the Hollywood gaffer and thrown away. It looked better, closer, but, for me, there was still too much light, too many crossing shadows; too harsh, not soft enough. Don and I discussed it, debated it, then argued about it, and finally he threw in the towel saying that, as he had suspected from the start, he was over his head and couldn't accomplish what I wanted. He simply wasn't experienced enough. And he quit.

I toyed with the cold, congealed gravy on my cold, stiff chicken-fried steak. Neither Don nor I had eaten much. It had been an emotional lunch. He wanted desperately to do the picture, and I desperately wanted him to do it. He was simply afraid to believe in himself, and, in the end, I could only convince him that I believed in him enough for both of us. We sent the rest of the crew home and Don, Bill Roper and I went back to the house to see if it was possible to please Joe Camp.

"I want it to look just like this," I said.

The three of us were standing at the bottom of the stairs in the dusty old mansion. The ambient afternoon light from two large windows cast soft but dark shadows across the room. It looked exactly as I had first seen it several months before. This was the look that had sold me on using the old house in the first place.

"Well, if you want it lit like God lights it," Roper said, "I suggest we put the lights outside where God puts them."

Donnie glanced from one of the large windows to the other and quite suddenly the sparkle was back in his eyes. He started spouting instructions and was gone in a flash to grab some of the other guys before they got away.

At the next round of dailies, Don Reddy got a standing ovation from the crew. The pictures on the screen, at last, were his. And, not surprisingly, they were terrific.

"If this were MGM, they'd dig me a hole!"

Frank was barking at no one in particular, but the line was to become familiar. He was lying on his 350-pound belly, scrunched as close to the camera as possible and I was sprawled on top of him. Jim, the focus-puller, was on his knees with his elbow jammed in the small of my back. Donnie was hunkered behind the eyepiece and Tony was wedged between the wall and the camera trying to place Benji's eye light right next to the lens. We had discovered early on that without the pinpoint of reflected sparkle created by this tiny light, Benji's eyes became dark, expressionless holes. It's amazing how much difference it made, and invariably, for maximum effect, the light needed to be exactly where Frank had settled in.

"Put it where Benji will be looking," Donnie would always say. It had to do with geometrical things, like angle of reflectance. But, of course, Benji, in close-up, would usually be looking at Frank and the ever-wagging finger from which he took his instruction. So, we spent months trying to repeal the physical law against two solid objects occupying the same space.

"Watch your finger, Frank. You're making shadows on the dog's face."

"I wouldn't know. I can't *see* the dog's face!"

"Can you move over a bit?"

"How's this?"

"No, his look's too far off."

"Try this."

"Too low. Can't you keep your hand behind the light?"

"If my dog can't see it, he's not going to do what Joe wants him to do! Move your damn light!"

"If the light's not there, it won't matter what he does!"

Normally, when tempers flare like this on a movie set, there'll be a methodical build to a final insult, a screaming retort and one or more of the parties will stomp off, adult-like, until he or she or they cool down. But there was nothing *normal* about our set. We were usually piled on the floor at Benji's eye-level, shoe-horned into some corner where nobody could move, much less stomp off, so there was little choice but to deal with the problem.

We spent the better part of three months like that, on our knees and bellies, stacked on top of each other, scrunched into impossible spaces attempting to look *up* at our fluffy hero. Placing the camera just slightly below an actor's eye-level tends to make him appear stronger, more in control, more heroic. But there's a hidden side effect. Even though Benji's size is clearly defined by shots with people and other animals, whenever he makes personal appearances, there are always those who are astounded that he's as small as he is. The low camera angles tend to create a larger-than-life feeling that outlasts the intellectual reality of, for example, seeing him easily cuddled in the arms of a pint-sized seven-year-old. It's not a new phenomenon among short actors.

The word *short*, of course, is relative. Placing a camera below a human's eye level, however short, creates no unusual problems. But Benji stands a mere thirteen inches off the floor. And much of the time he was lying down. New camera rigs and devices had to be designed virtually on a daily basis. How does a camera, for example, precede a dog at dog's eye level running down a narrow sidewalk *at thirty miles an hour?*

Back when the script was in the typewriter, I tended to worry more about story than production problems, managing to over-look—or possibly choosing to ignore—the simple fact that a heavy motion picture camera usually works better when attached to some-thing like a pan head and a tripod or camera dolly. The head allows the camera to be smoothly panned or tilted, but for the head to be stable, it has to be attached to something like a tripod. The shortest *something* known to the motion picture world prior to Benji was called a *high hat*, topping out about six inches off the ground. The pan head lifted the camera another eight inches, already above Benji's eye-level before adding the distance from the bottom of the camera to the lens.

Jim and Tony came up with an entire arsenal of creative new gear, from simple plastic lazy susans bought at the dime store for $1.98 to complex welded rigs that hung off the sides of camera dollies, dangled from pickup trucks, dropped off the bases of vari-ous pan heads, and circled birdbaths like merry-go-rounds. I be-

lieve we even had the first skateboard in the world. But it transported a camera, not a teen-ager. The lens was simply never
allowed to look *down* on Benji unless there was a special and
specific reason for it to do so.

Bruised knees, sore backs, and grimy clothes from lying in the
dust and dirt were the order of the summer. A few movies later on
Benji the Hunted, a camera assistant with a bias toward capitalism
discovered a prescription for part of the pain and made a few extra
dollars in the process. He purchased a dozen or so pairs of hard
plastic knee pads, the kind designed to protect the limbs of professional skaters, and sold them out immediately to crew members at a
good profit. Locals were probably wondering why in the world the
roller derby had invaded the woods of Oregon.

"Pull the light up just a bit, Tony, right over the lens. Get
closer to the camera, Frank." Don Ready was the speaker.

"Get a smaller camera," groused Frank.

"Get a smaller trainer," Donnie grinned.

Frank tried to squeeze closer to the camera and bring Benji's
look even closer to the lens. Our floppy-eared star was peering
through the branches of a large potted plant, supposedly watching
the goings-on in the room across the hall where family, friends and
police would be fretting about a kidnapping.

"It's not too late to put on a longer lens and back up a bit," Jim
suggested. "That would appear to bring his look closer and, more
importantly, it would get Tony off my back." Tony was now
straddling Jim like a horse, leaning across the front of the camera
with the eye light. We must've looked like one of those modern
sculptures, all arms and legs and no bodies.

"You know the rule," I grumbled.

The *rule* was no long lenses on close-ups.

Anyone who has ever played around with photography has no
doubt witnessed the compressing effect of a telephoto lens. We

learned early in the production that long lenses on Benji's face flattened his features, made them less dimensional, and eliminated the feeling of intimacy that could be achieved with a wider lens, up close, right in the bushes with him. If the lens is right there, the perspective is different. You can feel it. It puts you virtually inside Benji's head, examining and experiencing his every thought or reaction. If the shot is made with a longer lens from across the room, even though it's still a close-up, you are no longer right there with him, but now off, away, just an observer rather than a participant. The understanding of this phenomenon, I felt, was extremely important to the emotional magic of involving the audience totally with Benji and his dilemma.

Don Reddy understood, but the crew never really signed off on my relentless refusal to back the camera away, and this, over time, revealed a bizarre soft spot in the movie making process. The technical crew, it dawned on me years later, cannot judge the quality of its work based upon what the director wants. To do so, they would have to judge the movie itself, and if most of them began to relate the quality level of their own work to the ultimate quality of every movie they worked on, I'm afraid none of them would think very highly of themselves. Conversely, if a grip or an electrician only toiled on movies that he felt were going to be terrific movies, he'd soon be out of work. As a percentage of the whole, there simply aren't that many terrific movies around. So, for self preservation, someone who makes his living working on as many movies as possible must place his or her emphasis on tangible things, like speed and quota. Any crew can be proud of their day's work when they film more setups than they were supposed to. When they beat the clock. But keeping the camera so close to Benji often slowed the pace to a standstill and caused problems that dominoed in complexity. When you get that many people piled that close to a subject as small as Benji, it becomes virtually impossible to light the scene. With the camera across the room wearing a telephoto lens, there's no one in the way, blocking lights. When it's two feet from the subject, *everybody's* blocking the lights.

So, in a strange sort of way, my efforts to make the film better often worked counter to the crew's feeling of self worth.

Thank God I didn't understand all this at the time.

"Scrunch up, Frank," I said. "Right next to the lens."

Frank rolled a little and tried to hold his hand right next to the lens. "Look here, Higgins," he said.

"He looks confused," Donnie whispered.

"Damn right he looks confused," Frank blurted. "He's wondering what the hell I'm doing down here on the floor buried under all these people!"

"Perfect," I said. "Confusion is perfect for this scene." I tapped Donnie on the shoulder. "Roll."

For most of us, it was never dull, and rarely standing. Point-of-view shots became fond breathers because a camera looking at what Benji was supposed to be seeing meant that Benji wasn't in the scene, and Frank wasn't on the floor, and the eye-light was back in the truck. The few of us remaining around the lens could breathe a little easier. There was no fear of anyone getting squashed by Frank. And it was quieter. Frank has a catalytic effect upon noise levels, and he and I together seem to reach a critical mass.

The truly cherished commodity on the set, however, was the human actor, because an actor in the vicinity usually meant the crew would soon be standing up. Spirits would lift, knees would flex, and jokes would begin to flow.

That is until Chris Connelly and Mark Slade arrived.

They were both strong character actors from the world of television, but by no means stars. During their flight down together—I was told later—they jointly concluded that they were off to the sticks on a paid vacation. A lark of no consequence; making movies with amateurs. I'm sure we were an unimpressive group to two who were usually surrounded by hundreds on a television set. Our number was barely twenty. And I doubt that we were doing things exactly like they would be done out west. A certainty, according to Frank because we weren't digging him any holes; and I must admit, during the years that followed, I've never walked onto a Hollywood set and seen the director, cameraman, trainer, assistant cameraman and electrician in a heap on the floor. But the clearly focused, unnerving reflections of what these two actors felt about *this silly little dog movie* being made by a bunch of inexperienced Texans who had never even worked in Hollywood definitely affected morale on the set. They would swagger through the crew like a pair of prize roosters in the midst of ordinary hens, then stand off in a corner, joking and giggling about whatever was going on at the time. It was all folly to them and the crew quickly became impatient for me to do something.

The dilemma was that I had no confidence in my ability to deal with two apparently spoiled Hollywood brats. I had factored against such a need by hiring these two in the first place. Carolyn and I had spent hours watching them on television and had convinced ourselves that Chris and Mark were pretty nice people. Such a quality is generally difficult to hide, no matter what the acting assignment. But I was afraid we had miscalculated. To me, no actor's performance—or name—is worth the kind of misery some can dish out. Life is entirely too short. And for this first picture, it was terribly important to me that set chemistry be positive. Keep the problems technical, not emotional. Nothing can destroy the momentum of a team like a single temperamental ego. And now, apparently, unexpectedly, we had *two*.

I dreaded the confrontation that must come. What if they told me to stuff it? What if they walked off? Or what if I had to fire them? Everything they had filmed would have to be re-shot, which, of course, would mean more time, and more money. We had the time, but we certainly didn't have the money. So I procrastinated. Some of my finest creative work has been devoted to the invention of plausible, seemingly rational excuses for not doing something I needed to do, an exercise usually bred from fear of rejection. Not that postponement is wrong, per se. A valid argument can be mounted for not attacking until your guns are in place. But one must be careful not to secretly bury the guns, trying to slow down the process.

Tony finally brought things to a head one morning after a scene with Mark and Chris. He jerked me aside and informed me that he no longer intended to listen quietly to their slurs and innuendoes. Tony is, shall we say, a physical person, and his drift was clear.

Perhaps, I said, that very evening after wrap would be an ideal time to have a little talk.

Butterflies fought wars in my stomach for the rest of the afternoon. I had no idea what I was going to say. I didn't consider myself much of a talker, especially a spontaneous talker, and any form of intimidation usually begot lockjaw. I preferred letting results speak instead of words. But anything I had in the results column would surely seem insignificant to this pair. Somehow, I needed to win them over, to convince them that *Benji* would be something they could be proud of, and I had no idea where to start. *This is really stupid,* I thought. I had convinced some of Dallas' wealthiest that the picture was worthy of their investment, but I couldn't think of a thing to say to two barely successful television actors. Yet I knew I had to convince them, or fire them.

That would make Ed's day, I thought. The idea of telling him we had to re-shoot a week's work churned my butterflies into a frenzy.

Late that afternoon, Chris and Mark were told to relax for an hour while we worked with Benji. During that hour, the most incredible thing happened. When they were called back to the set, they came scuttling down the stairs, eyes wide and jabbering like kids who had just ridden their first pony. Chris took the last four steps in a single leap and grabbed me by the shoulders. "Joe, the stuff looks great! It's sensational!" He was screeching for all to hear.

I was lost.

"We've been up in the editing room looking at footage with Leon! It's unreal!"

They were both bubbling over like runaway porridge.

"Donnie, the shot from the landing is incredible! It's gorgeous!"

I glanced at Tony. He was as flabbergasted as I was.

"We need to apologize to you guys," Mark said.

"Amen," chimed Chris. "I'm sure we've been a couple of first class pricks."

Tony couldn't resist an affirming nod.

I couldn't resist a grateful smile.

"If Benji is through for the day, will somebody please get me out from under this table?!"

In the flurry and fluster, we had forgotten that Frank was still sprawled on his side, half under a table where Benji was supposed to be hiding.

Chris and Mark were first to the rescue.

Thin, delicate eyebrows arched skeptically over rolling eyes and the lady smiled sweetly. "I can't print that, Mr. Camp. Tell me about the story, and the actors."

She was giving me a clue, handwriting on the wall—or in this case the Dallas Morning News—but I wasn't listening. I was too astonished. I had just spent thirty minutes ranting giddily about the unique concept of a dog *acting*, about the incredible facial expressions Higgins was giving us, about those big brown eyes and the reams of dialog they were speaking, about the dog himself and how for the first time I had come to realize that the story we were telling wasn't purely the emotional petition I had once thought but, in reality, quite plausible. Dogs, I had discovered, *can* think rationally. And this particular one was extraordinary.

Not that others aren't. But most dogs who have the intelligence, attitude and temperament to do what Higgins was doing, never have the opportunity to learn and to gain the vocabulary that Higgins—and later Benji's—have had.

"Vocabulary?! That's ridiculous!"

I bit my tongue because we were on the air. This was later, a radio talk show in Norfolk, Virginia, with a host that went on to imply that I was as full of dark brown bull droppings as any Hollywood hype artist.

But Norfolk radio notwithstanding, Benji has a vocabulary. He thinks, and he understands concepts. Like the concept of *other*. If you ask for a foot, then ask for the *other* foot, he switches. If he walks off and Frank tells him to go the *other* way, he looks back to see *which* other way, then takes Frank's point and heads in that direction. He understands the concept of words like *slow, hurry, easy,* and *not,* no matter how the words are applied. When asked to perform a difficult task, you can actually witness the process as he studies the situation to determine the best approach. But none of this is particularly unusual. Sheep dogs in Europe tend entire flocks *by themselves* for months, keeping the sheep together, deciding when to move them from one pasture to another, even stopping the whole group to check for vehicles before crossing a road.

At a press conference in a Miami hotel suite, a dozen reporters watched Benji perform one of his standard show routines, completely unaware—until they were told later—that he had made a mess of it and would've never finished had he not been able to think it through.

He was wedged between two banister poles, pulling a coffee mug tied to a string of leashes up to the mezzanine level which overlooked the group below. A person, of course, would use two hands, one over the other, but Benji uses his mouth and a foot. He reaches down and pulls up a length, holds it tightly against the floor with his foot, then reaches down again and pulls up another length, holds it with his foot, and so on, until he has retrieved whatever is tied to the other end. As he performed, the leash slipped over the corner of the mezzanine floor and, because he was so snugly wedged between the banister poles, he could no longer reach it with the foot he had always used to hold it. I marveled as I watched the wheels turn. He pondered the situation for only a few seconds before he, quite logically, placed the *other* foot on the rope—the foot he had *never* before used to hold it—and went on with the routine as if nothing had happened.

Benji even understands what he's doing when he's acting.

"Now you've heard it all folks. The dog understands he's acting! I suppose he gets script approval!"

Chicago. Another talk show host.

One of the more important sequences in the picture involved Benji moping forlornly, aimlessly through town. He knew the children were in danger but was unable to communicate what he knew to the family, who had, in fact, scolded him for trying. This is the same sequence I had visualized months earlier sitting in the bar of the Hollywood Holiday Inn with those first Polaroid photographs. For the sequence to work, indeed for the entire *story* to work, these scenes had to generate unencumbered empathy and support for Benji's plight. He had to look as if he had lost his last friend. His desperation had to reach out from those big brown eyes and squeeze passionately upon the hearts of the audience.

It worked so well, that during the first rehearsal, I almost aborted the sequence. I was forty feet above the scene with Donnie and the camera in the bucket of a cherry picker—the kind utility companies use to fix power lines—and Frank was in the alley below *screaming* at Higgins, "*Shame on you!! Put your head down!! Shame, shame on you!!*"

Higgins looked as if he had, *in fact*, lost his last friend. It was perfect. I *believed* him. But I couldn't bear to see him hurt so from the scolding.

I asked Tony to lower me back to the ground and I walked into the scene and asked Frank to hold for a minute while we talked.

"What's the matter?" he asked, eyes wide and curious. "Isn't this the look you want?"

"It's perfect," I said. "But I don't feel right about getting it this way."

"What the hell are you talking about?"

"I don't feel right about you scolding Higgins like that."

Frank's eyes rolled heavenward. "Turn around," he said. "Does that look like a scolded dog?"

Higgins was aimlessly scratching his ear. He looked up at me and yawned idly.

"Watch closely," said Frank. He motioned Higgins onto his feet and began scolding him again. Our floppy-eared star's head dropped like a rock, his eyes drooped and he looked as pitiful as anything I had ever seen. Then Frank relaxed, chirped a simple "Okay," and as if he had flipped an emotional switch, Higgins blinked away the blues, had a good shake, wagged his tail, and awaited his master's next command. He fully understood what was going on, and scolding wasn't it. He might not have known the word, but he was, in the truest sense, acting.

He picked things up so quickly that he even astonished Frank on occasion. Like the time we realized he had deciphered what *cut* and *print* meant. Frank unraveled from beneath a pile of people and suddenly realized his dog was nowhere in sight. "Your dog's no fool," Tony chuckled. "Joe said 'cut' and he split for the air conditioning."

Attached to our portable air conditioner was a fifty-foot hose, fifteen inches in diameter, and attached to the end of that was a little cubicle enclosed on the top and bottom and two sides. This was Benji's home between shots. The air was necessary to keep him from panting.

Higgins learned very quickly that the air conditioner was *his* and that's where he was supposed to be when the camera wasn't rolling. It didn't take him long to figure out that the camera quit rolling whenever I said "Cut." So off he'd go, without a word from Frank. Whenever I said "Print," the shot was probably over, another one checked off the list, and Higgins would prance happily over to Frank's wife, Juanita, and gather up a few "Good boys."

But telling these stories, and a dozen others, left not the slightest dent in the structured armor of the Dallas Morning News reporter covering the newly emerging film production scene in north Texas. Movies, after all, are actors—*real* actors—and scripts, and cameras, and glitz. And that's what this reporter was going to write about in the newspaper. The story came out the next day, to our amazement, on the *front page!* It was all about a seven-year-old Dallas girl and a nine-year-old Dallas boy making their motion picture debuts. The dog was barely mentioned.

That was my first experience with newspaper writers and I should've paid more attention. It might've saved weeks of frustration a year later. I had thought, naively, that the uniqueness of *Benji* would speak for itself and the dog's ability to express emotion would propel him immediately into the hearts of audiences. He was the emotional focal point of the story, the three-dimensional character playing off the humans as virtual props. With *real* audiences, that's the way it worked. But not with the press. Early critics killed us. A trite and clichéd story, they said. The acting wasn't memorable. Neither was the directing. *And nobody talked about the dog!*

I was destroyed. How could I have been so wrong?! They were missing the point and perspective of the movie. The soul of our scruffy little dog seemed to be buried under the critical process, the charge to analyze, while critics searched feverishly—and in vain—for the souls of the *people*. "The people are incredibly one-dimensional," said one. *That's what they're supposed to be!* I wanted to screech. *The dog has the depth! The story is not the people, and not the kidnapping! It's the dog's struggle to communicate something to a group of humans with whom he has no way to converse!* But that's not the way they saw it. Their critical check list had been structured over the years, based upon all the movies that had gone before, all of which were anchored in the emotions and relationships of people, not dogs. Even in movies about animals, the concern, the compassion, was not with the animal, but with the kid who had to dispose of the animal because the animal was killing the chickens.

It took a full week to pull myself off the floor after the first bad reviews came in, and still another to push ego aside, analyze the problem, and figure out how to solve it.

But now I'm getting ahead of myself.

Theme from *Love Story* was playing on the car radio. I was intrigued by the way these classical strains tugged at my emotions and left me sort of sad and empty. I turned to see if Carolyn was listening, but didn't need to ask. The tears spoke the answer. She hadn't read the book and knew little about the film, but was responding to the music as if she were living it.

I told that story to Euel Box the first time we met. "That's the kind of music we must have for *Benji*," I said.

And with filming and editing on the picture complete, I was now telling him, quite seriously, that our movie was still only *half* done. The rest was up to him.

Like most of us on the picture, Euel lived in Dallas and had never worked on a theatrical feature before *Benji*. He had composed music for dozens of television commercials and hundreds of those radio station jingles that sing out call letters like they were classic lyrics to a hit record. But it was his enchanting theme for a jewelry commercial that had caught my ear several years before. The spot featured a young couple in love, walking in a park awash with springtime azaleas. Soft, romantic photography circled and swirled about them, eventually settling upon a close-up of the inevitable engagement ring, and a priceless, stunning reaction from the beautiful young girl.

This commercial could've easily fallen into the ranks of the dumb and clichéd, but the execution was perfect. The direction and photography were lusciously understated, and Euel's music was exquisite. I wanted to grab Carolyn, race out to the park and propose all over again. It was emotional magic.

Even then, long before *Benji*, I knew I didn't want to forget this composer's name, and that early decision resulted in one of the happy surprises of the *Benji* production.

But it wasn't easy, and it didn't come quickly. Still another testimonial for *perseverance*. First, I had to literally shake Euel out of a *kiddie music* gridlock. He knew that children would be in the audience and he was writing *down* to them, Mister Rogers-like.

After listening to the third or fourth piano demo, I took a deep breath and paced across the room.

"I've asked you to think of *Benji* as an *adult* movie that will also entertain kids," I said, "*not* the reverse. I've asked you to move *me* with your music and promised that by doing so, you'll also move my kid! I've asked you to look at the Disney classics! Listen to *Love Story!* Go back and listen to your own jewelry commercial music! But it's simply not working. Either you haven't heard a thing I've been saying... or perhaps I've made a terrible mistake."

Something clicked. No more Mr. Rogers.

But no Academy Award nominations either. And that, quite literally, was the next stumbling block. When Euel and I first talked about the movie, I had told him that the opening song was going to have to win an Academy Award nomination. He didn't think I was serious, of course, and when he finally realized that I was, he decided, most certainly, that I was crazy. I had done a study of movie songs that had been nominated for the Award, and, at the time, it was sort of a throw-away category. It seemed to me that this was an area in which we might have a realistic shot at a nomination; which, if achieved, would certainly bestow credibility onto our unknown movie about the unknown dog by the unknown company with the unknown director. I had no idea, until later, how much pressure this put on Euel and his writing efforts, compounded when I asked him to create a melody that would work both for the bright and cheerful (*Academy Award quality*) opening song *and* the slower, more poignant underscoring later in the film. I felt that subconscious familiarity with the melody line—from the opening piece—would strengthen the emotional impact of the slower, more plaintive pieces later in the film.

But trying to make a single melody accomplish two separate objectives, both very important, and both very different, caused more creative clog. Finally I told Euel to forget the romantic and poignant stuff for the time being and concentrate only on the opening song. It's funny how the mind works. Remove the barriers, tell that globular, gray, gelatinous mass it no longer has to make one piece of music do two jobs, and what comes out is a beautifully haunting melody that works splendidly both ways.

I'll never forget the night I heard the final recording. I had been in looping sessions all day while Euel, his wife Betty, and a large orchestra were recording music. I met Betty a block from the studio and as we walked I asked how the session had gone.

"Pretty good, I think," she said nervously, which is not exactly what I wanted to hear. We entered the control room where Euel and two engineers were mixing the day's sessions and, for a moment, everything seemed to freeze and get very quiet. Euel sat me down in a chair right between four huge speakers, asked Jerry Barnes, the chief engineer, if he was ready, apologized to me because I would be hearing a rough mix, not a final; then the tape rolled. I was listening to two of the three most important pieces of music in the film. Each had to reach deeply, sensitively into the emotion and squeeze softly with all its might. This kind of music you shouldn't even be aware of hearing, only feeling.

I didn't last long. Three, maybe four minutes and I had to leave the room. I scampered down the darkened halls of the deserted studio, turned a corner by a water fountain, and there I stood for a very long time, yes, with tears streaming down my face. I had never in my life wanted anything to be so good, and had it turn out even better than I could've hoped.

It must've been at least ten minutes before I could pull myself together and return to the control room. Euel and Betty and the engineers were all seated, just staring into space, sort of glassy-eyed, looks of devastation sagging on their faces. They were certain I had hated the music. Why else would I have simply gotten up and left like that?

I circled the room slowly, trying to portray the producer, the guy who was supposed to be in control, but the little boy crying happy tears in that theater back in Little Rock kept getting in the way. Words were difficult to squeeze out. "Until tonight, we had nothing but a bunch of film strung together," I stammered. "Now, at long, long last, we've got a *movie!*"

The smoke from a huge, black cigar lay heavy across the room, stirred only by the cigar itself as it leaped from mouth to hand, swirled and circled up from the chair, danced across the huge office, then paused to jab at the air like a driving piston.

Ed and I sat in stunned silence. There was a dank, black empty feeling oozing down over me. Cold and distant, yet agonizingly painful. The words spewing from the smoke of the fat man's cigar, were going astray, some hitting, some missing. I was drifting in and out. Had all of this been for nothing? The years of preparation? The experience? The planning? The dreams?

"Totally wrong for Paramount!" barked the mouth behind the cigar. "It's too damn sweet. And the music is... well... it's... it's too sticky... it's all wrong. If you cut the Clairol sequence, we might try something with Saturday matinees, but beyond that... I mean, at night it doesn't have a chance! Have you tried Disney?"

The words fell out of his mouth like crystal shattering on a tile floor. We had tried Disney. And Fox, and MGM, and Warner Brothers! And this simply couldn't be happening!

It's a good movie, I tried to reassure myself. It works. Reaction to the first screening had been terrific. The audience was mostly investors, friends and crew, but you could still tell, like the difference between a serious hug and a pat on the head. And at the exhibitor's convention in Dallas, theater owners had loved it, or so they had said.

Years of hopes and dreams, eons of study, practice and hard work had finally come together in a movie. A real movie that real audiences would cherish. I was certain of it. I had seen it in their eyes during the screenings. They laughed and cried, and burst from the theater with big smiles stretched across their faces. It was all working. Except for one thing. We couldn't get a distributor. No one wanted it. Not one. Zero.

11

FROM THE ASHES

"He who desires but acts not, breeds pestilence."
William Blake
The Marriage of
Heaven and Hell

I was in a daze, frozen in time. What was happening simply would not compute. My brain cells wouldn't handle it. Problems, roadblocks had become second nature throughout production, but the solutions were always stirred by a single focus. To prevent what was happening now from ever happening. To so thoroughly involve whoever saw the film in a subjective, emotional experience that there could only be one response.

But this wasn't it! This wasn't the end result we had worked so long and hard for; that we had overcome obstacle after obstacle for, obstacles that had seemed enormous, some literally. Like our blimped camera that was almost as big as Frank Inn. We were continually trying to stuff the two of them into tiny Benji-like corners. A week into filming, we had to dispense with the blimped camera altogether and go with a much smaller unblimped Arriflex that would fit into tighter spaces, which meant all the sound had to be reconstructed later because camera noise was on every track. Virtually every line of dialog in the film was looped—which means it was re-recorded in a sound studio, one line at a time, in perfect sync with the film; a long and tedious process.

One of the most memorable sequences in the film was almost thrown out because it didn't work; the group of soft-focused, fog-filtered scenes with Benji and Tiffany romping together in slow motion through Samuels Park—the same sequence that was postponed twice because of pesticides and sprinklers. When it reached the editing table, instead of a beautiful series of playfully romantic scenes revealing the changing relationship between the dogs, we had a slow, boring, completely unemotional sequence. Leon cut and re-cut, for more than a week, but the end result never changed. One day, out of sheer frustration, I went out and bought four movie soundtracks on cassettes. Perhaps the right piece of music would give it some life. We tried the themes from *Love Story* and *Godfather* and the footage still lay there dying. Then I shoved *Theme from The Summer of '42* into the cassette player, and miracles began to happen. Leon and I watched the sequence in awe. It was no longer simply a series of shots, but a beautiful and cohesive, emotional piece. It was, at last, working.

We transferred the cassette to magnetic film and the entire sequence was edited to that track from *The Summer of '42*. In fact, the last four bars, sort of a descending jingle bell effect, worked so well with the butterfly sequence, that I was never happy with anything else and ultimately asked Euel to copy those four bars as closely as law and conscience would allow.

This montage—labeled the Clairol sequence by the man from Paramount who wanted it removed from the film—ultimately became the piece everyone wanted to use to represent the movie. Local and network television talk shows selected it over other clips to use on the air, it was featured on two network television specials and it inspired a beautiful piece of original music from Euel Box that was nominated for an Academy Award and has been re-recorded dozens of times around the world. And we almost removed the entire sequence from the picture.

Again, persistence had prevailed. Never give up and you'll ultimately stumble onto every solution. That philosophy was my strength throughout the experience. I was certain it applied, no matter what. Any mountain could be scaled, any problem ultimately solved.

That was before *Benji* was turned down by every major distributor in the business.

They had told us earlier. All of them. But we didn't believe. A year before, Ed and I had flown to Los Angeles to meet distributors and introduce our plans for what we were certain would be the most unique movie about a dog ever made. We had thought it might help, later, to know some warm bodies behind the cold, intimidating block letters of the studio signs. But they all looked at us like we were crazy. First because we were making a *dog* movie—a *unique* dog movie is still a *dog* movie! Don't do it, they said in unison—and second because none of them, I assume, had ever had anyone in their offices who wasn't asking for something, usually money.

Bob Carpenter at Universal was the only distributor who ultimately saw the finished picture and truly loved it. And even he was afraid of it. Or, at least, afraid that he couldn't give it the attention he felt it needed.

"It's a very special movie," he said, "and if I could take it out there myself and handle it personally I believe I could make it a smash!" He leaned forward across the desk, soft-spoken and sensitive. There was no cigar. "Unfortunately, I can't do that. I have to stay up here in the black tower. And I can't promise you that my people in the field will feel like I do about it. This film will be hard to sell because, on the surface, people like to think all dog movies are alike. You've already experienced that talking to distributors. The public will be the same, and it's going to take someone who cares a lot to spend the time to develop the ways to convince them otherwise."

He leaned back in his chair and stared at the ceiling for a long moment. "Have you considered doing it yourself?" he finally said.

The question hit Ed Vanston in the face like the flat side of a well-hit hockey puck. Neither of us had ever considered doing such a thing. And Ed wanted to keep it that way. He had already risked his relationship with every friend he had by encouraging them to invest in, of all things, a movie. Now, he wasn't about to go back and tell them that nobody wanted the movie so we were going to add film distribution to our lengthening list of inexperienced firsts.

Me, on the other hand, I was sucking deep breaths trying to rush oxygen to the blood suddenly racing rampant through my head. My brain was on fire, spitting out thoughts and questions like a machine gun.

"There's no real mystery to it," Carpenter was saying. "It's just selling, pure and simple. Isn't that your background, Joe? Advertising and marketing."

"That's not really an option for us," Ed said quickly. "Our investors want to see some money coming in, not more going out."

"Well, if you change your mind, and need some questions answered, just give me a call."

When we arrived back in Dallas, I still hadn't said anything. I was trying to collect my thoughts and evaluate the idea and the alternatives. I didn't sleep that night. I couldn't quiet the gremlins racing around in my head. For two weeks, I had felt myself helplessly sinking lower and lower with every meeting. Our advertising to the trade throughout production and post-production had done exactly what we had wanted it to do. Every major distributor in the business except Columbia had called us. We hadn't had to initiate a single call. We had wanted them to come after us, instead of vice-versa, and it had worked. Only to have them all smile sweetly and say no thanks. All except Paramount. No sweet smile there.

I was as close to giving up as I have ever been. It all seemed quite hopeless. Before Bob Carpenter, we had seen everyone there was to see, and we only had one tiny little offer. An advance that barely covered the investor's commitment to the film from a mail-order record company named K-Tel. Their business was selling all the great musical hits of the century, *together for the first time on a single album,* usually promoted on late-night TV. They had the notion that they could use *Benji* to launch themselves into film distribution. I had not even considered them to be in the running, and didn't think Ed had, until I met with him the next morning.

"I think we should take the K-Tel offer," he said.

My jaw hit the floor with a clunk.

"It'll get the investors' money back and who knows, if we're lucky... I mean, K-Tel does know how to sell. Marketing *is* their business."

"They know how to sell schlock!" I blurted. "On late-night television!"

The war was declared.

I was in shock. We could get the investor's money back with a single television sale. How could $300,000 even be a consideration for throwing the movie away to an outfit like K-Tel?!

It was the biggest face-to-face fight Ed and I ever had. From his point-of-view, his arguments made implicit sense. From mine, he was cutting the throat of my baby, my dream, my career, and leaving them all in an alley to die.

We raise more money, form a company, and distribute ourselves, I bleated, pounding everything Bob Carpenter had said into every sentence. *The picture could be a smash if someone who understands marketing and really cares for the movie takes it out.* No one cared more than I did, and I had spent the past twelve years of my life in marketing and advertising. I understood it, and I wasn't afraid of it.

But Ed was. Film distribution was a major mystery to him. If it were that easy, everybody would be doing it. No way we could get a handle on something so complex in time for a summer release. And where would we get the money? He didn't even want to try. It was easier, the line of least resistance, to take the advance from K-Tel and run. At least his friends wouldn't hate him.

"But K-Tel knows nothing about film distribution!"

"Neither do you!"

The screaming went on for almost two hours. And it wasn't friendly. I wasn't about to put a stamp of approval on what I was sure would be the certain demise of our motion picture, and Ed wasn't about to tell his friends that to protect their investment they had to ante up even more, because Joe wasn't happy simply proving that one shouldn't produce movies without experience, he wanted to prove the same thing with distribution.

"For a little risk and a lot of work, we can have a twenty million dollar movie! All the Disney figures back that up! And this movie plays just like a Disney classic!" I screamed. "You've seen the reactions yourself!"

But I was screeching at a stone wall. He could see nothing but the $350,000 K-Tel had offered. I had never before experienced an Ed Vanston impervious to reason. Usually, he even *liked* a little risk if the rewards were great enough. But this time there was no moving him. The decisions of Twentieth Century Fox, Warner Brothers, MGM, Disney and Paramount were good enough for him.

"I'm sorry!" I screeched. "I've put too much into this. I cannot sit by and watch it be thrown away!"

Ed paused for a moment, his face flushed red, the veins of his neck pulsing. "You don't have any choice!" he said finally. "You don't control this company!"

I exploded all over his desk. "I have a choice! Do with the movie and this company exactly as you please, and if I ever have any money coming, which I seriously doubt, you have my home address!! I quit!" And I wheeled around and flung open the door scattering our horrified eavesdropping staff like a covey of quail.

I stomped across the hall into my office, slammed the door, and started slinging stuff from my drawers into an empty film box. I knew I was acting like a child, but I was powerless to do otherwise. Even if we couldn't raise any money, distributing the picture ourselves was still better than giving it to K-Tel. *Anything* was better than giving it to K-Tel! I had talked with their marketing guy at length who had promised me they would handle *Benji* with the very same skills and finesse used in their late-night record promotions on TV. These people were simply cut from a different mold and however successful that mold was for mail order records, they were *not* the people Bob Carpenter had described who could make *Benji* a smash hit. And no one else wanted it!

I was beginning to feel like that nut marching down the street claiming he was the only one in the entire squadron in step. How could I believe that all these experts were wrong? How could I be so cocksure against the word of so many? How much experience does it take to convince me that I should take another look? Was the movie really any good, and even if it was, could it be sold? Maybe people—real audiences—could never be convinced that it was something special, something unique, that it was not just another dog movie. Maybe the experts were right. After all, how could they have become experts if they couldn't even tell one dog movie from another? Maybe even Ed was right. Maybe it was impossible to learn the distribution business in three months.

I was trying to convince myself, but I simply didn't believe me. The jigsaw puzzle, I mused. One step at a time. It's an unknown, but there just isn't any mystery to it.

What would I do first? I mean, besides trying to find some people to hire? What, indeed? I thought about it as I dropped papers from my desk into a second film box. I would find out who books movies for Northpark, and go see this person. Ask him to screen the film and tell him we wanted it to play at the Northpark theater, which, at the time, was one of the two top theaters in town. Simple enough.

But it was silly to think about. I had just resigned from my own company. And, as it sank in, I could only regret why it happened, not the decision itself. Ed had seized control for the first time—even though, by stock ownership, he always had it—and he had made a decision that I was certain would destroy the chances for *Benji* to have any kind of success. I couldn't help but wonder just what the hell life was supposed to be all about. How could it all come to this? It didn't make any sense.

Just then, the door cracked open, barely enough for Ed to peek in.

"Is it safe to come in?"

"Probably not," I said sourly.

He eased the door open anyway.

"If," he began slowly, "we formed a distribution company, I suppose that company would get the fee that would've gone to Fox or MGM or whoever, right?"

"I've never heard of a distribution company working for free," I grumbled.

"And you really believe the picture can gross twenty million?"

"At least."

"How much do you think it would cost to capitalize the company?"

"I have no idea," I said. "But I've got a pencil, if you've got the time."

He tried to hide the flicker of excitement in his eyes as he closed the door and pulled up a chair. Then, he grinned.

"You don't ever let it get boring, do you?"

My office looked like a New York newsstand. Movie pages were stacked and scattered everywhere, recent Fridays, and Fridays months ago, from the newspapers of the top sixty or seventy cities by population in the country. And sheets upon sheets of numbers, grosses from the theaters in those markets. And stacks of booking sheets and advertising budgets to approve. And I had to leave for the airport in a matter of minutes.

This was what we later, facetiously, called our period of analysis. We were, in fact, market-testing the picture, we just didn't know it at the time. I was merely trying to match up the pieces of the puzzle, one by one, picking our way across the southern part of the nation, playing carefully selected markets that met carefully controlled criterion, analyzing each opening for improvement against the last and making changes to improve it even more for the next, creeping up on superb grosses, but not there yet.

With each improved report, Ed wanted to *break out*, as it's called, go wide, go national. But before we had even played our first theater, he had promised that we'd go slowly until I was certain we had all the answers. He pressed and pressured, but kept his word and left the decision with me as to *when*.

Many a movie, loved in previews and screenings, has bombed at the box office, because, even though adored by test audiences, the advertising and promotion didn't manage to sell enough early tickets for that all-important word-of-mouth to take hold and make the film a *must-see* picture before theater-owners jerked it from their screens and sent it packing. When a movie opens everywhere at once, in theaters all across the nation, it is virtually impossible to correct a problem if the advertising isn't working. Usually, there just isn't enough time to analyze the situation and implement solutions.

The classic example of a terrific save is *American Graffiti*, one of George Lucas' first pictures. In early weeks, the movie did very little business. The promotion wasn't working. But Universal was the largest studio in Hollywood, releasing more films each year than any other distributor. Since films are the lifeblood of a theater existence, the studio's ability to spit out quantity alone created a certain attention factor with exhibitors. Also, however, Universal had *The Sting*, with Paul Newman and Robert Redford, following *Graffiti* into many of the same theaters. I'm told, they were able to cause theaters to keep *American Graffiti* on their screens, despite the low grosses, by threatening to withhold *The Sting*. Eventually word-of-mouth began to accumulate, attendance multiplied, and *American Graffiti* wound up grossing very well.

We, of course, had no such power or influence. We were tiny and unknown, and there were no big movies following *Benji*. We had only the box office results of the picture itself with which to woo theaters so that's where we focused our attention. If *Benji* were going to be the smash Bob Carpenter had predicted, we *had* to have exceptional first-week attendance to ignite word-of-mouth into a spontaneous roaring bonfire or the picture would be out of the theaters before word could get around. For Mulberry Square, they wouldn't wait, like they did for Universal and *American Graffiti*. So, until we were absolutely certain we had the right mix of advertising and promotion to wrap first-week lines completely around the block, we simply couldn't consider opening nationally. We had come too far to let it all ride on a roll of the dice.

Benji had its world premiere at Northpark Cinema the last week in May. Not only was this theater one of the top two in Dallas, it turned out to be one of the top-grossing national flag-ships for the burgeoning General Cinema chain. Remarkably, the difficulty had not been in arranging for the theater, but in convincing Ed it was the right thing to do.

He had performed quick miracles raising the needed capital for the new distribution company with a combination of loans, sale of Mulberry stock, and peddling more of the only real asset we had, interests in *Benji*. By the time the production was finished and paid for and the distribution company was capitalized, Mulberry Square's profit participation in the picture had been reduced to a mere 16.5%.

Now, with his friends impaled even further on the financial hook, Ed was more anxious than ever to see some cash coming back. But before we could even start, we needed people; somebody who knew *something* about distribution. We explained our position to each and every job candidate: that we knew absolutely nothing about the process of releasing motion pictures, but we intended to know everything about it, and if we felt it was necessary, Ed and I would make final decisions on any issue that affected the picture's success. I wanted everybody to understand this up front.

We hired two men, very experienced in film distribution, but not long after, one was advised by his doctor that the pressure of his new job was going to be too much, and he had to resign. I don't blame him. I wouldn't have wanted to work for me during that period either. That left Jerry Kamprath as Head of Distribution. He had cold steel for skin and knew the business inside out. We fought until the day he left Mulberry, years later, but we respected each other immensely and were always the closest of friends.

The first item on the agenda, after Jerry was hired, was Northpark Cinema.

"That's where I want to play *Benji* in Dallas," I told him. "We need that theater to validate the picture."

It was a simple theorem. The public knew where the good pictures played, and where the rotten pictures played. Put a terrific picture into a lousy theater that usually plays lousy pictures, and no one's going to go. They will assume, usually correctly, if it's playing at *that* theater, it can't be very good. On the other hand, put the worst picture in the world in a theater like Northpark and it will still do at least *some* business because people assume that it must be good or it wouldn't be playing there.

Jerry thought I was nuts. He didn't think there was one chance in a hundred for a picture like *Benji* to play at Northpark.

"Just ask them to take a look," I said.

For political reasons, he also wanted to approach Interstate, another large chain that was particularly dominant in Georgia, Florida and the Carolinas. They owned the other top theater in Dallas and I told Jerry I would have no problem with that theater if we couldn't get Northpark.

Jim Tharpe, who went on to become head of all film-buying for General Cinema's 1400-plus theater screens and then became head of distribution at Dreamworks SKG, was then second in command in the Dallas regional office. The task of screening *Benji* fell to him, and he loved the picture. They happened to have three weeks open at Northpark from May 24 through June 13 -- too short a period for major distributors with big pictures, especially with kids still in school until May 31. Jim recommended to his boss that they give us those three weeks for *Benji* if we'd take the play-date without any advance or guarantee.

The conflict erupted when Interstate offered us eight guaranteed weeks and a cash advance of $40,000, not for their best theater, but for their worst, the struggling Village Theater. When Ed heard this, we were back at war.

"Forty grand is practically one-sixth of the original investment. From *one* theater!"

"But it's a lousy theater," I screeched. "We'll get our advance but we won't do any business, then no other theater in the country will ever want to see Benji's face!"

The Village was a second-run theater that Interstate was trying to build back to first-run status. But we total unknowns with a G-rated dog movie were going to have enough trouble getting people into a theater like Northpark. It would be foolish, I felt, to knowingly bury our picture under the second-run image of this theater. Jerry Kamprath joined Ed arguing *for* the Village. "It's a good offer," he said, "and Interstate has all those terrific theaters over in the Southeast!" But, to me, neither argument was sound. We needed to propel our picture into the marketplace with such impact that other exhibitors around the country would kill to get it? The Village simply wouldn't produce such avarice.

The tide of battle began to turn when I asked Ed to pause for a moment, forget the $40,000, and tell me when he was last inside the Village theater.

He couldn't remember.

"Why," I asked.

There was a long pause.

"Because they play lousy pictures?"

It was possibly the most important decision we made throughout the entire process. Northpark was such a good theater that it made up for a basket full of advertising and promotional mistakes, and *Benji* wound up doing very well. Not an A-plus, or even an A, but at least a B-minus, and at Northpark, a B-minus made theaters all over the country sit up and take notice.

"Where did that picture come from??"

"What is a *Benji*??"

"Where do I call to book it?"

Benji did well enough at Northpark to have the run extended a week, pushing back the scheduled picture, making a certain major distributor very angry. I had to smile. The distributor was Paramount. The same Paramount who had said we'd never have a chance in a regular run. *Benji's* first week at Northpark more than doubled the first week of Paramount's incoming picture.

But we still had a lot of work to do. We just didn't know how much until we moved out into other markets and were greeted, like a cold slap in the face, by stinging, terrible reviews, virtually across the board.

It took several days to patch my ego back together and try to figure out why. Reviews in Dallas had been terrific. But we had been working on the picture for over a year and had had ample time to chat with film writers and critics in the area about *Benji's* uniquenesses; about how the dog expresses emotion; about why we felt the picture was the reverse of all the dog movies that had preceded it because the *dog* was the three-dimensional character and the people were the props; about how the story was *not* about kidnapping but about the struggle of a small, helpless dog to communicate with all-knowing humans. In effect, we had unconsciously positioned the Dallas press to view the picture from an entirely different perspective than they normally view films; to throw away the critical rule book, or to at least revise it.

But out in the real world, critics were killing us. Somehow— and I still don't understand it—they were missing the entire performance and struggle of the central character while they searched in vain for a handle among the human actors and the kidnapping plot.

Of course, I couldn't be certain this was the problem, but it was the only conclusion that made any sense, so I called Frank and told him to put himself, Juanita and Benji on a plane, and we hit the road. The plan was for us to descend upon each market where *Benji* was going to play *before* any critic saw the picture; to put them face-to-face with Benji's big brown eyes and my discourse on the concept of the film *before* the critical norms took charge; to, as we had inadvertently done in Dallas, *unconsciously* position them before they ever sat down in the theater.

It wasn't easy because many critics have a rule that they will not do interviews until they have seen the movie in question, but at the time, we had very few prints of the film, and none to spare, and we used that fact, along with our acknowledged naïveté, to our advantage. With pleading, very few of them turned us down.

Of course, no self-respecting critic is likely to admit that an interview and a meeting with a dog could affect how he might feel about a given movie, but the demarcation line in our review scrapbook is unmistakably vivid. The minute we went on the road, the reviews of the picture changed dramatically for the better. There will always be some who simply don't like this type of film, never mind the perspective, but even those were hard pressed not to speak kindly about the dog's acting ability. In fact, overnight, the reviews rebounded from virtually no comments about the dog to so many terrific observations that we actually mounted a tongue-in-cheek campaign to get Benji an Oscar for his acting.

Traveling to each market became an integral part of the promotion of the picture. With very few exceptions, we did one city a day, usually arriving late in the evening and going quickly to bed, to arise before dawn for an early morning talk show, sometimes two, usually on opposite sides of town, then several radio shows, more television, a luncheon for newspapers—usually at a fancy restaurant with Benji sitting at the head of the table with a napkin tied around his neck, eating his medium sirloin from Frank's fork like the perfectly behaved gentleman he was. Afterward, Frank and I would do one-on-one interviews with the writers from the major papers, then on to more television and radio shows, and—as Benji's fame grew—maybe a personal appearance or two. Then back to the airport for a plane to the next city to do the same thing all over again the following day. This was our schedule, five days a week for the entire summer. I would leave Frank, Juanita and Benji on Friday evenings and fly home to spend the weekend analyzing the results of the latest advertising changes, to approve bookings in additional markets and the opening advertising budgets for each, incorporating the changes resulting from the previous week's experiments. I would stay through Monday morning to see figures for new openings over the weekend, then shortly after noon, I was back on a plane to rejoin Frank, Juanita and Benji for another week of promotion.

Gradually, as we moved from market to market, the grosses slowly improved. We only booked cities in which we could get Northpark-quality theaters that had played some of the same pictures. I had grosses for every film Northpark had played during the past year, and I compared ratios of *Benji's* gross to those pictures against the same ratio in other theaters to determine, with each promotional change, if *Benji's* performance was improving, and how much.

I began the summer believing *Benji* would have more appeal in rural areas than in the big cities, but I was wrong. I thought the picture would play better to blue collar than white, but I was wrong again. We thought, with adults, the over-fifties would pour out. The ones who had been complaining so about the lack of wholesome movies. But they didn't, in droves. We couldn't budge them.

We had to quickly find a way to convince adults, in large quantities, to give it a try or I knew the prediction by the man at Paramount would come true. We'd have no night business, and without night business, the picture wouldn't last in the caliber of theaters we wanted to play, and there would be no smash hit. *Benji* wound up with a national audience ratio of two adults to every kid and that's what really made it all work. Adult word-of-mouth. For the most part, they were young adults and parents, regular moviegoers, and it took a complete departure from usual movie advertising to create enough curiosity to get them into the theater. I think we were the first to film testimonials with young adults coming out of an actual screening, expressing what they felt—*felt*, not *thought*—about the film. And the communication worked. The adult audience began to grow. They weren't expecting much when they entered the theater but, when the movie actually entertained them, when it made them laugh, and cry, and feel good, they would burst out of the theater telling everyone in sight not to miss it.

Through June and July, we reworked our television commercials several times, we dropped radio advertising altogether, and we were constantly changing the way our television spots were scheduled on the air, adjusting the so-called *target audience*. Harland redesigned our newspaper ads more times than he would like to count and, with each and every adjustment, we were forever analyzing, studying, plotting and planning.

It was August 2nd, in Albuquerque, when we finally hit the critical mass. Sold-out signs and lines around the block. *Benji* became the second highest grossing picture in Highland Theater history.

It was almost time to celebrate. One more market to confirm the plan, to make sure that Albuquerque was not a fluke, then we'd be ready to go. Baltimore was next. It opened August 16 and exploded right through the roof.

And, suddenly, the summer was gone.

"You can't be serious??!"

Ed was screeching, and pacing, and waving his arms.

"Once a picture is out there," Jerry chimed in politely, "... well, it's... out there. You can't just put it away for nine months and expect to start over."

"Why not?!" I asked.

"I don't know. It's just not done. Never have I ever heard of it being done." Jerry was emphatic, but not loud. He rarely raised his voice. I wished for just a pinch of his restraint.

"So??" I fired back.

"We have to keep playing," Jerry said.

"No!" I bellowed.

Ed paused in mid-pace and pointed at me.

"No way I'm going back to all the investors and tell them they have to wait another year."

"If someone told you you could have a dime *now*, or a dollar next year, which would you take??" I exclaimed, trying not to out-shout him.

After Baltimore, for a fleeting moment, we had felt invincible, certain that the old wives' tale about grosses disappearing after Labor Day didn't apply to us. So we booked right into September... and fell flat on our face. The minute school started, *Benji's* attendance dropped out of sight, to less than twenty percent of the Albuquerque and Baltimore numbers. That left logic little choice. Why continue to waste the picture? With our marketing plan perfected and proven, we could put the film on the shelf for nine months, spend that time carefully setting the entire country, and open nationally in June to at least five times these terrible September figures.

Granted, it had never been done before, but so what? If it was right for us, why not? One last time I found myself fighting everybody in sight for what seemed to me to be the *only* reasonable alternative.

"How can you use national advertising when almost twenty-percent of the country is past history?" asked Jerry.

"We'll do a test," I said, "in a couple of markets we've already played, watching only weekend grosses, to see if the picture is finished, or if, perhaps word-of-mouth has made it even better. If the latter, we'll re-book every market we played this summer, along with those we haven't played, and this time we'll do them right!"

"You'll never get exhibitors to play the same picture again next summer!" Jerry was finally joining the scream fest. "It just isn't done!" To him, I was breaking every rule in the book, and he was the one who would have to relay those breaks to exhibitors. Ed was beginning to think I had been placed in this world simply to make his life miserable. How was he going to explain to investors who were hounding him that it would be another year?

But, in the end, both Ed and Jerry relayed this bizarre plan to their respective groups, and the test worked. The weekend figures in San Antonio and Fort Meyers, Florida were better than ever. So we set out to book the entire nation for the following summer.

Except for Los Angeles.

If we were to be successful in our Academy Award efforts for the song, I felt the validity and the exposure would have far greater value if it all happened *before* we opened the picture nationwide.

To qualify for the Awards, a film has to play in Los Angeles prior to the end of the year. We first looked at Christmas, but Jerry found that too many of the good theaters were already booked. So we decided on Thanksgiving. Kids had four to five days out of school, and we could play right up to the opening of the Christmas pictures. Not ideal conditions for maximum gross from the area, but, I felt, a terrific investment in the national run the following summer. And, with our test results, and a strong summer kickoff, I was certain we could re-book a second Los Angeles run in late July or August.

The heavy advertising for the picture at Thanksgiving would fall just a few weeks before Academy members would vote for award nominations. Concurrently, a trade advertising program drawing attention to the song would run in Daily Variety and Hollywood Reporter, and to increase interest and curiosity in the picture among adult Academy members, we mounted a second program in the trade papers presenting Benji for a best actor nomination. These ads were laced with accolades from critics all over the country, several suggesting that he was a better actor than many humans, and a couple actually endorsing him for the Oscar.

The effort had even more impact than we expected. The song was nominated. Johnny Carson began to make jokes about Benji in his monologue. The bid for the acting award was discussed on talk shows, and several situation comedies began to write in Benji jokes. This was a tiny, tasty clue to the kind of acceptance that was coming. But what all those comedy writers in Los Angeles didn't know was that eighty-percent of the nation had never even heard of Benji. I suppose they assumed that the film had opened *everywhere* when it opened in Los Angeles. Whatever the reason, it was of immense value, helping pave the way for the following summer.

The Los Angeles premiere was a spectacular event benefiting *Actors and Others for Animals*. I think every Hollywood star who ever cared for a furry little creature came out and, for a few glorious hours, we were swept away from the business at hand into never-never land. I suppose being a part of *any* Hollywood premiere would be exciting, but when your first is *your own*—and it happens *before* the cynicism sets in—it's like living a fantasy. Carolyn and I had never even ridden in a limousine before that night and I spent much of the evening not having the vaguest idea what to do or say. Especially after the movie, when compliments began to flow from people I had watched on movie and television screens for most of my life. I kept trying to make at least one reasonably intelligent remark, and kept saying the dumbest things.

The high point of the evening came when the organization presented me a plaque of appreciation. I stood staring out at all those extremely familiar faces, not seeing a one of them.

I've told this story enough to know the reaction, especially from the younger among you. But, I'm sorry. I couldn't help it. As a teenager, I was absolutely head-over-heels in love with this lady, and now, here I stood next to her, before all of Hollywood, with her hand on my back. Doris Day was *touching* me! Of course, a week later she wouldn't even accept a phone call, but at that moment, the world was in perfect harmony.

The entire evening went like clockwork, except I couldn't think of a thing to say when emcee and Daily Variety columnist Army Archerd questioned me for the TV cameras. But, all in all, the evening was terrific, topped only in my scrapbook by the Golden Globe Awards—the Hollywood Foreign Press Association's version of the Academy Awards—which always precedes the Oscars by a few weeks and is sort of a precursor of things to come. Virtually everyone who was nominated was there, yet, to our amazement, Benji was the celebrity of the evening.

Unlike the Oscars, where the party comes *after* the awards—when four out of five nominees are disappointed, if not outright angry—the Golden Globe Awards has their party *first*, when everyone is still giddy with anticipation. Then they eat, the award ceremony follows, and everyone goes home.

Carolyn kept reaching over and closing my mouth as we met and rubbed elbows with everyone who was anyone in the industry. From the moment we walked in, crowds formed around Frank and Benji and the "must" of the evening quickly became having a picture made with our huggable, floppy-eared hero.

I had convinced myself there wasn't a chance in the world for our song to win. This, after all, was Hollywood, and we were outsiders. So the plan was to have a good time and not worry about the award. And it worked, right up until the time Helen Reddy began reading the nominees. Suddenly all breath left me, my heart began to pound, and both hands reached for Carolyn. The competition was stiffer than I had anticipated a year-and-a-half before when I had first talked to Euel, including a strong entry from *Towering Inferno*, a top-grossing, expensive co-production from *two* studios. As Ms. Reddy tore open the envelope, I squeezed Carolyn's hand, and bit a hole in my lip.

"And the winner is... Benji's Theme: I Feel Love!"

I must've leaped four feet into the air, screeching like a maniac. Euel grabbed Benji from Frank to take him on-stage and as I was stumbling to get out of his way, I fell backwards right into Ernest Borgnine who was waiting by our table to be the next presenter. I turned to apologize and when I saw who it was, I couldn't say a word. I just pointed. He reached out and shook my hand.

"Congratulations," he said warmly, and I'll never forget the look in his eyes. Our entire table, including calm, sedate Ed and Jackie Vanston, had erupted as if we had single-handedly won the Super Bowl. The room seemed to gasp in unison at the outburst, but Mr. Borgnine's fleeting expression was one of approval, like the old patriarch wishing he could once again be so easily stirred, so young and innocent. Years later, on the film *The Double McGuffin*, I had the opportunity to remind Ernie of that and he remembered the moment fondly.

"This is Benji," I heard Euel say, "our inspiration." I turned to see the four of them leaving the podium together, Euel, Helen Reddy, Benji... and the glorious Golden Globe!

A few weeks later, we watched the song from *Towering Inferno* win the Academy Award; but our effort, the process, the Golden Globe Award, and the Academy nomination had served their purpose well. An entire world was now out there waiting for an inexpensive little movie about a special, scruffy little dog.

12

IN REFLECTION

"The reward of a thing well done is to have done it."

Ralph Waldo Emerson

During the following summer, *Benji* grossed thirty-three million dollars, roughly equivalent to one-hundred-and-eighty million today. Variety listed *Benji* as the number three grossing movie of the year.

Frank and I, Benji, Joe III, and sometimes Harland, Juanita, and Ben Vaughn, toured and talked in 120 cities and towns over the two summers, from Seattle to Spartanburg, from New York to San Diego. Frank and I were so practiced in how to throw the lead back and forth to make sure our points about the picture were heard that we actually took control of a couple of shows where the interviewer wanted to talk about everything *but* the movie.

We spent over five million dollars on advertising and promotion, almost all of which was on the come. That is, we didn't have it when we committed for it. But we had tested the picture so thoroughly that we knew we *would* have it, and when.

Jerry had recruited Carolyn into the distribution division and she was managing the movement of hundreds of *Benji* film prints, to and from theaters, back and forth across the country. She eventually became second in command of distribution, later ran our merchandising arm, and, finally, the entire company.

Even with everything finally going our way, that big summer was not without its problems. First, we couldn't book New York.

The powers that be wouldn't give us the quality theaters we wanted. It's not a *New York* kind of picture, they said. So we ran a full-page ad in the Sunday New York Times with a big picture of Benji and a dozen sensational quotes from critics around the country. What made the ad different from most movie ads were the bold, black letters across the bottom of the page: *Call your favorite theater for opening date!* By the close of business the next evening, *Benji* was booked in New York.

I still have the Variety headline *Jaws, Benji: Boffo in Gotham.* Our little mutt from the Burbank Animal Shelter—without a *New York kind of picture*—took the Big Apple by storm, setting two house records in the process.

The Detroit Free-Press ran an editorial cartoon with a shark swimming across the surface of the water, and a little fluffy dog swimming up from below, teeth at the ready, about to bite a chunk out of the belly of the big fish. Unfortunately, a bit exaggerated, but indicative of that elusive but all important momentum the picture had. Based upon our per-screen averages and our city-by-city totals, virtually everyone was convinced that *Benji* was the number-two picture of the summer, second only to the Great White Shark from Universal. The incredible race our little dog was running became the talk of the country.

Except in Boston and Philadelphia. There, the opening was delayed several times because General Cinema wanted to put the picture in a large group of sub-run theaters. The houses I wanted were each playing Disney pictures throughout the summer on one of their two screens and General Cinema's corporate policy was to *not* play G-rated pictures side by side in the same theater. I said no to the offered theaters for the third time, and left town for a week of promotion. When I returned, the sub-run theaters were booked, to open the following Friday, and advertising had already started. That Saturday, Jerry and I had our biggest fight ever!

He had booked the Boston theaters, even though I had said no, because he felt he had no choice. General Cinema had been incredibly helpful to us all across the nation. They had paid us early whenever we needed money. They had bent over backwards to put us in the theaters we wanted. But they weren't about to break corporate policy just for us.

"That's my point!" I said to Jerry. "It's just a picture to them. It's our entire future!"

I knew the industry was watching every opening to see if *Benji* was really phenomenon, or fluke. The figures most watched were the per-screen grosses; how well the picture was doing, on the average, per theater.

The sub-run theaters Jerry had booked had never generated the kind of averages *Benji* was producing, not even close, and I was afraid low numbers would burst that delicate bubble of momentum. We simply couldn't take the chance. Every opening had to be as good or better than the last.

I made Jerry pull the run. He came back downstairs after calling Boston and said we'd probably never play another General Cinema theater. He was going home to get drunk and he might not be back on Monday. He slammed the door as he went out.

He was there Monday, but instead of personally bringing down the weekend figures, as he usually did, he *sent* them down with a secretary. I didn't see him at all until I was racing out the door, headed for the airport. I crashed headlong into him and we both almost wound up on the floor.

"Boston called," he said.

"I told you the subject was closed!" My snap had an unnecessary bite.

"No it's not," he said. "They gave you the theaters you wanted."

I threw my arms around him, then disappeared out the door. I could've flown from Dallas without a plane. We opened the following Friday in Boston and did, in some cases, three times the gross of the Disney picture next door. Philadelphia opened the following week and set house records.

All in all, it was quite a summer.

So there we were, standing in the Piazza del Cinquecento in Rome. The Eternal City! Gaping up at a forty foot billboard, the proud parents of a brand new, floppy-eared international phenomenon.

I remember standing there for a very long time. Back in Dallas, the staff was already in pre-production on our next picture. Lawyers were finalizing Mulberry's purchase of Ed's stock. Jerry was negotiating with Japan for *Benji,* and, in California, Frank was hiring trainers for the eighteen camels we had just purchased.

But that's all another story, and at the moment, it was all 10,000 miles away. For the first time in years, Carolyn and I were in neutral, tingling with the triumph of the summer, our problems and plans stuffed somewhere in a suitcase on the train from Milano. Nothing that was about to happen depended upon us. I was there as the director, not the producer, or the distributor, or even the production company. The customs of the country and the business practices of the Italian distributor were as foreign to us as the language. For once, the reins were not in my hands and there was nothing to do but relax and enjoy it.

Those days in Rome were like a magic potion, the most carefree time we had spent in years.

But, with all the success, the summer had ended sadly. Our last scheduled stop on the promotional tour was Boston, and I would be returning early to Dallas, leaving Frank, Juanita and Higgins to finish the final day without me. Ironically, Frank was now calling Higgins Benji, but I never could. He responded to either, but he was always Higgins to me.

In each new city, as we traveled from interview to interview, from show to show, Higgins would make the treks lying in my lap, probably because the car was always crowded, and Frank didn't *have* a lap. It became a running joke that he would frump and growl until I scrunched into a position that was suitable to him, then he'd climb into my lap and go to sleep. I loved it, because I loved the dog.

As we made the mad dash to the airport in Boston, to put me on a plane to Dallas, Higgins had curled up in my lap as usual, and as I scratched his head, the strongest, strangest feeling suddenly consumed me. I knew, somehow, that this would be the last time I would ever see him.

It was rush hour and the Boston traffic was the worst I had ever witnessed. I was certain we'd never make it through the tunnel; that I would miss my plane, and I begged God to make it so. I desperately did not want to leave like this. I wanted to stay and break the spell, the feeling that was eating at my insides. But the driver performed miracles and we got there with mere minutes to spare. As our local representative was dragging me bodily out of the car, I hugged Higgins, he licked me in the ear, then I raced off through the airport, blinking back tears all the way to the plane.

Two weeks later, at the age of fifteen, he was gone. I can remember very few moments in my life that hit me as hard. After the call from Frank, I shut my office door and cried. Later that day, I called Frank back and told him I wanted to tell the press. It was *Higgins'* movie, the *only* movie he'd ever make, and his fans deserved to know.

"You just can't do that," said Frank. "Not now. Not yet. The movie is still playing all over the country. Think of the kids who are seeing it today and how they're going to feel if you tell them tomorrow that Benji is dead."

I hung up the phone and just stared at the huge framed photograph of Higgins consuming the wall across from my desk. It had been a birthday surprise from Carolyn and was a magnificent, majestic reproduction. It didn't seem fair that he should go without a word. But, Frank was right, and we wound up waiting for almost a year before telling anyone. By then, a puppy Higgins had sired had picked up her Daddy's reins to carry on. This would be the first dog actually named Benji and, without *any* doubles, would bless us with three more *Benji* movies—including one with virtually no humans at all—four television specials and a network series.

I reach for words, but find it impossible to describe the feeling of being able to appear on a street corner virtually anywhere in the free world, say one word, and see eyes light up with so much love and affection. To have been able to pass through this life and leave behind something that makes people feel so good keeps me forever aware that it has been a worthwhile trip. And makes me ever mindful that God is at work in our lives, even when we feel the most abandoned. For now I knew why I had been turned down for entrance into UCLA. Notwithstanding how much I would need Carolyn, I would also need the advertising and marketing I learned at Ole Miss, and later at the two advertising agencies, when the picture was turned down by all those Hollywood distributors. And had it not been turned down, you would have never heard of Benji, because no large Hollywood distributor, with ten to twenty pictures in the pipeline, could possibly take the time that we took to get the marketing right. *Benji* would've been gone before he ever got started. Two of the most devastating times in my life, and both *had* to happen for you to know our floppy-eared superstar.

"Benamino! Te Amo!"

The child's voice rang through the piazza.

"Benamino! Benamino!" another squealed.

Carolyn and I turned from the huge billboard to watch Frank and Juanita emerge from the terminal into the gathering swarm of

Italian mothers and children. I silently wished that Higgins could've been there to share this spontaneous show of affection. His stand-in and very best friend, Scamper, was fielding the kisses and squeezes from the squealing throng. We stood there for a very long time, waiting for the crowd to dissipate, but it just kept getting larger and larger.

"Must be a star," Carolyn said.

"Overnight success," I whispered.

She smiled, and I reached for her hand. It was a warm autumn day. A light breeze was blowing. We were half a world away from home, standing in a beautiful Roman piazza, absorbing, seeing, realizing for the very first time, the results of our labors... and it felt good.

AFTERWORD

With the release of *Benji Off the Leash* in 2004, the original *Benji* movie has spawned a total of seven theatrical motion pictures, several television specials, books, toys, a series, and *benji.com*, which continues to bring the films and programs starring those famous brown eyes, past and future, to millions. In short, that first motion picture enabled a dream career that somehow has yet to go away and for which I feel truly blessed. Only last year Oprah named Benji her favorite onscreen animal. This, thirty-five years after that first movie. And Benji's efforts to get homeless pets adopted, and the many requests for appearances and speaking engagements continue to take us all over the world.

Was it all worth it? All the time and effort? The heartaches?

If someone had convinced me back in the beginning that it would take so long and be so difficult I might've had second thoughts. But not today.

We're one of the few tiny little production companies who owns the copyrights to all of its movies and programs except two. Twentieth Century Fox financed *Oh Heavenly Dog*, and even though we produced *Benji the Hunted* independently, Disney distributed it and thus controls it. I voted against this but was outvoted 2:1 in our general partnership. All of the other properties, including the Benji trademarks, Mulberry Square Productions owns and controls. And Benji continues to earn today.

More importantly to me had it not happened the way it did there would've been no Benji and those millions who grew up loving our floppy-eared hero would've never known him. And I would've missed so many wonderful experiences like the joy of introducing that young boy in Paris to Benji, and all the affectionate emails we still get every day which keep me so aware that it's been a worthwhile trip.

Could our model be replicated today? Not, perhaps, exactly the way we did it. But it could be figured out. Start smaller and move slower. The times, costs, and players have changed. But mostly that's good news because today's technology provides so many more ways to be successfully independent than have ever been available to any of us before. The internet, DVDs, direct digital downloads, global social networking all provide a more direct access to the ultimate consumer than ever before possible. All you need is the tenacity to never give up and the passion to drive that tenacity. And, of course, a good product that people like.

That Benji was a unique and emotionally involving piece of entertainment played a huge role in the picture's success. At the time good filmmakers did not make family entertainment so a really good piece of family entertainment was in itself unique. How well Pixar, and Spielberg , and Lucas understood this.

Another beauty of today is that *every*body doesn't have to like your project. At the studios they pretty much have to look for projects that they hope everybody will like. You don't have to. There are ways to speak directly to virtually any group or market segment through the internet. You are only limited by your creativity and your passion. And your willingness to keep going when those doors are slammed in your face.

These are exciting times.

I would like to share the joy of *Benji's* success with everybody who helped to make it happen, especially my mother and father who, for better or worse, molded me into what I am today. I wish they could've lived to read this. Dad, I am still doing what I would do if I didn't have to make any money at it whatsoever.

And God, of course, who has the most extraordinary way of taking charge just when you've reached your limit of confusion and frustration.

And I am eternally grateful to Joe III, Brandon and Carolyn, for each of whom the cost of my commitment was extreme. I love them dearly. As, now, I do Kathleen, my second wife and life, and her three children, my new step-children.

We're supposed to change, you know, as we grow older, as we mature. So we try to do so, many of us, but I'm not sure we ever do, really. We manage to cover up a bit, to try to be what we want others to *think* we are. But, inside, I'm still that same kid sitting in the theater in Little Rock. I still want to run for a closet to hide my tears, I'm still ill at ease with people I don't know, and I still gawk at movie stars. I suppose that's why I so enjoyed writing this book. Maybe everyone should write one, because to make it communicate—if, indeed, it does—I had to dig deeply and speak honestly. I had to reintroduce myself, and get to know me again. And, for that, I thank *you* because you are the book's reason for being.

Life is but a series of choices. I hope these words have demonstrated to you, in real life example, how your dreams can become reality by making the right choices and sticking with them: the choice of following your passion at all cost: the choice of persistence, of never giving up, because you can never fail unless you quit; the choice to learn, to seek knowledge and wisdom, and to turn your back on the naysayers. You are the driver of your destiny. Only you can accept the challenge and make your life extraordinary.

It's not easy, after all these words, to find just the right ones with which to close. One thing I haven't talked much about is *losing*. It's a risk that must be taken in any serious effort to accomplish a difficult goal. You have to step out on the end of the diving board and leap off into the deep water. Neither winning nor losing ever happens when you're sitting in the stands. You must be in the arena. Teddy Roosevelt said it better than I ever could. His credo has never failed to fuel the fires that continue to burn inside me, and I read these words often:

"It is not the critic who counts, not the man who points out how the strong man stumbled or where the doer of deeds could have done better. The credit belongs to the man who is actually in the arena; whose face is marred by dust and sweat and blood; who strives valiantly; who errs and comes short again and again; who knows the great enthusiasms, the great devotions and spends himself in a worthy cause; who, at best, knows the triumph of high achievement and who, at worst, if he fails, at least fails while daring greatly, so that his place shall never be with those cold and timid souls who know neither victory nor defeat."

My fondest hope is that the chronicling of this story and the choices made might inspire you to invade Mr. Roosevelt's arena, to believe—yes, passionately—in yourself, to banish the naysayers, to promise yourself you will not give up, *ever*, to climb upon that white horse and charge off after things worthwhile... and to leave this world a better place for the effort.

I wish you Godspeed.

"We needed a dog whose face would communicate genuine, honest emotion; a dog who could show anxiety, fear, happiness, warmth and love."

Joe Camp

"Benji is able to sulk, skulk, peek, pause, do double-takes, worry, frown, scowl and glint in sly triumph. He is so wordlessly articulate that he should do a film without any two-footed creatures at all trying to steal scenes from that small and extraordinary dog with the soulful eyes."

Charles Champlin
Los Angeles Times

Also by Joe Camp

National Best Seller
The Soul of a Horse
Life Lessons from the Herd

The Soul of a Horse Blogged
The Journey Continues

The Benji Method
*Teach Your Dog to do what
Benji Does in the Movies*

Coming:

Born To Be Wild
The Soul of a Horse

The Soul of a Happier Healthier Horse
No Stalls – No Shoes – No Sugar

For more: www.14handspress.com

WHAT READERS AND CRITICS ARE SAYING ABOUT JOE CAMP

"Joe Camp is a master storyteller." *THE NEW YORK TIMES*

"This book is absolutely fabulous! An amazing, amazing book. You're going to love it." *JANET PARSHALL'S AMERICA*

"One cannot help but be touched by Camp's love and sympathy for animals and by his eloquence on the subject." *MICHAEL KORDA, THE WASHINGTON POST*

"The Hollywood glamour days are almost secondary, the theatrical drama virtually anti-climactic. In a strange, strong, compelling sense, the book is not about the making of a Hollywood movie. It is about faith....having faith in what you can do, in hanging on. The conscientious reader wanting much more than the typical Hollywood celebrity story need not despair or search any longer. He or she will find it in what Camp has written." *JACK L. KENNEDY, THE JOPLIN INDEPENDENT*

"I wish you could *hear* my excitement for Joe Camp's new book. It is unique, powerful, needed." *DR. MARTY BECKER, BEST-SELLING AUTHOR OF SEVERAL CHICKEN SOUP FOR THE SOUL BOOKS AND POPULAR VETERINARY CONTRIBUTOR TO ABC'S GOOD MORNING AMERICA*

"Joe Camp is a gifted storyteller and the results are magical. Joe entertains, educates and empowers, baring his own soul while articulating keystone principles of a modern revolution in horsemanship." *RICK LAMB, AUTHOR AND TV/RADIO HOST "THE HORSE SHOW"*

"This book is fantastic It has given me shivers, made me laugh and cry, and I just can't seem to put it down!" *CHERYL PANNIER, WHO RADIO AM 1040 DES MOINES*

"Joe Camp is a natural when it comes to understanding how animals tick and a genius at telling us their story. His books are must-reads for those who love animals of any species." *MONTY ROBERTS, AUTHOR OF NEW YORK TIMES BEST-SELLER THE MAN WHO LISTENS TO HORSES*

"Joe speaks a clear and simple truth that grabs hold of your heart." *YVONNE WELZ, EDITOR, THE HORSE'S HOOF MAGAZINE*

"Joe Camp has done it again. He grabs our attention right away, makes us laugh, cry, and believe in the possibility of all good things. A smart man, with a true gift of storytelling, Joe Camp brings us along for the ride, inspiring this reader to stay true to her passions. We laugh, struggle and cry with him. A really good read!!!!! Thanks, Joe!!" *MARJORIE SAMUELS - READER*

"I got my book yesterday and hold Joe Camp responsible for my bloodshot eyes. I couldn't put it down and morning came early!!! Joe transports me into his words. I feel like I am right there sharing his experiences. And his love for not just horses, but all of God's critters pours out from every page." *RUTH SWANDER - READER*

"I love this book! It is so hard to put it down, but I also don't want to read it too fast. I don't want it to end! Every person who loves an animal must have this book. I can't wait for the next one !!!!!!!!!" *NINA BLACK REID - READER*

"I LOVED the book! I had it read in 2 days. I had to make myself put it down. Joe and Kathleen have brought so much light to how horses should be treated and cared for. Again, thank you!" *ANITA LARGE – READER*

I LOVE the new book... reading it was such an emotional journey. Joe Camp is a gifted writer." *MARYKAY THUL LONGACRE – READER*

"I was actually really sad, when I got to the last page, because I was looking forward to picking it up every night." SABINE REYNOSO - READER

"*The Soul of a Horse Blogged* is insightful, enlightening, emotionally charged, hilarious, packed with wonderfully candid photography, and is masterfully woven by a consummate storyteller. Wonderful reading!" HARRY H. MAC-DONALD - READER

"I simply love the way Joe Camp writes. He stirs my soul. This is a must read book for everyone." *DEBBIE K - READER*

"This book swept me away. From the first to last page I felt transported! It's clever, witty, inspiring and a very fast read. I was sad when I finished it because I wanted to read more!" *DEBBIE CHARTRAND - READER*

"This book is an amazing, touching insight into Joe and Kathleen's personal journey that has an even more intimate feel than Joe's first best seller." *KATHERINE BOWEN – READER*

For more about Joe Camp
please visit one of these websites:

www.whoneedshollywood-thebook.com

www.14handspress.com

www.thesoulofahorse.com

http://thesoulofahorse.com/blog

www.benji.com

Email Joe at: joe@benji.com
Comments and questions welcome.

17743598R00157

Made in the USA
Lexington, KY
27 September 2012